"This book shows why so many people see Hans Loewald as the unmatched innovator in Freudian psychoanalysis and the most profound extender of its possibilities. Loewald brings out a whole new dimension of the Freudian mind. If you are disappointed that the Freudian discovery seems to miss the hopeful vibrance of human life, you will be amazed to see what Loewald draws from the tradition.

If you're a clinician whose old terms seem a little stiff and mechanical, your professional adventure will be refreshed when you see those terms spring to life. Loewald worked quietly without proselytizing, but his writing and teaching have kindled wide enthusiasm, and a Hans W. Loewald Center has formed, where scholars and practitioners will explore applications of Loewald's outlook to the nature of mind and mankind, the workings of treatment and the wider use of theory.

Experts here discuss the mental blending of past, present, and future. His application to interdisciplinary areas such as sociology, anthropology or feminism are profound. There are comparisons of his relationship to theorists such as Laplanche and the Italian Field Theorists. Other topics include Loewald's theory of language, his reflections on religion, on the arts and culture.

Despite his courageous independence, Loewald was the most self-effacing of pioneers, and the editors anticipate our personal curiosity by including something of what it was like to be treated or supervised by Loewald as a clinician. To get a fuller sense of Loewald as a person, we hear from his family as well.

This book, and its companion, *The Legacy and Promise of Hans Loewald*, are a treasure trove for Loewaldians, and a prospectus for those who have wondered what all the fuss is about. It announces a new era of innovation that might, indeed, go far to secure a future for psychoanalysis."

Lawrence Friedman, M.D., *Clinical Professor of Psychiatry,*
Weill-Cornell College of Medicine;
Psychoanalytic Association of New York (PANY)

"Loewald writes poetically: 'We would say that the patient instead of having a past, is his past. He does not distinguish himself as a rememberer from the content of his memory.'

This wonderful book conveys how the language of Loewald speaks to us profoundly, enlightens us, helps us clinically and theoretically, and conveys also that psychoanalysis may be approached in many different ways. Loewald has engaged Freud in such a complex fashion that we too become deeply involved with his investigation. I believe that everyone in the psychoanalytic field is looking towards the future, can benefit from this exciting, new encounter with Loewald."

Haydee Faimberg, M.D., *Training and Supervising Analyst, Paris*
Psychoanalytical Society (SPP); author of The Telescoping
of Generations *(2005); winner of the Sigourney Award for*
Outstanding Achievement (2013)

The Emerging Tradition of Hans Loewald

Alongside its companion volume, *The Legacy and Promise of Hans Loewald*, this book addresses the current lack of familiarity with the ideas and life of the eminent psycho-analytic teacher and scholar, Hans Loewald (1906–1993). It provides an account of the evolution of his ideas across different disciplinary fields.

Contributors to this volume take a broad look at Loewald's impact on the fields of sociology, anthropology, and feminism, language development, as well as delving into his work's significance for the sublimatory potential of religion, music, the arts. This volume shows how Loewald's thinking about internalization can adapt to our ever-changing social and cultural environment, even offering a Loewaldian lens to understand the contemporary use of psychedelics in mental health treatment. Ultimately, this book demonstrates that, after Loewald – as would have been his wish – for those who read him, psychoanalysis as an approach to mental health can never languish in stasis.

Animating this powerful, yet contained and complex man, there are contributions from his family, students, and analysands, and an introduction to the new virtual Loewald Center, making this volume essential reading for any psychoanalyst or psy-chotherapist working today.

Rosemary H. Balsam, F.R.C. Psych., M.R.C.P is Associate Clinical Professor of Psy-chiatry, Yale Medical School; Staff Psychiatrist, Yale Department of Student Mental Health and Counseling; and Training and Supervising Analyst, Western New England Institute for Psychoanalysis.

Elizabeth A. Brett, Ph.D., is in private practice in New Haven, Connecticut and a train-ing and supervising analyst at the Western New England Institute for Psychoanalysis.

Lawrence Levenson, M.D., is Training and Supervising Psychoanalyst and For-mer Chair of the Education Committee at the Western New England Institute for Psychoanalysis.

The Lines of Development

Evolution of Theory and Practice over the Decades Series

Series Editors: Joan Raphael-Leff, Aleksandar Dimitrijević and Norka T. Malberg

The Anna Freud Tradition
Lines of Development – Evolution of Theory and Practice over the Decades
Edited By Norka T. Malberg, Joan Raphael-Leff

Fairbairn and the Object Relations Tradition
Edited By Graham S. Clarke, David E. Scharff

The Winnicott Tradition
Lines of Development-Evolution of Theory and Practice over the Decades
Edited By Margaret Boyle Spelman, Frances Thomson-Salo

The W.R. Bion Tradition
Edited By Howard B. Levine, Giuseppe Civitarese

The Lacan Tradition
Edited By Lionel Bailly, David Lichtenstein, Sharmini Bailly

The Klein Tradition
Lines of Development—Evolution of Theory and Practice over the Decades
Edited By Kay Long, Penelope Garvey

Ferenczi's Influence on Contemporary Psychoanalytic Traditions
Lines of Development—Evolution of Theory and Practice over the Decades
Edited By Aleksandar Dimitrijević, Gabriele Cassullo, Jay Frankel

The Marion Milner Tradition
Lines of Development: Evolution of Theory and Practice over the Decades
Edited By Margaret Boyle Spelman and Joan Raphael-Leff

The Legacy and Promise of Hans Loewald
Edited By Rosemary H. Balsam, Elizabeth A. Brett and Lawrence Levenson

The Emerging Tradition of Hans Loewald
Edited By Rosemary H. Balsam, Elizabeth A. Brett and Lawrence Levenson

The Emerging Tradition
of Hans Loewald

Edited by
Rosemary H. Balsam, Elizabeth A. Brett
and Lawrence Levenson

Routledge
Taylor & Francis Group

LONDON AND NEW YORK

Designed cover image: Main image: Hans Loewald in the 1980s; Left column: HL about 11 or 12 years old; HL in his 20s; HL, Child Guidance Clinic, University of Maryland, early 1940s; HL on vacation, 1950; HL in Baltimore. All by permission of the Loewald family.

First published 2025
by Routledge
4 Park Square, Milton Park, Abingdon, Oxon OX14 4RN

and by Routledge
605 Third Avenue, New York, NY 10158

Routledge is an imprint of the Taylor & Francis Group, an informa business

© 2025 selection and editorial matter, Rosemary H. Balsam, Elizabeth A. Brett and Lawrence Levenson; individual chapters, the contributors

British Library Cataloguing-in-Publication Data
A catalogue record for this book is available from the British Library

ISBN: 9781032685168 (hbk)
ISBN: 9781032685144 (pbk)
ISBN: 9781032685151 (ebk)

DOI: 10.4324/9781032685151

Typeset in Times New Roman
by codeMantra

Contents

Acknowledgments

I, RB, have been honored, blest, and companioned to have as my co-editors my loved colleagues Betsy Brett and Larry Levenson. They were and remain a delight on this journey on behalf of Hans. Anne Rodems, our friend and WNE administrator, was invaluably knowledgeable in helping us organize and transport our efforts across the interspace pond to Routledge.

We thank Paul Schwaber, my husband, for his loving support at all times and his deft and helpful editing skills. We all want to thank our families and close friends for their emotional encouragement. Our colleagues at WNE have uniformly been supportive and excited for us and the new Loewald Center, and some have expressed their vast admiration for Hans through their brilliant essays in this volume. From the bottom of our hearts we thank our magnificent contributors – Larry Friedman for this Preface, our supportive colleagues for their promotional statements, and all of our dear friends who so willingly poured their passions, ideas, and scholarship into these chapters; Nancy Chodorow (our adopted WNEnglander) and Jonathan Lear (our own WNEnglander) for loyally allowing us to publish their plenary talks from the Inaugural Conference of LC in April 2022. We thank Margery Kalb too, whose enthusiasm and creativity in building the Loewald Center are recoded here, and whom we applaud.

And now we together would like to thank, first among our issue editors, Joan Raphael-Leff, who was responsive to the idea of including Hans Loewald in their issue series within their noble array of psychoanalytic ancestors whose work is still seminal. The seeds of this book happened in 2017, during her visit to WNE. She was a long-admired heroine of RB for her work on women, and they finally met. The idea for this book was born. Norka Mahlberg, her issue co-editor at the time, was a member of WNE and fully aware of our pride in Loewald. Her support has been and is much valued, and that of Aleksandar Dimitrijevic. Their affirmation has been crucial to this publication.

We also would like to thank Routledge's Kate Hawes and her team who came on board for the actual publication. We have appreciated their helpful interchanges along the way.

Next we want to express our deep appreciation and ongoing pleasures in our colleagueship with the Loewald Center – Margery, Seymour, Gil, Chris, Doris, Matthew Masha, Natasha, and Angela and Guy.

Most importantly, we would like to thank the Loewald family for everything they have helped us with, especially Liz and Caroline, who, in consultation with their other family members, have so generously been enthusiastic about our efforts in supporting our requests and sharing information. As you will appreciate from reading this book, Hans was not the only gifted author with this last name! We are deeply grateful to them for their personal essays on these pages.

About the Editors and Contributors

The Editors

Rosemary H. Balsam, F.R.C. Psych., M.R.C.P., is a British medical doctor and an American psychoanalyst. She grew up in Northern Ireland, graduated Medical School at Queen's University Belfast, studied psychiatry, and moved to join the faculty of the Yale School of Medicine. She is Associate Clinical Professor of Psychiatry, Staff Psychiatrist in the Yale Department of Student Mental Health and Counseling, and a training and supervising analyst at the Western New England Institute for Psychoanalysis, New Haven, CT. Her special interests are female gender developments; young adulthood and the body in psychic life, psychoanalytic education and Hans Loewald's work. She was a member of the Executive Committee of the Loewald Center. She has written award-winning papers and books and lectured nationally and internationally. On the editorial boards of PQ and Imago, she is a former book review editor of *JAPA*. Her books are: *Becoming a Psychotherapist: A Clinical Primer; Psychodynamic Psychotherapy: The Supervisory Process; Sons of Passionate Mothering; and Women's Bodies in Psychoanalysis*, and her latest papers have been on Misogyny and the female body and Abortion. In 2018, she was a recipient of the Sigourney Award for Outstanding Psychoanalytic Achievement.

Elizabeth A. Brett, Ph.D. is in private practice in New Haven, CT and a training and supervising analyst at the Western New England Institute for Psychoanalysis. She is currently a lecturer in the Department of Psychiatry, Yale University School of Medicine and, for many years prior, an associate clinical professor of Psychiatry (Psychology) and recipient of the Outstanding Clinical Faculty Award. She conducted empirical research on combat trauma and has written research papers as well as articles on psychoanalytic perspectives on trauma. Related to this work, she served as President of the International Society for Traumatic Stress Studies. Her current scholarly interests include psychoanalytic theories of therapeutic action and technique. She is a member of Board of Directors of the Loewald Center.

Lawrence Levenson, M.D., is Training and Supervising psychoanalyst and former Chair of the Education Committee at the Western New England Institute for Psychoanalysis. He teaches individual psychotherapy and group psychotherapy at Yale University Health Services. He is a past recipient of the Menninger Prize from the American Psychoanalytic Association, and has been a Kohut Visiting Scholar at the University of Chicago and Visiting Scholar for the annual Paul Gray visiting scholar weekend. He currently is Treasurer and Board Member of the American

Board of Psychoanalysis. He is a member of the Executive Board of the Hans W. Loewald Center.

Preface

Lawrence Friedman received his M.D. from Temple University in Philadelphia, did Psychiatry Residency at the Yale University Graduate School of Medicine, and worked as Lieutenant Commander in the United States Naval Hospital, Yokosuka, Japan. He is currently in private practice of psychoanalytic psychotherapy. He is Clinical Professor of Psychiatry at the Weill-Cornell Medical College in New York City **and is** on the faculty of the Psychoanalytic Association of New York (PANY) affiliated with NYU Grossman School of Medicine. He is an honorary member of the American Psychoanalytic Association, the New York Psychoanalytic Institute and Society, and the Psychoanalytic Institute of New York. He has written and published a great deal on the theory and practice of psychoanalysis. Two of his books are *The Anatomy of Psychotherapy* and *Freud's Papers on Technique and Contemporary Clinical Practice*. His accolades include the Sigourney Award in 2012, for outstanding contributions to psychoanalysis.

Contributors

Angela Cappiello, M.D., Ph.D. is a psychiatrist and psychoanalyst in Hamden, CT. She is a training and supervising analyst at the Western New England Institute for Psychoanalysis, an assistant clinical professor in the Department of Psychiatry, Yale University School of Medicine, and a former program committee chair of the Hans Loewald Center. She has explored the concept of creativity in women, addressing the embodiment of both feminine and masculine elements as central to the development of generative authenticity. Her scholarly interests include the function of dreams in the psychoanalytic process, the history of Italian psychoanalysis, and most recently, the interface between Loewald concepts and the post-Bionian analytic field theory.

Nancy J. Chodorow, Ph.D., is Professor of Sociology, Emerita, University of California, Berkeley, Training and Supervising Analyst Emerita, Boston Psychoanalytic Institute and Society, and Faculty, San Francisco Center for Psychoanalysis. Her books include *The Reproduction of Mothering*; *Feminism and Psychoanalytic Theory*; *Femininities, Masculinities, Sexualities: Freud and Beyond*; *The Power of Feelings: Personal Meaning in Psychoanalysis, Gender and Culture*; *Individualizing Gender and Sexuality: Theory and Practice*; and *The Psychoanalytic Ear and The Sociological Eye: Toward an American Independent Tradition*. She is honored in *Nancy Chodorow and The Reproduction of Mothering: Forty Years On* (ed. P. Bueskens).

Giuseppe Civitarese, M.D., Ph.D., is a training and supervising analyst of the Italian Psychoanalytic Society, in private practice, in Pavia, Italy. He is a recipient of the 2022 Sigourney Award for Outstanding Psychoanalytic Achievement, and the 2022 Gravida Lavarone Prize. His recent books include *Psychoanalytic Field Theory: A Contemporary Introduction*, 2022; *On Arrogance: A Psychoanalytic Essay*, 2022; *The*

Hour of Birth: Psychoanalysis of the Sublime and Contemporary Art, 2020; *Vitality and Play in Psychoanalysis (with A. Ferro)*, 2022; *Sublime Subjects: Aesthetic Experience and Intersubjectivity in Psychoanalysis*, 2018. He has many more books, co-edited books, and journal publications to his credit, and he has lectured and taught internationally and extensively. A full list of his publications is available at www.giuseppecivitarese.name.

Caroline Loewald Farnham, L.C.S.W., was educated at New York University and Smith School for Social Work. Her thesis was award winning. She is in private practice and a mental health clinician at Student Health and Wellness at the University of Connecticut, Storrs. She taught graduate students at both the Universities of Connecticut and Saint Joseph. Her interests are in trauma work and non-profit community mental health.

Barbara Rosen Garber, M.A., raised in New York City, lives in Southern Vermont with her husband, and is a painter, printmaker, and installation artist. Educated in Sarah Lawrence College, and New York University, she has had fellowships from the Virginia Center for the Creative Arts (1990, 2000), the Sanskriti Foundation in New Delhi, India (2004), and was artist in residence at the American Academy in Rome, 2011. Grants include Vermont Arts Council, the National Endowment for the Arts. Garber has exhibited her work widely, for example, in The Drawing Center, NYC; the Berkshire Museum, MA; the Portland Art Museum, ME; Art in General, NYC; and The Brattleboro Museum and Art Center, VT. Recent exhibits are *Free Fall*, a drawing installation, Brattleboro Museum &Art Center, 2017, *Composition for a Yellow Wall*, Public Art Project, Dartmouth Hitchcock Medical Center, Lebanon, NH, 2015–2016.

Tsilia Glinberg, M.D., is an assistant clinical professor of Psychiatry in the Yale Medical School, working in a Yale behavioral health clinic and teaching. She is also in private practice. Dr. Glinberg received her medical degree in the former Soviet Union, Republic of Ukraine and worked for a year of internship in general medicine and infectious diseases at a hospital in the city of Mykolaiv on the Black Sea, before emigrating to the United States in 1972.

Gretchen Hermes, M.D., Ph.D., M.T.S., is the medical director of the APT Foundation, a cornerstone treatment facility for individuals with substance use disorders in New Haven and the Yale Addiction Psychiatry Fellowship's site director at the foundation. Her current research at the Yale Stress Center focuses on the effects of adrenergic receptor agonists on drug craving. She completed theological studies at Harvard Divinity School, psychoanalytic training at the Western New England Institute for Psychoanalysis where she serves on faculty and is Chair of the Continuing Education Committee. Her latest publication is Hermes G, Fogelman N, Seo D, and Sinha R, Differential effects of recent versus past traumas on mood, social support, binge drinking, emotional eating, and BMI, and on neural responses to acute stress. *Stress*, (6):686–695, 2021.

Oscar F. Hills, M.D., is a general psychiatrist and psychoanalyst in private practice in New Haven and a training and supervising analyst and current chair of the Education Committee at the Western New England Institute for Psychoanalysis.

He served for many years as Firm Director of Acute Psychiatric Services and Chief of the Psychiatric Emergency Room at the West Haven VA Hospital and retains an interest in providing a wide range of mental health care.

Margery Kalb, PsyD, is a psychologist, psychoanalyst, and supervisor in private practice in New York City. She is Faculty and Supervising Analyst at NYU's Postdoctoral Program in Psychotherapy and Psychoanalysis, where she is also emeritus Chair of the Contemporary Freudian Track. She is Co-Editor of two books: *Ghosts in the Consulting Room* and *Demons in the Consulting Room,* and author of numerous theoretical-clinical papers on ghosts, encompassing themes such as development, internalization, interpsychic and intersomatic communications, values/morality, and loss and mourning. She is a co-founder of the Hans W. Loewald Center.

Elizabeth Loewald, M.D., is now retired in Maine. She did her B.A. in Berkeley, CA, and graduated from Johns Hopkins Medical School. She is a writer and poet. The widow of Hans Loewald, M.D., she was on the faculty of the Yale Child Study Center and in private practice in child psychiatry. Her recent memoir (2022) *The Tree Grows Standing Still.*

Richard L. Munich, M.D., trained at Yale and The Western New England institute for Psychoanalysis, served in the US Air Force, and held various positions at the Yale Psychiatric Institute, the West Haven Veterans Hospital, the Westchester Division of New York Hospital. He was a training and supervising analyst at the Columbia University Center for Psychoanalytic Training & Research. He was Medical Director and Chief of Staff of The Menninger Clinic. His publications include articles on symptom formation, psychotherapy for difficult patients, hospital psychiatry, and aspects of leadership and group dynamics. He is currently located at the Psychoanalytic Center of the Carolinas.

Jenifer Nields, M.D., is an assistant clinical professor of Psychiatry at the Yale University School of Medicine and a member of the Western New England Psychoanalytic Society. She serves on the Group for the Advancement of Psychiatry's Committee on Psychiatry and Religion, and is a graduate of the New Directions program in Writing with a Psychoanalytic Edge. She has published numerous papers and book chapters on psychotherapy, supervision, psychoanalysis and religion, and the neuropsychiatric aspects of Lyme disease. Dr. Nields is in private practice in Fairfield, CT.

Nancy Olson, M.D., is a psychoanalyst and assistant professor of Psychiatry, Yale School of Medicine. After undergraduate and graduate studies in art history, she received her M.D. and psychiatric training from Yale, and her analytic training at the Western New England Institute for Psychoanalysis. She has explored psychoanalysis and art in a series of essays: "Cubism, Freud and the Image of Wit," "Pictures Into Words: Visual Models and Data in Psychoanalysis," "Bachelard Revisited," "Marion Milner: Psychoanalysis Unvented," and "Rebecca in the House: Musings on Identification."

Lorraine D. Siggins, M.D., grew up in Melbourne, Australia, graduated medical school, and came to Yale for psychiatric training. She is Clinical Professor Emeritus

Psychiatry at the Yale School of Medicine, and until recently, the director of Mental Health and Counselling Center at Yale University. She is also a training and supervising analyst at the Western New England Institute for Psychoanalysis. She has published and lectured on mourning, ritual, young adult development, and anorexia nervosa, and is on Editorial Board of *PQ*, and formerly on the editorial boards of *JAPA* and *APA*. Among her honors are the Sabshin Award for teaching, from the American Psychoanalytic Association, the Stephen Fleck prize for clinical excellence, and a teaching award from the faculty of the Yale Department of Psychiatry. An Opera lover, she has participated in lecture series at Glimmerglass Opera in Cooperstown, New York.

Doris K. Silverman, Ph.D., is a faculty member and supervisor at the NYU Postdoctoral Program for Psychotherapy and Psychoanalysis; a training and supervising analyst at IPTAR; on the editorial boards of *Psychoanalytic Psychology, Psychoanalytic Dialogues, International Psychoanalytic Journal, Psychoanalytic Review,* the *Journal of the American Psychoanalytic Association*; a former editor of the Newsletter and Newsmagazine of the International Psychoanalytic Association. Her interests are infant research and psychoanalysis, symbiosis, female development, sexuality and gender, attachment theory, and the use of empirical data to augment our therapeutic skills. Her co-authored book is *Changing Conceptions of Psychoanalysis: The Legacy of Merton M. Gill*, Routledge, 2001: recipient of the Scientific Scholar Award, American Psychological Association; the Linda Neuwirth Memorial Award, IPTAR.

Jeanine M. Vivona, Ph.D., is Professor of Psychology at The College of New Jersey. She is a member of the Editorial Boards of the *Psychoanalytic Quarterly* and *Psychoanalytic Psychology*. She has twice been awarded The *JAPA* Prize, for her 2006 article, "From Developmental Metaphor to Developmental Model: The Shrinking Role of Language in the Talking Cure" and for her 2012 article, "Is There a Nonverbal Period of Development?" She is currently working on a book focused on language and the therapeutic process, to be published by Routledge as part of the Psychoanalysis in a New Key series, edited by Donnel Stern. She maintains a private practice of psychoanalytic psychotherapy and supervision near Philadelphia.

Series Editors' Foreword

The history of psychoanalysis is one of re-visiting, rewriting, and re-integration. Hans Loewald's life and work are an example of such processes at an individual level, as he navigated the spiral of a tumultuous, at times persecutory, yet also reparative external world. These volumes demonstrate the legacy of a highly creative yet disciplined theoretical writer and clinician. Loewald's writing is poetic yet well-structured and clear in delivery, both relational and developmental in a way that was ahead of its time. As illustrated by these volumes, his writing and life's work have inspired many analysts to explore beyond the corseted bounds of ego psychology while respecting and conserving its value both theoretically and clinically.

Furthermore, as many psychoanalysts know, making a difference in the lives of colleagues and patients' lives does not require too much fanfare. What matters is the capacity not only to connect with ideas but also to approach discourse and exploration with respect, dedication, and generosity. The chapters in these volumes illustrate the multiple applications of Loewald's work to interdisciplinary thinking while still maintaining a focus on the ever-evolving interaction between primary relationships and the many iterations of the self. Such is the case for many writers in this book whose professional and personal trajectories were impacted by what seems to be Loewald's kind and collegial manner, which remains a staple of the Western New England Psychoanalytic Society and Institute to this day.

These two volumes are the last in our series 'Lines of Development' – the evolution of tradition, theory, and practice over the decades, celebrating the lives of psychoanalytic 'giants' and their legacy.

Generally, chapters are commissioned rather than reprinted and drawn from an international pool of experts in this field, rather than just those 'close to home.' Series editors Norka Malberg, Aleksandar Dimitrijevic, and Joan Raphael-Leff helped each volume in the series to follow a similar basic presentation adjusted to the needs of any specific tradition. This included a **Historical Frame** giving an overview of the tradition, its origins, historical milestones, influences, viewpoints, and inspirations for contemporary development. **Clinical Applications:** to illustrate the evolution of theory and the expansion of original concepts and applications to clinical work with children, adolescents, adults, families, and/or groups (in different parts of the world). **Outreach:** how this particular school of thought has informed the work of allied professionals and thinking in other academic disciplines and social systems outside the consulting room. Finally, **Personal Reflections:** pertinent historical recollections from active participants in the process of growth and development of its ideas.

These two volumes on Loewald differ from the overall format of other books in this series. The three co-editors are situated in one location in New Haven, CT, rather than different countries or transcontinental locations which we advocated for other volumes, to ensure a wide variety of contributors from around the world. Nonetheless, the chapters in these two books are organized with the overall philosophy of this series, bringing to the reader a survey of the author's main contributions while exploring how they emerged in the context of his personal and professional life. The reader will take a journey through the landscape of the relational, the mystical, and the divine, the creative therapeutic dyad, Loewald's life, and his voice as it resonates in the work and lives of former supervisees, training analysands, and newcomers who find their voice in the writings of a quiet yet revolutionary mind.

Lastly, this series began as a way of preserving Anna Freud's work and legacy, a quiet yet productive force in the world of psychoanalysis. For instance, although Anna Freud's thinking about 'the best interest of the child' was influential in psychoanalytic and legal circles in the United States. However, like Loewald, their unassuming and humble manner restricted wider recognition of their ideas in our contemporary world. We trust that, as with Anna Freud's volume in this series, these two books will serve to illustrate the robustness of Loewald's theoretical ideas and their clinical application, lending themselves to discovery, revisiting, creative rewriting, and re-integration.

Norka Malberg, Barcelona, Spain
Joan Raphael Leff, London, UK
Aleksandar Dimitrijevic, Vienna, Austria

Preface

For many of us, Loewald's paper on the therapeutic action of psychoanalysis burst like lightning on the gloomy riddle of how the same psychoanalytic truths that explain why patients stay stubbornly sick, will explain why a non-directive treatment will make them well. I once enthusiastically explained at a conference how Loewald brilliantly solved the riddle that had defeated all the other wise men.

I knew Loewald would see a transcript of the proceedings, and when his envelope arrived a few days later I fancied he had written something like, "I'm glad you found my work helpful." Maybe he would make a minor correction; it would show that I'd gotten him right, or at least not significantly wrong. Instead, after some courteous comments the note urged me to develop my ideas further. *My ideas! Not his!* What a classy way of saying: "Nice try, kid, but no cigar." It seemed that he wasn't about to endorse my explanation of his argument. Or so I thought. And so it may well have been. But long afterward, on re-reading my text and hearing about Loewald's famous disinterest in building a worshipful following, I see it differently. Now I think of his interchange with me as a perfect example of his attitude toward laborers in the field of psychoanalytic theorizing. I had addressed him with awe and gratitude. He encouraged me to follow my thoughts and go on working. That was it. No subtle welcome to his "school," for instance, by a seductive correction. He had done *his* work, and he was pleased that it had spurred *mine*. It was the ongoing aliveness of question and answer, problem and solution that was the point of psychoanalytic theorizing. He feared that psychoanalysis would die from contempt of theory as he saw it beginning. It was more important that I (and many others) keep thinking than that I prized his thinking. Which means that Loewald would have been happy that this book brings his work into relationship with many of our most prominent theorists and with many other realms of human experience. There are agreements and differences and, most encouragingly, new horizons sighted from his platform.

How, we may wonder, without a "school" to join or a special technique to reveal, has Loewald been able to engage so many diverse analytic enclaves and human studies? Aside from the appeal of his humane outlook and evocative presentation, what is there about Loewald's thought that attracts such widespread interest? Many unique features come to mind, but if I were to pick a prime generality, it would be this: Loewald models a vastly freer relationship to our heritage in Freud's theory. Why is that liberating? Hasn't there been abundant revision and critique after the movement's early years? And don't all the commentators feel they have a deep understanding of the theory's limits and possibilities? But it has not been easy – nor would one expect it to be – for us to take the honored Freud-ghost home, so to speak, and chat with it informally on an intimate basis.

In effect, that's what Loewald was bold enough to do. As one of the greatest masters of Freud's theory he felt free to liberate latent meanings that had been packed into the beloved – but overly familiar – Freudian idea as it echoed his own sense of things (and as often showed up explicitly in Freud's late text). He invoked the freedom to think along with Freud on equal terms. It took courage. Taking to one's own home an idea that belongs to everybody will seem confusing to many if not downright scandalous. Over time, however, I think Loewald readers sense the special pleasure in feeling at home with the revered Freud ghost, and able to collaborate on a comradely basis. For example, one's common sense is allowed to raise awkward questions about the indivisibility of mind, or the way ideas and wishes relate to each other by absorption and discrimination rather than by blunt combat. Loewald's respectful Freud scholarship legitimizes that freedom. For example, it brings out aspects of Freud that had not been developed; it allows antithetical perspectives to be tried out. That's how Loewald thought theory should always be learned, by doing it oneself along with one's predecessors. I'm pretty sure this volume would have pleased him with its variety of voices and reactions to his work.

What is an example of Loewald's comfortable relationship with Freud? His greatest liberty goes far beyond adding this or that useful idea or replacing some terms. Loewald dares to project before our eyes a *whole new portrait* of the Freudian mind – the mind as an undivided continuum of action. He places that image, like a translucent overlay, on top of Freud's familiar checkered landscape, which is the Freud that we have always known and still need – all of us including Loewald – in order to find our way around the continuum of mind.

It's a brave thing for a theorist to do. After all, psychoanalysis came into being to account for a network of conflicting aims, and it's not easy to find either a network or a conflict in an undivided continuum. But on the other hand, no one actually believes you can slice the mind into semi-autonomous parts. The mind seems to be more a "doing" than a container for smaller things to hang out in. Hence the frequent caveat of analytic writers: "Do not understand our substantial nouns and dramatic verbs too concretely." But Hans Loewald did not content himself with a cautious caveat. He continued to go along with the common sense view of the mind's immateriality just as long as he could while still navigating the specifics of Freud's theory. And so we see him continue to use – but soften up – our well-worn psychoanalytic terms – the precious terms that anchor the network of wisdom that has served us so well. He puts those terms to work where they can be given a live meaning that fits a flowing continuum of mental activity like the mind. He will no longer ask that we pretend that aspects of mind are like organs, each dedicated to distinct and contrasting purposes.

We can feel subtle liberation in this change. One of the hidden functions of high theory is to create a desirable cognitive attitude in analysts and patients. While the sharp classical intrapsychic divisions lend firmness to the model, they fill the atmosphere with a grim, liturgical solemnity. Loewald's Holism softens the stiff "disciplinary" quality of the classical Freudian distinctions. There are fewer Either/Or' s such as: "It's either a libidinal or a self-enhancing aim" (Loewald suggests they go together). Or: "One is either bravely facing up to a conflict, or dodging a decision by a distraction." (Loewald holds that the "dodge" may actually be the more progressive move.)

In the absence of reified mental entities about which to reason, the faculty of intuition is welcomed back in crucial junctures, for instance Loewald asks analysts to sense the type of immediate impact a fruitful intervention has had on a patient. He draws a picture of mind stuff interacting in mind-like ways, for example, by absorption and discrimination rather than by head-on collisions. And we're comfortable with effects emerging from earlier states and, not only from separable causes.

Not even the separate moments of time stay neatly divided in their deadly erasures and replacements. The human mind makes moments come together in lasting durations as steady stages for the dramas of life and culture to make their point, and to allow concepts to spread themselves out for science to deploy. We can even find a specious present lasting from past to future in a single vision of eternity and timelessness.

Improved reality testing has always been an aim of psychoanalytic treatment, but that aim could never be clearly defined because, as perceived, human reality always wears an intuitive, subjective gloss. What psychoanalysts mean by reality had to wait for a holist like Loewald to spell out. So Loewald was able to give reality testing a natural meaning for the first time.

Objective and subjective meanings are blended in human reality and it's hard to separate them in theorizing. The awkwardness troubled both Freud and Loewald yet both accepted the linguistic inconsistency *faut de mieux*. The practical necessity of hybrid descriptions proved to be more realistic than either a purely objective or purely subjective description alone. It makes for a more life-like model of the mind and we feel freer to "handle" it in our theorizing. I suggest that this greater acceptance of necessary linguistic *inconsistency* is what allowed Loewald to express theoretically what we all know tacitly about our mind. And when Loewald carefully superimposes his more holistic view on top of Freud's extensively articulated theory, the view is truly exhilarating. We now have exciting new ways to exploit psychoanalytic theory within the clinical realm and in all human realities.

Lawrence Friedman, M.D., New York, U.S.A.

Introduction

All of us influenced personally by this great scholar of psychoanalysis, we three editors want to present a comprehensive set of essays based on the work of our distinguished late colleague, the psychoanalyst, Hans Loewald (1906–1993).

We present two books that hopefully could be read together, or can stand alone. They will have the same introduction as they were created at the same time, except for the details of the content of each. The other volume is called *The Legacy and Promise of Hans Loewald*. This volume is called *The Emerging Tradition of Hans Loewald*.

"The Legacy" tells about Loewald's work, the history of its reception in North American psychoanalysis, its foundational philosophical influences, and its clinical dimension. His obituary concludes this work. The "Emerging Tradition" locates his oeuvre as forming a tradition that stands among the other major figures of our field, represented in the volumes of Routledge's "Lines of Development" series. "The Emerging Tradition" explores Loewald's interdisciplinary application and potential contribution to sociology, anthropology, comparative theories such as Italian field theory, Bion or Laplanche, language theory, music, religion, art, creativity, culture, feminism, and gender studies; to the latest neurobiology and psychodelic treatments; and to ideas of the origins of life. His person is animated at the conclusion of the work by his students, analysands, colleagues, and family members.

We want to showcase his thinking about psychoanalysis, as reflected by all these contributors who are significant authors in our field, and who have found different aspects of his work vital to their own understandings of analysis. We passionately want to demonstrate the value of Loewald's thinking as a contribution to the contemporary field of psychoanalysis. Hans Loewald's efforts to re-interpret Freud always sought for even more complexity and subtlety within the initial expansive framework already provided. We want to show elaborations of Loewald's work that allow one to see how quietly influential he has become, although somewhat vaguely, implicitly, and disparately focused within the general literature at the present time. We would like his explicit influence on our field to become more recognized and familiar to readers. With these rich essays we therefore hope to encourage and invite the field to focus more intensely on his work, to search its depths for guidance, inspiration and help in grasping what may well be at stake for a newer world of the present century, with its huge changes in global communication, baffling uncertainties and instabilities, and more questions than answers in every walk of life.

These essays demonstrate Loewald's thrust in opening aspects of a theory of mind that readily can include processes that are founded on psychic development through every phase of the life cycle; a theory of mind that concerns itself with origins, love, aggression, and nature; with living, imagination, and culture; that shows psychoanalysis as a clinical therapy, enriches and is enriched by philosophy, science, religion, and the arts. His open analytic thinking transcends and does not exclude any particular school of psychoanalysis. Loewald currently, we believe, offers many useful conceptual tools for the consolidation and advancement of analytic thinking further into the 21st century and the future.

The significant books by Loewald and on Loewald are few and listed below. The last book on Loewald was published over twenty years ago – a collection of his work published in 2000, edited by Norman Quist, with a brilliant and helpful introduction about the essence of his thought, written by Jonathan Lear. That book was based on his collected works that had been published by Yale Press in 1979, together with two of his monographs: *Psychoanalysis and the History of the Individual: The Freud Lectures at Yale University* (1978) and *Sublimation: Inquiries into Theoretical Psychoanalysis* (1988). In 1991, Gerald Fogel published a book that contains some key commentaries on Loewald's work. Here is a list of the few books:

Loewald, H (1979) *Papers on Psychoanalysis.* New Haven, CT: London Yale University Press.
Fogel, G (ed.) (1991) *The Work of Hans Loewald: Introduction and Commentary.* Hillsdale, NJ: Jason Aronson.
Loewald, H (2000) *The Essential Loewald: Collected Papers and Monographs.* (with an Introduction by Jonathan Lear) ed. N. Quist. Hagerstown. MD: University Publishing Group.

There have been some panels in the national analytic scene over the years. For example, one occurred at the Western New England Institute for Psychoanalysis, where Hans was present, to celebrate his birthday. It was published by the *Psychoanalytic Study of the Child* in 1989, Vol 44. A panel at the American Psychoanalytic Association was published in the *Journal of the American Psychoanalytic Association*, 1996, Vol 44; and another one was published in the same journal in 2008, Vol 56. The last one, again by the Western New England Institute, was published in the *Psychoanalytic Study of the Child* in 2018, Vol 71. Each panel noted that he was a major creative thinker who had, up to that point, been undervalued, and predicted the field's major future appreciation for his contributions.

There is specific evidence about a gap between the awe that his stature inspires (in the abstract), if mentioned at conferences, and yet, a notable lack of teaching and reading his actual work. Looking at the statistics on the PEP web archive. Donald Winnicott, for example, the most popular writer, has many thousands of all his papers downloaded per year. Thomas Ogden, as an example of a contemporary influential writer and thinker, has statistics also in the thousands, for several papers. Loewald's "On the Therapeutic Action of Psychoanalysis" (1960) – the paper by far the best known and read – is comparable in downloads to Ogden's third- or fourth-tier papers. His other papers fall off precipitously. We assume that these downloads reflect especially the papers that analytic teachers assign for classes, rather than necessarily for personal research. We worry that a lack of exposure to his work may leave too many analysts uninformed about his interesting approaches and exciting ideas that they may actually find ground-breaking.

We believe there are many reasons for the enthusiasm that his name inspires, yet it co-exists with a neglect of his oeuvre. The usual suspects are that he gives exceptionally few clinical examples; his technical language is too close to Freud's; and he is dense and overly intellectual to read. We agree only that he gave few case examples. There are other factors as well. Loewald had a long-standing antipathy for fostering any "school" of followers devoted to him alone. Unlike Melanie Klein, Heinz Kohut, or Jacques Lacan, say, he shied away from such promulgations on his own behalf. He did not travel to promote his ideas and teach his point of view like Anna Freud, Wilfred Bion, or the contemporary Kleinians. Winnicott was often on radio broadcasts in the United Kingdom, which may have contributed to his household name recognition. Mitchell, the relationists, Ogden, and others are modern users of the internet, where their work is helpfully disseminated. Not so Loewald. Consequently, he has remained "local," is best known within the United States, and likely more on the East Coast, where he made his home. The time has come to launch efforts to draw attention to the attractiveness and usefulness of his ideas and approach, despite his self-limiting activity during his lifetime.

In 2021, just before the Covid pandemic, some colleagues from the IPTAR called us at WNEIP with a thrilling invitation – to join with them in founding and creating a "Loewald Center" (the LC). Margery Kalb, Gil Katz and Seymour Moskovitz from the LC, and we three from WNEIP, with Doris Silverman, Matthew Von Unwerth and Christopher Christian from IPTAR, formed the founding Executive Committee of the new LC. After multiple delays due to trying to conduct it in vivo but finally deciding on a Zoom event, we had our Inaugural Conference in April 2022. We were delighted with the enthusiasm of presenters and also our responsive national and international audience. The organizational structure of this virtual center, beyond its foundation now, is a work in progress. It is dedicated to promoting the style of open thinking that Loewald brought to our field and that is generative toward innovations that are based on past substantial thinking. Some series of successful presentations have occurred in the past year. We encourage readers to look at the website, loewaldcenter.org, to find out what is going on.

For those who already know his writings, we hope you join in future discussions of the chapters of both of these books that we have edited simultaneously and feel encouraged to use and build upon his work. And for those readers who have not encountered him before, we wish you joy in the discovery of a great mind, and a creative master of psychoanalysis.

The Content of This Book

This book is divided into two sections. Part I is called *Developing Loewald*. And Part II covers *Personal Loewald*.

The Preface has been written by Lawrence Friedman, whose first introduction to Loewald's ideas on therapeutic action "burst like lightning on the gloomy riddle of how the same psychoanalytic truths that explain why patients stay stubbornly sick will explain why a non-directive treatment will make them well." With his signature verve and cogency, Freidman's expansive appreciation opens the way for the plethora of creative ideas that will follow, inspired by Loewald, as was Friedman.

"Developing Loewald" opens with Nancy Chodorow's morning plenary lecture to the Inaugural Conference of the Loewald Center on April 21, 2022. This is an inspiring and illuminating account of the steps of her own involvement with Loewald's writings, from her early Berkeley doctoral thesis that became her famous "Reproduction of Mothering" book of the feminist era of 1978. The telling of her own career traces how adaptable and well-suited Hans Loewald's work on human development is for use in anthropology, sociology, and feminism. She has applied Loewaldian theory in her own ground-breaking work on gender, and she credits his influence as a factor in attracting her to add psychoanalytic training to her knowledge base about individuals, in the latter portion of her career. The next chapter is by Guiseppe Civitarese and Angela Cappiello, who join together to look closely at post-Bionian field theory, reformulations of the concept of sublimation by Loewald in his last work and by Civitarese in a recent series of articles. Loewald had anticipated some aspects of Bion's and post-Bionian theories of the field, and in this essay, the authors use moments of engagement in a clinical vignette to examine the similarities between Loewald's "oneness regained" and Civitarese's elaboration of the concept of "at-one-ment." The post-Bionian theory of the analytic field examines Loewald's thought and mutually allows itself to be examined. The fruitfulness of this dialogue demonstrates the relevance of Loewald's theories for contemporary psychoanalysis. Doris Silverman continues the international dialogue by comparing the theories of Hans Loewald and Jean Laplanche. These two sophisticated scholars and abstract theoreticians prized Freud's model of the mind and his commitment to the power of sexuality in shaping it. In their approach to theoretical psychoanalysis, there are overlapping agreements as well as wide disparities. Their divergences lead to alternative ideas in their clinical thinking about development. Silverman underscores these differing ideas in a clinical example illustrating the polymorphous perverse features of infantile sexuality as interpreted by these two men. Jeanine Vivona does an exquisite job of looking closely at Loewald's uses of language, affording his readers a sense of how to be as an analyst who thinks as he does. For Loewald, language participates in meaning and relating from the beginning of life and, conversely, personal patterns of relating are written into language. Because the medium of psychoanalysis is speech, these patterns and meanings are active in the interpersonal actions of talking and listening at the heart of psychoanalysis. The author demonstrates correspondences between Loewald's theory and contemporary understanding of infant development regarding the inherently experiential and relational nature of language. By situating experience within language, Loewald offers psychoanalysis an understanding of speaking and listening that invites us to move forward toward a more integrated and whole version of our field. The missing link in Nancy Olson's chapter, "A Missing Link: Hans Loewald and Marion Milner," found and brilliantly explored by Olson, is the similarity between Loewald's thought and that of Milner in their concern with the maternal-infant field in development and recapitulated in analytic treatment. In her essay, Olson contributes valuable biographical material about Milner, including the influence of American management consultant Mary Parker Follet on Milner's thinking. Milner and Loewald, Olson shows, share a view of the individual in creative relation to the world beginning in the early maternal-infant matrix. Olson concludes: "Milner says: 'Without our own contribution we see nothing.' Thus Loewald's close reading of Freud gives us a new Loewald and a newly meaningful Freud." Twenty years ago, Jenifer Nields published an important, much-cited article in which she showed that Loewald's understanding of ego development offered a way to conceptualize religious experience as an enrichment, rather than, as Freud held, a defensive regression of the ego. In her chapter, Nields builds on and expands her earlier contribution, demonstrating parallels between Loewald's theory of ego development and the human experience of the divine as represented by the three Abrahamic religious traditions. Nields ends her chapter with a discussion of music in which she proposes that Loewald's thinking helps us to understand how music, like religion, has the potential to represent a movement toward transcendence. Lorraine Siggins also deepens the study of Loewald's interest in religion as an aspect of psychic life by discussing three papers – a very early paper (1953) that was part of a lecture series on "Christianity and Psychoanalysis," given in Washington, DC, and a second paper, written more than twenty years later (1978) – one of the Freud Lectures at Yale university. She then takes up his wonderful and mysterious late paper, "Psychoanalysis in Search of Nature" (1988). The discussions show his deep interest in religion. Gretchen Hermes shows us the exciting 21st century vast reach of Loewald's theoretical relevance to the neurobiology of the new treatments that use psychedelic drugs under controlled conditions, to induce regressive, ecstatic states, and also the ecstatic states of drug addiction. She uses the voices of participants, those writing about their experiences on drugs, psychoanalysis, and everyday life to demonstrate the deep resonances with Loewald's theories of the desire for archaic merger and transcendence, and the resource and sustenance that this well of creativity can have for ego functioning at a higher level. Oscar Hills brings this section to a close with his piece "Origins (Life after Oedipus)." Hills takes the reader on an exhilarating, wide-ranging intellectual excursion into ways that Loewald's thought mirrors advances in the physical and natural sciences. Drawing upon the views of recent scientific and philosophical thinkers, Hills shows their convergence with Loewald's world view. The powerful case vignette that ends the paper brings Hills's thinking about Loewald, science, and origins into a clinical context. As much as any chapter in this volume, Hills's essay demonstrates how Loewald's writings inspire novel, intrepid, engaging (and witty) scholarship among his psychoanalyst readers.

Part II, "Personal Loewald," is about the man himself as a father, teacher, analyst, and husband. There is a beautiful essay first, from his youngest child Caroline, about what it was like to have Hans as a father, and his influence upon her. This precious piece brings him to life. These contributions from family members are exquisitely experience-near in living with and loving Hans. It is true that he hated Heidegger's Nazism. Lying under the piano while Mother played Beethoven as a "memory" is apparently murky, but he did love music. We know that in his theory building, early perceptual tonalities and mourning were crucial states of mind. A few other brief and moving comments by analysands Barbara Rosen Garber and Tsilia Glinberg, and supervisee Richard Munich, show how he touched us professionally during his life. Looking toward our engagement in his future influences, Margery Kalb, who receives all our thanks and credit as visionary and driving force for the Hans W. Loewald Center has contributed an expanded version of the introduction she delivered at the inaugural conference of the Center. Her essay is at once an exuberant celebration of the creation of the Loewald Center and an elegant exposition of Loewald's thought.

She elaborates on ways that Loewald was a quiet revolutionary and creative synthe-sizer in his theoretical-clinical thinking and posits that in his very specific ideas about development Loewald offers a legacy that is uniquely suited to serve as a touchstone for contemporary applications of psychoanalysis.

As the final voice in our book, we have words of blessing for these forms of struc-turing his magnificent work with an eye to the future, from his second wife, Elizabeth, who is now one hundred years old. She is a lively presence, residing in Maine. She writes of a brief and lyrically intimate encounter with an aspect of Hans. She is a writer, poet and was a child psychiatrist, who shared an office suite with one of the editors (RB), in the same building as Hans, at 65 Trumbull St. (an 1893 late 19thc. Ro-manesque Revival house, in New Haven, Ct.). Recently she finished and published an elegant and moving memoir of her life, "The Tree grows by Standing Still: A memoir."

We have thus chosen to share something personal about who he was, to bring these two books to a close.

Rosemary H. Balsam, M.D., F.R.C.P. (London); M.R.C.P. (Edinboro)
Elizabeth A. Brett, Ph.D.
Lawrence Levenson, M.D.
Western New England Institute for Psychoanalysis,
255 Bradley St., New Haven, CT 0510, USA.

Part I

Developing Loewald

Chapter 1

On the Therapeutic Action of Reading Loewald, Then to Now

Nancy J. Chodorow

For some of us, academics, analysts, and those who are both, the discovery of Hans Loewald was transformative, and with each encounter we discover more. Here is a capacious thinker, who ranges from precise attunement to what it means, emotionally and existentially, for a person from infancy to old age to be centered upon, to fine-tuned insight into what constitutes an intersubjective encounter. From Loewald, we have a portrayal of an ego and reality that unfold from the infant's initial creation of meaning to the challenges of self-recognition and self-acceptance brought by the lifelong "waning of the Oedipus complex." In this chapter, I describe my own formulations and readings of Loewald over the years, focusing on Loewald's psychoanalytic vision, and how this vision, in all its facets, helps to found intersubjective ego psychology, an American independent tradition.

I am lucky, at least so far, to come from a family with some longevity, and to have been given permission throughout to follow my intellectual passions. I am a sociologist who became a psychoanalyst, which for many years was not easy on either side of that professional divide. I first read and fell in love with Loewald in 1971, and now, thanks to the devotion (to use Loewald's words, the love and respect) that many of us feel for Loewald, and thanks to the tireless commitment of some, psychoanalysis and the academy have a Loewald Center. We can *center upon Loewald*. For each of us who has known, or known about, Loewald for many years, it is overwhelming, as we (as I) reflect upon and try to convey all that we admire and love in Loewald's writings. I was thrilled the one time that I met Loewald, someone whose writings I had drawn upon throughout my career. In 1985, I was invited by Robert Wallerstein to a small conference, about twenty people, at the Menninger Foundation in Topeka. In the group photo, Loewald is found with Serge Lebovici and Eric Trist just in front of him, and John Bowlby and Joseph Kovacs just behind (Figure 1.1).

For me to fulfill the challenge of writing about Loewald, what finally seemed doable was to take a page or two (or many) from Loewald himself, to think, as Loewald did, developmentally. I thought about his first writing, "Ego and Reality" (1951/1980), where he avers that the child creates self and other, drives and ego, from her own subjectivity, through to "The Waning of the Oedipus Complex" (1979/1980), and then to *Psychoanalysis and the History of the Individual* (1978) and *Sublimation* (1988), how we transform our lives in our personal historical setting, through our emotion- and transference-creating minds. My solution was to look back on my own developmental history with Loewald, my discoveries and rediscoveries from first reading through rereading and writing on Loewald over the course of a long career. I look back on a lifetime with Loewald.

DOI: 10.4324/9781032685151-2

Figure 1.1 At 1985 Menninger Foundation Conference in Topeka, Kansas. Nancy Chodorow on right. Reprinted by permission of the Kansas State Historical Society.

I remember well where I first encountered Loewald. As a graduate student, I was fortunate that the Boston Psychoanalytic Institute decided – I know not how, but I am sure that Loewald would agree that this should be part of every psychoanalytic institute's community presence – to offer a free bi-weekly seminar for local graduate students. In that seminar, we were assigned "Internalization, Separation, Mourning and the Superego" (1962/1980). As I sat at a table in the reading room at Harvard's Widener Library along with another seminar member, my colleague looked up and rasped, in a reading room voice but with great excitement:

> Nancy, listen to this!! Loewald says, 'The deepest root of the ambivalence that appears to pervade all relationships, external as well as internal, seems to be the polarity inherent in individual existence of individuation and 'primary narcissistic' union….' He's talking about the *meaning of life*!

My reflections here are dedicated to the memory of this ancestor, never a ghost, Hans Loewald, who met me just exactly where I needed to be met some fifty-plus years ago, and who has accompanied me internally, at the appropriate developmental level, ever since.

I begin with my 1974 dissertation, "Family Structure and Feminine Personality: The Reproduction of Mothering." I notice the obvious: this was a psychoanalytic feminist dissertation on female development, mother-daughter relations, and what I named the reproduction of mothering, presented to a department of sociology. "Internalization,

Separation, Mourning and the Superego" is in the bibliography, but unfortunately (internet Luddite that I am), I do not know how to search for the cite or quote in the text itself. In *The Reproduction of Mothering* (1978), there is a chapter, "Post-Oedipal gender personality," in which I discuss how Oedipal resolution is both tenacious and might shift. Here, we find a footnote (p.164):

> I have discussed the resuscitation [of the Oedipus complex] in adolescence for girls. Bibring describes a similar process in pregnancy, as does Benedek for "parenthood as a developmental phase." Loewald suggests that the process of analysis also leads to the reexternalization of internalized or introjected objects and their reworking through and reinternalization, in such a way that there is often a radical change in mental structure.

The citation remains "Internalization, Separation," though the bibliography lists "On internalization." We do not even find "The Waning of the Oedipus Complex."

My next book is published in 1989. *Feminism and Psychoanalytic Theory* is a collection mainly of feminist papers that draw upon British object-relations theory. These papers were all written before I began analytic training. There is a chapter on Herbert Marcuse and Norman O. Brown called "Beyond drive theory: Object relations and the limits of radical individualism," and another entitled "Toward a relational individualism: The mediation of self through psychoanalysis." "Relational individualism," we see in retrospect, foreshadows both relational psychoanalysis and what I eventually name intersubjective ego psychology, with Loewald a founding theorist. My introduction describes the trajectory of my writing, its origins in Marxism and the New Left, psychoanalytic sociology and anthropology, and my looking to psychoanalysis to understand sexuality and gender. I describe a turn to what I call "psychoanalysis-in-itself": "[I am] hooked, have fallen intellectually in love" (p.8). I oscillate among feminism, psychoanalytic feminism, and psychoanalysis, and I name those who currently influence my thinking: Klein, Winnicott, and Mahler. Then, seemingly out of nowhere, Loewald (Chodorow, 1989, pp.10–13):

> Among psychoanalysts, Hans Loewald perhaps best expresses an evenhanded ability to see fully the promises and limitations of what we conventionally think of as early developmental and later developmental stances like connection and separation. He wants us to rethink these stances and to move beyond associating them with regressive and progressive moments in human development and human psychological life. He also ties these more directly than either Mahler or the object-relations theorists not only to powerful affects but also to drive derivatives. In a relatively early paper, he writes:
>   As we explore these various modes of separation and union, it becomes more and more apparent that the ambivalence of love-hate and of aggression-submission (sadism-masochism) enters into all of them and that neither separation nor union can ever be entirely unambivalent. The deepest root of the ambivalence that appears to pervade all relationships, external as well as internal, seems to be the polarity inherent in individual existence of individuation and "primary narcissistic" union.
>
> (1980, p.264)

Such a reading of development and psychic life enables Loewald to resolve a number of theoretical and clinical problems. He can move beyond the traditional privileging of Oedipal development as a more advanced stage without reverting to the sometime anti-Oedipal tendency of cultural critics and feminists who tend to see only pre-Oedipal modes of connectedness as a model for a desirable human life. He overcomes the tendency in object-relations thinkers and other theorists of early development like Mahler and Kohut to be unable to integrate their approach into Oedipal theory. These theorists tend simply to add on classical assumptions about Oedipal drive, ego and superego development to their broadly object-relational theories, based on different metapsychological premises, of early development, and to hold an implicit developmental model that the analysis of pre-Oedipal issues in adults is a residual necessity for those patients who need to be brought up to the Oedipal stage. For Loewald, "Oedipal" projects of individuation and morality and "pre-Oedipal" concerns with boundaries, separation, connection and the transitional space continue throughout life:

[psychoanalysis] seems to stand and fall with the proposition that the emergence of a relatively autonomous individual is the culmination of human development. How this may come about, and what interferes with such an outcome, resulting in psychopathology, is a most important aspect of psychoanalytic research, reconstruction, and treatment....

On the other hand, owing in part to analytic research, there is a growing awareness of the force and validity of another striving, that for unity, symbiosis, fusion, merging, or identification – whatever name we wish to give to this sense of and longing for nonseparateness and undifferentiation...

The Oedipus complex is a constituent of normal psychic life of the adult, and as such is active again and again. A psychotic core, related to the earliest vicissitudes of the ambivalent search for primary narcissistic unity and individuation, also is an active constituent of normal psychic life.

(Loewald, 1980, pp.401–403)

Returning from Loewald, I continue (Chodorow, 1989, p.12):

Echoing both Freud, in his invocation of the Oedipal killing of the father and subsequent instigation of guilt, and Klein, in his focus on the desire to repair or atone toward the other rather than simply to criticize and undermine the self, Loewald describes the psychoanalytic contribution to our understanding of morality:

'If without the guilty deed of parricide there is no individual self worthy of that name, no advanced internal organization of psychic life, then guilt and atonement are crucial motivational elements of the self [Loewald, 1979, p.394].'

My own recent thinking about the psychoanalytic contribution to our understanding of self, meaning, and experience is indebted to Loewald. This growing appreciation of his writing may be partly a result of my psychoanalytic clinical training, which has focused me more on the psychoanalytic dialogue and less on the psychoanalytic story of development and the early dialogue of mother and child. Loewald's writing bridges and sees as parallel these two sometimes disparate dialogues. He indicates for us the often-missing connection between psychoanalytic practice, psychoanalytic theory, and the potential uses and applications of that theory in other fields.

Loewald is certainly familiar to psychoanalysts, as he has been a consistently productive and wide-ranging psychoanalytic writer for several decades. He is highly respected within the profession but until recently has not been particularly lionized, adulated, or seen as a theoretical leader [At this point, I footnote Arnold Cooper and suggest that Cooper's is, "to my knowledge, the first article to make Loewald's work its explicit subject." I add "Like Cooper, I quote extensively from Loewald, because the power and profundity of his approach is found not just in the gist of what he says but in his precise literary usage." [I continue],

[Loewald] is not associated with a specific theoretical tradition and is not seen as an independent innovator, maverick, or rebel. There are no (at least not yet) "Loewaldians," as there are Winnicottians, Kohutians, or Mahlerians. Indeed, he himself seems to be an insistent synthesizer rather than polarizer within psychoanalytic discourse, committed to and able to maintain himself as a drive theorist, ego psychologist and object-relations theorist who respects self psychology, while also remaining fully enmeshed in the clinical situation that ultimately provides psychoanalysis its truths. Psychoanalytic feminists and other psychoanalytic social or cultural critics have not drawn much upon his work. Here, I cannot do justice to the Loewaldian *oeuvre*, but I indicate some of those directions in his thinking that I think show most promise for an expanded psychoanalytic sociology and psychoanalytic understanding of the life course, and, thereby, an expanded psychoanalytic feminism as well.

Loewald seems particularly able to capture the ways that unconscious processes resonate with conscious, and thus give conscious life depth and richness of meaning. As he does so, he gives us a vision of intersubjectivity deeply imbued with multiply tiered ways to understand and experience self and other. Against those who would maintain a negative view of transference as something that interferes with the reality of daily life, as well as those who would idealize the unconscious, he argues:

far from being... 'the enduring monument of man's profound rebellion against reality and his stubborn persistence in the ways of immaturity,' transference is the 'dynamism' by which the instinctual life of man, the id, becomes ego and by which reality becomes integrated and maturity is achieved. Without such transference – of the intensity of the unconscious, of the infantile ways of experiencing life that have no language and little organization, but the indestructibility and power of the origins of life – to the preconscious and to present-day life and contemporary objects – without such transference, or to the extent to which such transference miscarries, human life become sterile and an empty shell. On the other hand, the unconscious needs present-day external reality (objects) and present-day psychic reality (the preconscious) for its own continuity, lest it be condemned to live the shadow life of ghosts or to destroy life.

(1960/1980, p.250)

Similarly, he links, rather than opposes, fantasy and reality, and claims that these give meaning one to the other – here, a favorite Loewald citation by me and others:

But fantasy is unreal only insofar as its communication with present actuality is inhibited or severed. To that extent, however, present actuality is unreal too. Perhaps a better word than 'unreal' is 'meaningless.' In the analytic process the infantile fantasies and memories, by being linked up with the present actuality of the analytic situation and the analyst, regain meaning and may be reinserted within the stream of total mental life. Thereby they may resume that growth process (an element of which we call sublimation) which was interrupted or interfered with at an earlier time, leading to neurosis. At the same time, as the present actuality of the analytic situation is being linked up with infantile fantasies, this present gains or regains meaning, i.e., that depth of experience which comes about by its live communication with the infantile roots of experience. The disruption of that communication is the most important aspect of the problem of defense, of repression, isolation, etc.

(1975/1980, pp.362–363)

As I conclude my discussion of Loewald, I briefly reintroduce feminism, saying "This connection of transference and current relationship, of fantasy and reality, of rational and irrational, itself turns back upon the psychoanalytic enterprise (and upon any enterprise, like that of psychoanalytic feminism, that draws upon psychoanalysis)." (Chodorow, 1989, p.13). After one sentence, however, I return to Loewald:

While it has been [psychoanalysis's] intent to penetrate unconscious mentality with the light of rational understanding, it also has been and is its intent to uncover the irrational unconscious sources and forces motivating and organizing conscious and rational mental processes... unconscious processes became accessible to rational understanding, and at the same time rational thought itself and our rational experience of the world as an 'object world' became problematic.

(Loewald, 1979/1980, p.402)

Without a break, with no sense of contradiction, I return to feminism: "This volume traces my thoughts about the relations between feminism and psychoanalytic theory over the past twenty years...." (1989, p.13). In 1989, then, the object world and Loewald on the one side and psychoanalytic feminism as a complementary other.

Before moving decades, I notice an important parallel track to reading Loewald: teaching Loewald in the university. My initial recognition of Loewald came not from my analytic identity but from the fact that I, like my library reading partner, had early on discovered Loewald's intellectual kinship with my sociology professors at Brandeis. These were German-Jewish refugees with theoretical origins in phenomenology and social-philosophical thought (see Coser, 1984). They were respectful of psychoanalysis (this would also have been true in other social science departments that welcomed refugee intellectuals – NYU, The New School for Social Research, UC Berkeley). Some were Western Marxists interested in theories of subjectivity and intersubjectivity.

At the University of California, Berkeley, I taught Loewald to graduate students. Loewald had himself recognized the linkage between his own thinking and that of the social sciences. As he reminded me when we met, he had invited Talcott Parsons to a conference on internalization (see Loewald, 1973/1980, p.69). My students, qualitative sociologists whose work was based on interviewing or participant observation, wanted to know how to think about the people they would interview or observe and how to conceptualize the research encounter, its intersubjectivity, its transference and countertransference. They recognized Loewald's formulations as theirs. How rewarding, to teach Loewald to students in the social sciences, for them to understand his intellectual roots, how much he thought in ways akin to some of the mid-century sociologists. Here, Loewald might be describing the social scientist at work:

> The scientific fiction ... of a field of study to which we are in the relation of extraneous observers cannot be maintained in psychoanalysis. We become part and participant of and in the field as soon as we are present in our roles as analysts. The unit of psychoanalytic investigation is the individual human mind or personality. We single it out – for reasons deeply rooted in that human mind of which we ourselves are specimens – as a subject worthy of study, as a universe in its own right.... The object of investigation, the analysand, as well as the investigator, the analyst, although each has a considerable degree of internal psychic organization and relative autonomy in respect to the other, can enter a psychoanalytic investigation only by virtue of their being relatively open systems, and open to each other.
>
> (1980, p.278)

I have another teaching memory, in another academic domain. For several years, I co-taught a graduate seminar, "Psychoanalysis and literature," with the late Janet Adelman, psychoanalytic Shakespeare scholar and author of *Suffocating Mothers: Fantasies of Maternal Origin in Shakespeare's Plays, Hamlet to the Tempest* (1992). Our seminar proceeded as we started with our sole Freud reading, "Mourning and Melancholia," and then progressed to Klein with *King Lear*, Winnicott with *The Winter's Tale*, and, finally, Loewald with Toni Morrison's *Beloved*. Ghosts into ancestors.

The Therapeutic Action of Reading Loewald from 1989 to 1999, from Feminism and Psychoanalytic Theory to the Power of Feelings: Personal Meaning in Psychoanalysis, Gender, and Culture

In *The Power of Feelings: Personal Meaning in Psychoanalysis, Gender and Culture* (Chodorow, 1999), Loewald is second only to Freud in index citations. I describe him as a beacon of clarity, brilliance, and inspiration, documenting as powerfully as anyone what I am increasingly trying to clarify about psychic life and development, and leading eventually to my naming of intersubjective ego psychology: how can the analyst be both deeply involved and yet always attentive to the *patient*'s transference, fantasy and personhood, to the *one-person* elements in psychoanalysis and psychic life? In a chapter on transference called "Creating personal meaning," I write (p.18):

> Loewald begins his discussion of transference from the analytic encounter itself, foreshadowing a perspective that has moved to the forefront of American psychoanalysis. Against a traditional view of the uninvolved, neutral, evenly hovering analyst he poses an inevitably two-person relationship constructed through the feelings and intellect both parties bring to the encounter. In his classic paper, "On

the Therapeutic Action of Psychoanalysis," he speculates about why this interaction, which takes place on many levels of psychic integration and disintegration for both patient and analyst, has been overlooked:

Apart from the difficulty for the analyst of self-observation while in interaction with his patient, there seems to be a specific reason, stemming from theoretical bias.... The theoretical bias is the view of the psychic apparatus as a closed system. Thus, the analyst is seen, not as a co-actor on the analytic stage in which the childhood development, culminating in the infantile neurosis, is restaged and reactivated in the development, crystallization and resolution of the transference neurosis, but as a reflecting mirror, albeit of the unconscious, and characterized by scrupulous neutrality.

(Loewald, 1960/1980, p.223)

The analytic encounter, in Loewald's view, is characterized by transference and countertransference, the analyst's as well as the patient's emotion and fantasy: "The analyst's emotional investment, acknowledged or not by either party, is a decisive factor in the curative process.... If a capacity for transference... is a measure of the patient's analyzability, the capacity for countertransference is a measure of the analyst's ability to analyze" (Loewald, 1986, pp.285–286).

Whether countertransference is seen as the analyst's reaction to the patient's transferences, as any feeling or reaction on the part of the analyst to the relationship or to events within it, or as the analyst's transfer of unconscious to conscious or past to present in the analytic encounter and in the creation of the analytic space, the recognition and theorizing of countertransference move us further toward seeing the inevitably object-relational character of transference, the complex and continual creation of interpersonal and intrapsychic meaning, within the analysis and by implication within life. As Loewald puts it, transference and countertransference are "two faces of the same dynamic, rooted in the inextricable intertwinings with others in which individual life originates and remains throughout the life of the individual in numberless elaborations, derivatives, and transformations" (Loewald, 1986, p.276).

The concluding chapter of *The Power of Feelings* is entitled "Psychoanalytic Visions of Subjectivity." I allude to Freud's "where id was, there ego shall become" and "making the unconscious conscious," and I consider Erikson, Ogden, and Winnicott. But I return to Loewald. Chapter epigraphs (p.239) bring together a writer on music and Loewald (I did not know at the time of Loewald's pianist mother). In *Opera and Its Symbols*, Robert Donington claims, "I shall be concerned particularly with layers which may underlie our conscious experience, giving it an added glow." Similarly, Loewald avers, "Our present, current experiences have intensity and depth to the extent to which they are in communication (interplay) with the unconscious, infantile, experiences representing the indestructible matrix of all subsequent experiences" (Loewald, 1980, p.251). I write, in 1999,

About fifteen years ago, I began to keep track of particular psychoanalytic formulations that I called "meaning of life" statements. These were rarely topic statements of articles or books. They were more often buried within paragraphs – yet they summarized an entire conception of how life is or should be. I found them in formulations concerning the intrapsychic goals of analysis, in conceptions of the psychoanalytic encounter, and in accounts of individual development within an interpersonal matrix. I had first, while a graduate student, noticed Loewald: 'The deepest root of the ambivalence that appears to pervade all relationships, external as well as internal, seems to be the polarity inherent in individual existence of individuation and 'primary narcissistic' union' (Loewald, 1962/1980, p.264, quoted in Chodorow, 1999, p. 242).

After quoting a few other analysts, I return to Loewald, saying (Chodorow, 1999, pp.244ff, with internal citations of Loewald):

Winnicott has been almost lionized for his contribution to psychoanalytic visions of subjectivity, but I begin with Loewald. Loewald, followed especially by Bollas and Mitchell, develops an interpretation of the relations of unconscious and conscious that turns Freud's work (and a rationalist ego psychology) on its head. For Loewald, a meaningful human life is founded not on the absence or overcoming of the influence of the unconscious but on its presence and integration. Unconscious fantasies expressed in dreams and transferences enrich life and give it meaning. If, as Freud puts it, the psyche is composed of two records, one unconscious psychic reality and fantasy, and the other conscious, rational, pragmatic life, then the classical position wishes to replace the former by the latter, whereas Loewald advocates a constant intertwining of conscious and unconscious, of transference and reality, such that in the desirable case, any single thought or feeling creates and embeds itself in both realities.

In his influential paper, "On the Therapeutic Action of Psychoanalysis," Loewald notes that Freud used transference in three ways. Conventionally, transference refers to the transfer of relations with infantile objects onto later objects. A second meaning involves the transfer of libido from ego to objects. Finally, transference refers to the way that unconscious ideas transfer their intensity onto preconscious and ultimately to conscious, ideas. Dreams, which allow unconscious, intensely charged thoughts to enter consciousness through their connection with day residues, provide a model for this third meaning. Loewald claims that transference in all three senses is normal and desirable, but it is the third meaning that most concerns him. Although psychoanalysis discovered through the study of neuroses and dreams how preconscious and unconscious interact, the ways they do so 'are only the more or less pathological, magnified, or distorted versions of normal mechanisms' (Loewald, 1960/1980, p.248).

Loewald takes the position that without transference – the same processes of attribution and affective coloration that were originally seen as problematic in the psychoanalytic situation – there would be no personal meaning. Precisely through the infusion into the present moment of our unconscious as we have created it and our past as we have experienced it and made it ours, we most fully live our present and are conscious. Loewald's formulations seem particularly capable of capturing how unconscious processes resonate with conscious ones, and how, when they are integrated rather than repressed, they give conscious life depth and richness of meaning. As he, most radically, puts it: 'the integration of ego and reality consists in, and the continued integrity of ego and reality depends on, transference of unconscious processes and 'contents' on to new experiences and objects of contemporary life.... There is neither such a thing as reality nor a real relationship, without transference. Any 'real relationship' involves transfer of unconscious images to present-day objects. In fact, present-day objects are objects, and thus real, in the full sense of the word... only to the extent to which this transference, in the sense of transformational interplay between unconscious and preconscious, is realized' (Loewald, 1960/1980, pp.252, 254).

In his famous analogy for the gains that come from the transference of unconscious meanings to conscious phenomena, Loewald describes the turning of ghosts into ancestors. Ghosts of the unconscious "taste blood" and awaken when they find something familiar in conscious and preconscious life – the day residues that enable dream formation, for example. But, as Loewald puts it 'those who know ghosts tell us that they long to be released from their ghost life and led to rest as ancestors. As ancestors they live forth in the present generation, while as ghosts they are compelled to haunt the present generation with their shadow life. Transference is pathological insofar as the unconscious is a crowd of ghosts...: [In analysis] ghosts of the unconscious, imprisoned by defenses but haunting the patient in the dark of his defenses and symptoms, are allowed to taste blood, are let loose' (Loewald, 1960/1980, p.249).

[I continue] Although transferences, like ghosts, need to emerge and become visible, they are not something to be gotten over, something that interferes with the reality of daily life. Loewald makes a strong case for transference – here I again quote Loewald, that life without transference is sterile and an empty shell:

Loewald thus makes our capacity for transference directly into a virtue. Transferences – our psychological shifting between past and present or unconscious and conscious – gives vibrancy to life. The role of transference is not mainly to limit, drag down or negatively shape experience, though of course it can do so, and clinical psychoanalysis addresses this negative shaping. Transference also makes experience fuller, as it helps to shape and give meaning to interpersonal and intrapsychic experiences and encounters. What matters is not the presence of transference, but whether transferences are incorporated into psychic life in a way that gives texture and richness to experience, whether one lives one's transferences or is lived or driven by them. At the same time, Loewald provides an argument against idealizing the unconscious – as many psychoanalytic social critics have done. When he says, 'The unconscious needs present-day external reality (objects) and present-day psychic reality (the preconscious) for its own continuity, lest it be condemned to live the shadow life of ghosts or to destroy life' (1960/1980, p.250), he has clinical as well as well as visionary goals in mind.

Loewald revalues fantasy as well as transference. For Kleinians, transference is the vehicle for expressing unconscious fantasy, those constructions of self and object that we create through projections and introjections and other modes of mediating and shaping experience. In the ego psychological view, unconscious fantasy opposes reality and intrudes into conscious life (as well as into psychoanalytic theorizing). It is mainly a derivative of drives that express instinctual wishes, though it also receives some input from ego and superego reaction, and its existence is evidence of repression and psychic conflict (see Arlow, 1969). In both views, an important goal of analysis is to reestablish the linkage between fantasy and reality. As Loewald puts it, 'In the analytic process the infantile fantasies and memories, by being linked up with the present actuality of the analytic situation and the analyst, regain meaning and may be reinserted within the stream of total mental life' (Loewald, 1975/1980, pp.362–363).

Reality, then, is not intrinsically meaningful. In Loewald's view, unconscious fantasy gives this reality personal meaning: 'Fantasy is unreal only insofar as its communication with present actuality is inhibited or severed. To that extent, however, present actuality is unreal too. Perhaps a better word than 'unreal' is 'meaningless'' (*ibid.*, quoting Loewald, 1975/1980, p.362). The point, therefore, is not to overcome fantasy: 'At the same time as the present actuality of the analytic situation is being linked up with infantile fantasies, this present gains or regains meaning – i.e., that depth of experience which comes about by its live communication with the infantile roots of experience' (*ibid.*, quoting Loewald, 1975/1980, p.363). There comes to be a resonance between fantasy and reality, then, the former deepening and enriching the latter, the latter keeping us rooted and connected in the world.

As with transference, ghosts haunt us, but the ancestors are there to quicken us. In contrast to those psychoanalytic cultural thinkers who suspect that claims for psychic health or integration through analysis may become socially normative and who prefer Freud's theoretical pessimism, Loewald makes direct, optimistic claims about psychic health: 'Psychic health has to do with an optimal, although by no means necessarily conscious, communication between unconscious and preconscious, between the infantile, archaic stages and structures of the psychic apparatus and its later stages and structures of organization' (1960/1980, p.254).

In 1999, just as *The Power of Feelings* appeared, Loewald becomes, if it is possible, even more central to my reading and thinking. That year, the philosopher and psychoanalyst Joel Whitebook invited me and Stephen Mitchell to give plenary addresses at a conference on Loewald. My presentation was called "Loewald's vision of subjectivity," and Mitchell also had "vision" in his title. We drew upon almost the same quotes, Mitchell concluding that therefore, Loewald is fundamentally a relational psychoanalyst, and I, that therefore, Loewald is fundamentally an ego psychologist. Mitchell's *Relationality* (2000) has a section called "From ghosts to ancestors: The psychoanalytic vision of Hans Loewald," and I published an article, now a book chapter, called "The psychoanalytic vision of Hans Loewald" (Chodorow, 2003).

The American Independent Tradition

Invited in 1999 by Adrienne Harris and Stephen Mitchell to contribute to a special issue of *Psychoanalytic Dialogues*, "What's American about American Psychoanalysis?" I observed that Loewald, along with Erik Erikson, could be read to have created an American independent tradition: an ego psychology that was driven by unfolding ego and relational capacities but that was also fundamentally intersubjective, based in recognition, self-recognition and the person in interpersonal and social-cultural history. I named it intersubjective ego psychology. Psychoanalytic visions of *intersubjectivity*. Just as British independent analysts of Loewald's generation – Winnicott, Milner, Sharpe, Little, the Balints – noticed meaning of life elements that went beyond the theoretical or clinical, so also Loewald (and Erikson).

Loewald and Erikson, both European refugee-immigrants with almost identical life spans (Erikson, 1902–1994 and Loewald, 1906–1993), co-founded, I claimed, an American independent tradition. Here, we find Loewald contributing a more fine-tuned (and *how fine-tuned*!) formulation of intersubjective ego psychology, yet we also find, in *Psychoanalysis and the History of the Individual* (1978) that Loewald gives us a sense of the sociohistorical beyond, just as, in "The waning of the Oedipus complex," he gives us an account of that which is in between – this in-between perhaps especially important to a psychoanalyst who is also a social scientist, and to all of us in this day and age, as we so painfully and with rueful regret, at our long years of ignoring the social, wonder how we can best bring back society and culture to our understanding and fostering of the life history and lived experience of the individual. In "The Waning of the Oedipus Complex," Loewald tells us:

> Responsibility to oneself, within the context of authoritative norms consciously and unconsciously accepted or assimilated from parental and societal sources, is the essence of superego as internal agency.... self-responsibility.... involves appropriating or owning up to one's needs and impulses as one's own.... Such appropriation... in the course of which we begin to develop a sense of self-identity, means to experience ourselves as agents, notwithstanding the fact that we were born without our informed consent and did not pick our parents.
>
> (1980, p.392)

Here, Loewald, European born co-creator of the American independent tradition, meets Erikson on the ground of ego integrity, as well as identity. Erikson (1950, p.268) has described ego integrity as "the acceptance of one's one and only life cycle as something that had to be and that, by necessity, permitted of no substitutions: it thus means a new, a different love of one's parents." Erikson adds, "an individual life is the accidental coincidence of but one life cycle with one segment of history" (*ibid.*).

In *The Psychoanalytic Ear and the Sociological Eye: Toward an American Independent Tradition*. I write (2020, p.ix):

> We find in Hans Loewald and Erik Erikson two self-identified ego psychologists, deeply attentive and attuned to the intrapsychic and the development of self and ego capacities, yet each making central the relationship to the other, drawing thereby from the concerns of American interpersonal-relational psychoanalysis. Loewald gives us an intersubjective conceptualization of development and analytic process, through consistent attention to the asymmetrical mother-child pair and analytic dyad and to the role of each asymmetry in individual development and psychic change.

I continue (2020, p.1):

> Both Loewald and Erikson begin from self-identification as ego psychologists, but each brings in, foundationally, something of the relational-interpersonal. Loewald gives us the most comprehensive and finely detailed description that we have of intersubjectivity in the analytic dyad and the psychoanalytic process, while among Erikson's eight stages, basic trust, intimacy, generativity, and ego

integrity point especially to the intersubjective (this last, a relationship with the self). Throughout, Erikson attends to the sociohistorical and to personality and culture. Each nods to the other's terrain, Erikson with his eminently intersubjective eight stages, and Loewald with his later writings on life history and the history of the individual, as well as in his conceptualization of the child's being centered upon by her mother.

Moving toward now, it becomes impossible to quote so extensively from my reading of Loewald. Along with my chapters on the American independent tradition, my love and respect for Loewald are found in an entire section of *The Psychoanalytic Ear* (2021) called, like Mitchell's, "The Psychoanalytic Vision of Hans Loewald." Chapters include "The psychoanalytic vision of Hans Loewald," "Reflections on Loewald's 'Internalization, separation, mourning, and the superego,'" and (quoting Cooper) "A different universe: Reading Loewald through 'On the therapeutic action of psychoanalysis.'"

From that first paper to a one-time meeting until now, the therapeutic action of a lifetime of reading Loewald continues. I turn to the epigraphs and opening or closing paragraphs in my own 'Psychoanalytic Vision of Hans Loewald.'

My chapter, "The psychoanalytic vision of Hans Loewald" begins (as for so many!) with the epigraph: "Our present, current experiences have intensity and depth to the extent to which they are in communication (interplay) with the unconscious, infantile, experiences representing the indestructible matrix of all subsequent experiences." I open (p.93):

> Hans Loewald bequeaths us a vision of the psyche and psychic life, of the psychoanalytic process, and of the clinical and human goals of psychoanalysis. In all these realms, he holds, without apparent contradiction, two doubled perspectives. First, he is emphatically ego psychological and emphatically object relational, and second, he maintains a doubled commitment, to both the first topography and the structural theory. His views throughout are undergirded by a bidirectional developmental perspective that centers on differentiation and integration.

I conclude (pp.110–111):

> Loewald's doubled vision emphasizes both the intensity and depth and the range of experience. Assessments of intensity and depth are found in Loewald's conceptualizations of the integration of preconscious and unconscious and of fantasy or transference and reality. Range is found in his vision of the oscillation between subject-object unity and oneness, on the one hand, and oedipal differentiation and object love, on the other. Subject–object oneness is rooted in primary emotional and irrational ways of being that we also elaborate into religious feeling. It is reflected in an affectively charged and evocative language that we find in poetry. Oedipal differentiation enables scientific and other secondary process thought, as well as adult sexual and parental relationships that recognize the individuality and distinction of the other.
>
> Intensity, depth, and range characterize experience as we conceive it both from a radical subjectivist position and from the point of view of object relations.

Oedipal emancipation, necessary to full individuation and individuality, goes along with the irremediable continuity of the mother–child (and analyst–analysand) matrix, a relational setting that forms the basis from which experience grows. Loewald, as always, condenses his complex theoretical vision of the psyche and his psychoanalytic vision, as both life goals and analytic goals, in phenomenologically immediate terms: 'Our present, current experiences have intensity and depth to the extent to which they are in communication (interplay) with the unconscious, infantile, experiences representing the indestructible matrix of all subsequent experiences' (Loewald, 1960/1980, p.251).

My next chapter, "Reflections on Loewald's 'Internalization, Separation, Mourning, and the Superego'" returns to that paper that I first read long ago, in the Widener Reading Room. The meaning of life. My Loewald epigraph reads,

Whether separation from a love object is experienced as deprivation and loss or as emancipation and mastery will depend, in part, on the achievement of the work of internalization. Speaking in terms of affect, the road leads from depression through mourning to elation.

I conclude (p.123):

Loewald's writing hovers between the topographic and the structural, and he does not want us to choose one over the other. "Therapeutic Action" seems to have as one goal a conceptualization of therapeutic action and psychoanalytic process that restores the topographic theory to its rightful place, implying an argument, elaborated in later Loewaldian writings, that we cannot understand the mind or conduct analysis without having a firm grasp of the topographic theory. By contrast, "Internalization, Separation, Mourning, and the Superego" advocates for structural theory, but for a structural theory that has different emphases than *the* structural theory of id, ego, and superego, intersystemic conflict and defense.

For Loewald, internalization is the basis of structure formation, and structuralization is a psychic *process,* rather than an outcome. The three structures of the mind are differentiated not so much by how they interact intersystemically as by differences in quality and mode of functioning. In turn, these three structures can be understood only by considering them in terms of the mental processes that each exhibits – qualities and modes that include many elements best described by the topographic and drive theories. "Internalization, Separation, Mourning, and the Superego" does not have the words *structuralization* or *structure* in its title, but its project, here as elsewhere in Loewald's writing, is the creation of an alternative intersubjective ego psychology and structural theory within American psychoanalysis. Loewald does not *say* that he wants to revolutionize the theory. He just does it.

Finally, I turn to the paper where so many Loewald readers begin, in a chapter entitled, in recognition of Arnold Cooper, "A Different Universe: Reading Loewald through 'On the Therapeutic Action of Psychoanalysis.'" In what may be may be the first paper ever published on Loewald, Cooper uses the phrase "a different universe" to describe Loewald's originality and depth. Cooper, I note, "writes that Loewald's view of therapeutic action 'places therapy in a different universe from that dreamed of by Strachey'" "(I quote Cooper, p.126)". I continue, "Bluntly and with wonderment, Cooper remarks that 'the source for Loewald's vision' is an intellectual mystery" (*ibid.*, p.127), and we notice, once again, Loewald's vision. My epigraph reminds us of Loewald's claim, so counter to the accepted wisdom of his time, that transference brings us "the intensity of the unconscious" without which life is "sterile and an empty shell." I conclude (pp.141–142):

> A close reading of "On the Therapeutic Action of Psychoanalysis" shows how this paper, in its careful and elegant construction, unfolds a comprehensive and richly detailed account of all elements in the psychoanalytic process that together create therapeutic action. The paper opens a window into Loewald's work and into the history of psychoanalysis, providing a multifaceted prism through which the reader can further shape an analytic identity and stance.
>
> I have tried to show that Loewald integrates, in noncontradictory ways, many positions that we have historically polarized. He is an ego psychologist who advocates for unconscious-preconscious linkages and primary process, by implication retaining the topographical perspective. He shows that ego and object, as well as ego development and the development of object relations, go hand in hand. Finally, his emphasis on object relations and interaction underpins a fully subject-subject view of the analytic encounter and of analytic change. Loewald [creates].... a different universe within which we can understand the psychoanalytic process, therapeutic action, and the analyst's stance, as we also seek to understand that "universe in its own right," the individual mind.

How do we step outside Loewald's writing, in which every sentence invites the reader to think, where concepts and formulations move and inspire our clinical and intellectual conscious and preconscious and our unconscious fantasy and affect?

Some of these questions, I imagine, led to the creation of a Loewald Center, a Center for a "Loewaldian" community of analysts, social scientists, philosophers, and literary scholars who have been inspired by Loewald's vision. We recognize Loewald and recognize ourselves in his writing and teaching, and in doing so, we help to expand an American independent tradition. We did not pick our parents, but we can continue to develop a sense of self-identity and agency, on our own and with others, reading Loewald.

References

Adelman, J. (1992). *Suffocating Mothers: Fantasies of Maternal Origin in Shakespeare's Plays, Hamlet to the Tempest*. New York: Routledge.

Chodorow, N.J. (1989). *Feminism and Psychoanalytic Theory*. New Haven, CT: Yale University Press, and Cambridge, UK: Polity Press.

Chodorow, N.J. (1999). *The Power of Feelings: Personal Meaning in Psychoanalysis, Gender, and Culture*. New Haven, CT and London: Yale University Press.

Chodorow N.J. (2003). The Psychoanalytic Vision of Hans Loewald. *International Journal of Psychoanalysis*, Aug; 84(Pt 4):897–913.

Chodorow, N.J. (2020). *The Psychoanalytic Ear and the Sociological Eye: Toward an American Independent Tradition*. London and New York: Routledge.

Coser, L.A. (1984). *Refugee Scholars in America: Their Impact and Their Experiences.* New Haven, CT and London: Yale University Press.

Erikson, E.E. (1950). *Childhood and Society.* New York: Norton.

Loewald, H.W. (1951/1980). Ego and Reality. In *Papers on Psychoanalysis*, pp. 3–20.

———— (1960/1980). On the Therapeutic Action of Psychoanalysis. In *Papers on Psychoanalysis.* New Haven: Yale University Press. pp. .221–256.

———— (1962/1980). Internalization, Separation, Mourning and the Superego. In *Papers on Psychoanalysis*, pp. 257–276.

———— (1973/1980). On Internalization. In *Papers on Psychoanalysis*, pp. 69–86.

———— (1978). *Psychoanalysis and the History of the Individual.* New Haven, CT and London: Yale University Press.

———— (1979). The Waning of the Oedipus complex. In *Papers on Psychoanalysis*, pp. 384–404.

———— (1980). *Papers on Psychoanalysis.* New Haven, CT and London: Yale University Press.

———— (1986). Transference–Countertransference. *Journal of the American Psychoanalytic Association*, 34(2):275–287.

———— (1988). *Sublimation. Inquiries into Theoretical Psychoanalysis.* New Haven, CT and London: Yale University Press.

Mitchell, S.A. (2000). *Relationality: From Attachment to Intersubjectivity.* Hillsdale, NJ: The Analytic Press.

Chapter 2

Loewald's Sublimation or Oneness Regained

Giuseppe Civitarese and Angela Cappiello

The working hypothesis of this essay is that Hans Loewald anticipated elements of the concept of sublimation recently developed in several writings focused on the post-Bionian analytic field theory. This essay will proceed in four parts: we will briefly mention the theory of sublimation in Freud and give a summary of our own theory of sublimation; we will discuss some facts of Loewald's vision on sublimation, underlining the convergence with our conception; we will illustrate some "moments" of sublimation in a clinical vignette, understood as *at-one-ment* or, in Loewald terms, as "oneness regained" (Loewald, 1988, p. 81), that are crucial in the weaving of the emotional links; finally we will make some conclusive remarks.

Reinventing Sublimation

The Freudian concept of sublimation is firmly rooted in our everyday language. That someone could unconsciously renounce their own libidinal impulse by diverting it to a socially acceptable neuter aim, particularly as an artistic achievement, is well established. All that said, the notion of sublimation is also a Cinderella of the Freudian theory as Laplanche and Pontalis (1967) accurately report in their dictionary of psychoanalysis. As Loewald ([1952] 1980, p. 449) puts it: "the nature of the processes indicated under the title sublimation, have thus remained obscure," and further on, "sublimation is one of the most obscure and vague concepts in psychoanalysis" ([1978] 1980, p. 578).

Does sublimation employ sexualized or de-sexualized drive energy? Is it a defense or an alternative to defense? Does it involve Eros or Thanatos? Is it useful or useless in clinical work? Is it about ordinary or exceptional creativity? Is it overly infiltrated by ideology or not? Is it singular or plural? The only handhold, however uncertain, for a definition of sublimation seems to lie on an extrinsic and "sociological" criterion of the concrete artistic realization, as an elevated, honored state, actualized in the artistic masterpiece.

Freud's concept of sublimation reflects a one-person psychology model, based on a complex hydraulic system of psychic energies, of undoubted historical value, but that nowadays finds less relevance in clinical work. However, the topic of sublimation continues to fascinate us. If we read it under the light of the aesthetic of the sublime, the pool of theory of the aesthetic creativity developed during the Romantic period, we could certainly interpret sublimation as a true theory of psychic birth. Sublimation and sublime have the same etymology, both terms indicate a process of elevation that

DOI: 10.4324/9781032685151-3

implies pleasure and occurs within a social frame. While for Freud, the concept of sublimation is built into his metapsychological framework of drives and defenses, for the aesthetic of the sublime, sublimation begins with the feeling one experiences facing ineffable beauty.

For a more detailed analysis of the interconnection of the two concepts of sublime and sublimation, we recommend the work of Civitarese (2014, 2016, 2018, 2020, 2022a, 2022b). Here it is enough to say that the aesthetic experience in art and in psychoanalytic practice is concerned with the social constitution of the individual, especially understood at its pre-reflective, non-verbal or intercorporeal level. It is at this level that, thanks to the encounter with a receptive other, the turbulence of sensations and proto-emotions become soothing rhythms, proto-ideas or sensible ideas at first and, once words are added, concepts. Typically, in the paintings of the Romantic age, we find a subject facing an object both terribly threatening and of incomparable beauty. It is the history of both psychic birth and aesthetic conflict (Meltzer and Harris Williams, 1988).

The work of art though, does not just give us a theory but is an incarnation of what speaks to our emotional body. It does not only explain what it means to encounter the object, and to feel the spiritual growth, it also lets us recognize it through a bodily experience. Two different individuals meet, negotiate the mutual emotional distance, are able to weave affective links; an area of identification-like-a-becoming-the same that brings organization and structure, is created. A similar thing happens when we formulate concepts that belong to all of us and allow us to understand each other. The growth as an individual (or improvement through psychoanalytic therapy) means to create as many links as possible, to expand as we can, this field of belonging or undifferentiation which creates the capacity to think and communicate.

The concept of sublimation reveals the path from animality toward the height of rational thinking. It coincides with the process of widening the shared area that allows human beings to resonate one with the other. The essential element is language. Without language neither concepts, nor thoughts would exist, and consequentially there would be no individual per se. This is the visible part of the process: the construction of links through language. But it is not all. The aim toward the top, toward the summits of rationality could evade the connection with the body which is what happens in different ways and intensities with all our patients. We would be in the presence of individuals who suffer from a certain degree of depersonalization or splitting between mind and body. What is the point then? It is to consider that *a similar process of sublimation occurs also at the level of the body and through the language of the body*. Even at the level of the body, semeiotic "concepts," schema, habits, sensible ideas, etc., must be created. After all, Freud directs us on the right path when he connects sublimation with the vicissitudes of the libido, the drive that aims to meet the object.

In substance, *sublimation defines the construction of links* that creates what Merleau-Ponty (1964, p. 155) calls "the sublimation of the flesh" a process that leads from matter to the highest levels of human spirituality, that does not have a defensive value, but rather a construction of the psychic. Such a process is possible thanks to the instinctual propension of human beings to enter into emotional resonance. Bion (1961, p. 153) describes it as "instantaneous, inevitable, and instinctive," and adopts the chemical metaphor of "valency," that is the ability elements have to establish bonds and thus constitute more complex units. It is not as much a forced renunciation of the physical orgasm, rather the capacity to tolerate the frustration elicited by the temporary absence of the object, that for Bion is at the origins of the thought (1962a; Civitarese, 2019a). As such, *sublimation is no longer a phenomenon within the frame of the conflict of drives, but rather within the dialectic of being.* Each link is a further organizational element that the subject capitalizes on by experiencing a feeling of pleasure. It is the pleasure of differentiation, remaining at the same time a member of a transcendental field that itself is part of what we call subject. *Sublimation then is the name we give to the development of a conceptuality that gradually becomes more abstract and therefore more powerful, but that also proceeds at the sensorial-emotional-semeiotic level, and not only at the abstract-logic or semantic level.*

For the analyst, it is crucial to be aware of this process that occurs in parallel with the rational thinking. Therefore, it is important to theorize the nature of the social transcendental field that is at the basis of the subject. In therapy, this is the area that the analyst aims to expand. When Ogden (2019) compares the epistemological with the ontological paradigm, we could say that he also contrasts the epistemological sublimation with the ontological sublimation (of *being* or *becoming*).

The analyst is with the patient to secure as many links as possible in this area: the *emotional links.* It is from the emotional links more than the logical ones that the feelings of ourselves and our existence derive. Those are the links that when stable and intense are transformed in the affective links that play out in the most intimate relationships. It is the crisis in this vital area of our existence that motivates people to ask for analysis. This could also very well proceed through the construction of logical-linguistic links (when one agrees with another in judging something) but always verifying that they are not split by the true sublimation as the process of becoming *one* from *many* in the inter-corporeal area. If the new links were only in the linguistic-abstract realm, they could perpetuate the psyche/soma split we were talking about. As we know from life experience, links based on an explicit agreement are weak, the emotional links are the extremely strong ones.

In fact, in Bionian terms, the *at-one-ment* between mother and baby is *a form of primordial abstraction* and occurs first in the dimension of the purely sensory and indistinct, and then in the affective space, which nonetheless is always a symbolic space if we take in account that sociality is provided for the couple-system by the mother.

The important point is that every emotional link coincides with a process of growth of the transcendental field of the subject, that is, the social, unconscious, undifferentiated, common area that represents its invisible face, but also and simultaneously of its visible, conscious, differentiated, personal side. For us, it is important to keep in mind this other side of the subject, because it is so counterintuitive. This way, we avoid the trap of the subject-object split, and we can more easily monitor how the process of sublimation is proceeding. How? During the session, oscillating between a vision of two separate subjects who interact between them, and a vision of two subjects who form a group aiming moment by moment to self-interpretation and this way attaining to exist.

At the level of psychoanalytic models, we have moved from a relational model, where it rules the split *you/I* to a field model, where the key vertex is *we*. It is similar to the oscillation between the profiles of the vase or vice versa the ambiguous or bistable figure of Rubin. The two visions cannot be simultaneous but when there is one, the other does not stop to exist. In fact, it is a matter of viewpoint.

In other terms, we need a metapsychological concept of common, intersubjective, relational[1] or shared, unconscious that correlates to the clinical metaphor of the analytic field, whose function could be understood looking at the system and its emerging properties. It is clear that this way of reinventing the concept of sublimation is based on a radical social conception of the birth and the development of the psyche. It is also evident that in clinical practice we end up favoring models that inform us as accurately as possible on how and if the process of building new links is unfolding, and what is the connotating sign-whether *L, H* or *K* (Bion, 1962b)-in a certain context. For this purpose, the theory of the analytic field has put in place various technical-theoretical tools that are extremely effective, accurate and versatile.

If now we look a little closer at the concept of link, we realize that the construction of a link coincides with the process of formation of symbols. The prototype is the primary symbol that is generated at the moment in which through projective identification the mother represents/*becomes* the child and vice versa, without cancelling the respective differences, and therefore is actualized in a dimension that, without complete exclusion from the symbolic registry, is primarily aesthetic, meaning based on feelings. The creation of this first symbol is the foundation of any subsequent symbolizations that involve other objects in the world. From birth on, in the process of interaction with the object, the "sublimating factor" resides in the transmission of the creativity of the object, its capacity of reverie, to the rising subjectivity of the child; in other words, the maternal capacity to provide the infant the opportunity of absorbing these functions, enabling the capacity to think and individuate, and therefore promoting psychic growth.

From this point of view, sublimation is a process of containment that unfolds thanks to the maternal capacity of reverie and to the alpha function, but also to the spontaneous capacity of the child to "contain" the maternal anxiety giving her the impression of being healthy, a "socialist" drive, or a "truth drive" as Grotstein puts it (2004), what that urges a mutual recognition/reconciliation. In this sense, rather than a diverted satisfaction from the libidinal drive, sublimation expresses that unique human capacity of cooperation and linking.

The specificity of sublimation is found in its way of showing that becoming a subject means syntonizing with the Other and gradually forming concepts that are more and more a distillation of things, filtering what is inessential. Furthermore, a sublimation supporting the process of personalization (Winnicott, 1945) shows that this process of simplification, which is at the basis of the most sophisticated forms of thinking, must not dissociate the emotional from the intellectual. On the contrary, ideally, sublimation proceeds in parallel, along lines that are both logical and sensorial, rational and intuitive, intellectual and physical.

Therefore, if we continue referring to the artwork, we do not mean that sublimation actualizes in a particular artistic activity, instead we intend art as a metaphor of a process of developing of the subject, able to think abstractly, not dissociated from the subject's bodily roots. "The intercorporeal truth" becomes the vital lymph that feeds and promotes growth and freedom of the individual.

Loewald on Sublimation

Let's turn now to Loewald, to some aspects of his theory on sublimation that resonate with what we have discussed so far. In his "uncanny mix of loyalty and subversion"

(Lear, 2012, p. 169), Loewald invents a new concept of sublimation that makes use of Winnicott's ([1951] 1975) concept of transitional phenomena and the phenomena without acme, phenomena that do not depend on libidinal gratification.

The use that a child makes of a toy is a prototypical example of this dimension of being. The essential characteristic of the transitional object is that it does not make sense to ask whether it has been found or created and by whom. An essential indivisibility with respect to the subjects that give it life is inherent in the experience of the transitional area. In reference to this area, Loewald (1988, pp. 23–24[2]), citing Winnicott ([1953] 1967) uses expressions such as "a separation that is not a separation but a form of union"; a union that is "a reconciliation of polarities, of separateness"; " a unitary field that undergoes differentiation"; "mother-infant matrix"; "in genuine sublimation this alienating differentiation is being reversed in such a way that a fresh unity is created by an act of uniting… differentiated unity."

For both Winnicott and Loewald, the transitional phenomena express a dialectic relationship between mother and infant, conveying both unity and separateness. "The mouth breast combination" is a discovery of what existed before "but had remained unknown" (p. 76). It is as the Barangers ([1961–1962] 2008) specify about the shared unconscious fantasy that underlies their conception of the analytic field: it is neither the patient's nor the analyst's alone. The fantasy would not exist without the participation of both, although outside of it, each remains the same. The transitional phenomenon per se, is nothing but the experience of *making links with the objects*, of "relating to objects" (p. 25). Winnicott (1967) uses a splendid metaphor when he compares relatedness to the kind of electricity that seems to generate in meaningful or intimate contacts, similar [Loewald adds] "to waves, oscillations, vibrations in a *magnetic field*, not like a discharge phenomenon" (p. 25, italics added).

The electricity is both in the mother and the baby and allows them to turn on the light of love, but it could not be *only* in the mother or the baby. We can see that what Winnicott theorizes to explain transitional phenomena, and more so Loewald, is a shared undifferentiated transcendental field that relates to some newly generated, differentiated aspects of the subject, and furthermore it is the necessary sine qua non.

The subjects that are created in this space, in turn are needed to create it, but they do not control it. It is difficult to capture the dialectic between subjectivity and intersubjectivity because unlike the pole of subjectivity that is *visible* and obvious, the pole of intersubjectivity as a medium, allows the separation between subjects and therefore the subjectivity (self-consciousness) is *not visible* (Civitarese 2023). It is as if we realized the separation of the two banks of a river and not the river as a shared element and the responsible agent of their separateness.

As Heidegger wrote (cit. in Williams, 2017, p. 119), trying to clarify the difference between the concept of Being and the concept of the incarnation of Being in concrete individuals, it is the same difference that runs between the light that comes from a bulb and the electricity. The metaphor is prosaic but effective, and in line with similar metaphors of Winnicott and Loewald on electricity and magnetic field.

Through our senses we can see discontinuity, not continuity. However, as analysts we are called to "repair" the destructions at this shared level of psychic fabric; otherwise, we would not need to formulate the concept of unconscious.

Now, that the link implies a being the same, an identification, may not be as obvious. It becomes *a being at one*, if we think that the link is always an affective link, a libidinal link. The link always expresses an aspect of belonging, a co-existence. Loewald ([1973] 1980, p. 83) describes identification as both that merging of subject and object that eliminates differences, but also as the "waystation" on the track of subjectivity and separateness. Identification is a step on the path toward "internalization" in which new identities of both subject and object are formed and reconstituted. With internalization, a redifferentiation has taken place; it defines a transformation in which old identities are renounced. It follows that establishing a bond, identifying oneself with another as becoming-identical, coincides with the expansion of an area of the transcendental field that underlies transitionality (in play, art, religion, science etc.).

The origins of the English word *link* are both from late Middle English denoting a loop, a bend, and from the Germanic *gelenk* "joint." The Italian word for link, "legame" derives from the Greek *ligein-* that means "fold," "tie." The etymology is interesting because it brings us to the image of fold, that according to Deleuze (1968) stands for the reflexivity that pervades matter and then "specializes" (evolves) in self-reflectiveness of the human subject. But the image of "fold" represents again both difference but also identity because the fold could never free itself in an absolute way from the background it emerges from.

There could be no mutual understanding between two distinct subjects if their exchange were based only on the externalization and transmission of content from the interiority of one to the interiority of the other. On the contrary, it is possible because the channel of communication, as for the placenta in the womb between mother and fetus, has been already given, and it is an undifferentiated, common dimension of co-existing. The way in which psychoanalysis theorizes this area already with Freud is the communication from unconscious to unconscious. The formula is enlightening but dissatisfying if read as an interaction between two unconsciouses, each sealed within an isolated subject. It is more convincing to hypothesize a relational shared unconscious, intersubjective, where specific waves flow and vibrate across the two of its places.

This is no small innovation because it configures the same radical reversal of perspective that takes place with Husserl's philosophy, for example, and in different ways with that of Heidegger and Merleau-Ponty: the Cartesian anthropology of the Cogito and the isolated subject is replaced by the Heideggerian analytical-existential anthropology of the subject always seen as situated in the environment. Citing Lafont (2005, p. 273),

> from the private perceptions of isolated subjects there is no way to explain how these subjects could achieve a shared perspective *about the same objects*. The order of explanation is actually the reverse: the subject–object perspective is only possible as a result of success in achieving a shared subject–subject perspective.

This perspective, however, is not only to be gained; in a certain variable measure, we could speculate that it has been always present.

Loewald, commenting on Winnicott's (1967) quote of Hartmann's term neutralization, remarks that neutrality does not allow the question "subject or object" and makes reference to the etymology of neuter *ne u*ter, "not either," and adds "neutrality implies absence of discharge" (p. 25). It appears that each time Loewald moves away from the Freudian viewpoint of sublimation, so strictly based on the drives theory, as a partially diverted, channel of instinctual forces, Loewald underlines that satisfaction is not exclusively bound to sexual discharge and it may be achieved by means other than elimination (or reduction) of a state of tension or stimulation. If there is such a thing as a life instinct, its "aim" would be satisfaction through the attainment of higher, more differentiated, unities... (p. 27). Here Loewald invites us to share a passionate journey that pulls us away from the classical concept of sublimation as a defense and takes us to a theory of sublimation as a "reconciliation" not at the service of the Id but the Ego. It is not only the satisfaction of the libidinal drive that is important, but also the development of the Ego that is key. "We are reminded that the formation of an ego... can be described as a sublimatory process and that a distinction between sublimation and ego formation is not easily made" (p. 42). The fabric of the Ego is woven by making links with objects. Therefore, these objects must be left "unchallenged," per Winnicott as well, "in respect to the question of subjectivity and objectivity." In Winnicott's words (1958), as quoted by Modell, "ego relatedness" takes precedence over the forces of the id" (Modell, 1991, p. 467). We can almost visualize the image that Loewald is proposing. Links are binding, but one cannot say that the connection derives from one or the other. At the same time, when prompted, the function of linking is to hold together without any lacerations, just like the mountaineers are tied together by a safety rope when climbing a cliff. Obvious are resonances with Bion's (1962b) concepts of content/ container as the mechanism that allows new links to form; or with the Kleinian concept of "reparation" (Klein, 1940).

Loewald's idea of "differentiated unity" is another way to express the essential dialectic of identity (intersubjectivity) and difference (subjectivity) that constitute what we call subject. However, it is obvious that the scandalous and invisible element that-following-Winnicott, Loewald reveals is the paradox of something (space, object) we cannot say whose it is, because it is at the same time subjective and objective, of both the individual and the group formed together. The process of subjectivation can only be understood if, as mentioned above, we postulate those characteristics of the common area. Brilliantly, Loewald puts forward the hypothesis that such transitional space (shared, intersubjective, indistinct) does not represent a developmental phase to overcome during the growth of the individual, but it is always there as the psychic matrix of the human being, "as an active ingredient or constitutive element of the individual experience" (p. 33).

Sublimation, Loewald summarizes, "is not a form of defense" (p. 33). If sublimation is not a defense, then what is it? It is here that the term sublimation brings us to the long and noble pathways of the speculative thinking of philosophers such as Hegel but also to psychoanalytic thinking. The Bionian *at-one-ment*, for example, obviously derived from *atonement*; or, in Loewald terms, *reconciliation*. In Loewald's book on sublimation that was published in 1988, we glimpse some of the essential elements of the field theory. In fact, the inaugural essay of the post-Bionian field theory of Bezoari and Ferro was written in 1989. When nowadays the question is raised of why a reverie could not represent a countertransference phenomenon, here with Winnicott and Loewald, besides Bion, we could simply answer that "the question is not to be formulated" (p. 23). It is not because the question does not make sense in the absolute, but because it is a question that does not account for of the different theoretical frameworks from which those two concepts (reverie and countertransference) originate. If, the transitional object (link, area) is defined as *an agreement between the two of us*, then wanting to break this intrinsic unity is misleading. Reconciliation is the concept that better expresses the way in which an agreement is reached to weave a new psychic fabric, or to repair tears that could have happened in some areas. Referring to Hegel, one could say "recognition," but it is evident that the act of reconciliation, which obviously is mainly unconscious, is a constitutive element of what we mean by "recognition" (Hardimon, 1994).

Recognition, reconciliation, internalization, etc., are all expressions that help to understand how from the multiplicity we can extract some shared, common unitary elements. It is in the nature of a symbol to reunite. The concept of sublimation, that comes from a metaphor borrowed by chemistry to designate the transition of a substance from a solid state to a gas state, indicates the wonder of the ascending process from the concrete to the symbolic, from the body to the spiritual. In other words, abstraction is in the sense of *abs-trahĕre*, to forgo differences and detect similarities, to identify what is in common to different entities, what becomes the symbol that reunifies in a concept. Immediately, this is also a model of therapeutic action, that also resonates with Loewald's (1960, p. 32) definition of therapeutic action: "infantile object and contemporary object may be united into one—a truly new object as both unconscious and preconscious are changed by their mutual communication." It is not simple at all, because the nature of the symbols to institute in order to become subjects is duplex-not only at the representational or linguistic level, but also at the corporeal level, symbols such as schema of action, habits, affective invariants, etc.

Following Winnicott, Loewald aims for a concept of pleasure that is separate from the sexual discharge, but based on the creation of links and therefore, to be understood not as instinctual forces aim-inhibited. Loewald, in fact, refers to "the pleasure of the nonclimactic intimacy of being in love, or in that binding of tension involved in higher psychic organization" (p. 30). It is not any longer the vertical dimension of sexual and orgasmic sublimation; rather it is the horizontal dimension of sociality that must not be challenged by the question of subjectivity and objectivity. It "is not satisfaction in the form of the removal of the state of stimulation, rather [...] the perpetuation of tension, of the excitation inherent in the living substance [...] a relatively permanent phase or form of bound energy" (pp. 30–31).

It brings to mind the puppet-toys that Meltzer (1975) describes to explain "the disassembly" of an autistic defense whose different elements are kept together by an elastic cord that runs internally. The puppet sags sadly and disjointedly if the tension of the elastic cord is released.[3]

The level of theoretical eloquence that transpires in Loewald's writing is extraordinary; for example, when he describes that the perpetuation of tension lives "in transindividual and endopsychic binding" (p. 31). That is to say the individual and the group are not antagonistic, one against the other, but rather divergent perspectives just like the vase and the profiles. We would like to reiterate that the subjective polarity of the ego is made of infinite identifications with the group, the ego is intersubjectivity (Green, 2002) and internal "groupality." If one grows, automatically grows the other, unless traumatic events cause a collapse of the ego-group into ego-mass. Given this increasingly "transitionalist," intersubjective or "from the field" view, should not we focus the attention less on the casualistic explanation of the connections between biography and symptoms and more on the creation of links, the refined weaving of the psychic matrix in the *here and now*—the being and becoming?

Ruby and Rambo

We will now present a brief excerpt from an analytic encounter to illustrate some "moments" of sublimation, understood as *at-one-ment* or, in Loewald terms, as *oneness regained*. We will comment on how, in our opinion, in the here and now of the session, analyst and analysand oscillate between interacting as two separate subjects, and at a deeper, intersubjective level, as two subjects who form a group aiming moment by moment to self-interpretation and this way attaining to exist. These elements of sublimation are essential in the weaving of the emotional links.

In the past few months Lisa has talked about the loss of a sweater that her mother, who has recently died of Covid, has knitted for her. She is distraught for the lost sweater. It represents memories of her childhood, her conflictual relationship with her mother, her love for her, and her recent death.

In the following session, Lisa comes in proudly pointing out the sweater she is wearing.

A: *It is nicely knitted. I like the image of the cat and the colors. It seems comfortable and warm. Oh!... I did not realize... it is your old sweater, the one you were looking for...! You have found it! Lost and regained.* [The analyst plays the role of a Greek chorus (Civitarese and Boffito, 2023), as a background and a facilitator of the emotion expressed by the patient. With no need to make explicit the unconscious sense of the fragment of narrative that opens the session, the analyst listens as if the story were written by herself together with her analysand, measuring the affective temperature of the relational moment, discovering a sense of pleasure and intimacy, a being together with the other. In the meantime, the cat comes forward (unveils itself) as a significant character of the narrative.]

L: *Yes. It is cozy. I finally found it in the lost and found at the gym. My mother knitted it... the cat on it... it is my cat growing up. She was Ruby. Now I have Rambo. He is my new cat. I found him. He was lost wandering in the streets of my neighborhood. I adopted him a few weeks ago. It is a full-grown cat. He is huge.* [It is not just one cat, now we have two cats on the stage of the analytic theater, Ruby and Rambo. The analyst interprets them as affective holograms (Ferro, 2009) in the analytic field, as figures that hypothetically could signify the climatic transformation occurring during the session. At times they function in a Ruby mode, other times, in a Rambo mode. Ruby, the cat knitted by her mother, metonymically has a function of contact (texture, colors...), while Rambo functions in the field as a character expressing resentment for having been abandoned, but also found and adopted.]

A: *It may have been hard for him out there.* [From a merely psychotherapeutic point of view, this comment could be seen as based on a reality level or simply a punctuation of the analytic conversation. But it could also be seen as an interpretation *in* the transference. From the viewpoint of the analytic field, it is as if the analyst said: "I realize how much we suffer when we feel as we abandon each other."]

L: *I took him off the street, I saved him. He was lost... he did not belong to anyone. Rambo came over and sniffed me as if he knew me. I am so thankful I found him. He is so friendly.* [The patient, as the speaking person of the unconscious narrating couple takes charge to comment that at times the separation feels like a permanent loss, but also there is a field function of re-finding-adopting. At this moment, it is as if Rambo became a bit of Ruby].

A: *New and old coming together, it is a reconciliation that opens your heart.* [It is as if the analyst had in mind Loewald's concept of reconciliation. She celebrates the reconciliation in the here and now. In doing so, the conscious goal is to reso-nate with the patient's emotion–as a way of letting her know what she is feeling. A new link is created, but it needs to be confirmed by the upcoming signals in the analytic field.]

L: *I am recreating a new family for myself here. Alex commented that Rambo looks like a racoon.* [We could understand Lisa's comment as a shared unconscious reply that signals the climatic transformation, as more familiarity-intimacy. The link strengthens. Not only Rambo becomes a racoon, but we also do not know how Alex feels about it. It is an animal known for its adaptability but also it is not domesticated.]

A: (I think of the raccoon as the dark side and Rambo as a symbol of animality). [Now we know that the analyst is thinking of wilder-animal-instinctual aspects that permeate less domesticated aspects of the relationship. Could that be a signal that with the re-union not all the separation issues are gone?]

L: *He is huge. You can almost feel afraid of him. Alex had bad cats before who scratched and bit him, but Rambo is the kind of cat that he's going to get along with. I'm ex-cited. Alex is going to move in with me. After our appointment today I am going to help him to get the last of his stuff and then he's going to stay here, and my family will be complete. I baked bread. It smells good....* [In fact, arrives the fear! As Freud says, the more you love, the more you are afraid. More intimacy means more dan-gers. Not only with Rambo, but also with Alex: another re-union that inevitably has its dark side. Dealing with the weaving of affective links, if these links are au-thentic, both analyst and patient feel pleasure, excitement, but fear of "not getting along." At this level no asymmetry exists, the love connections don't allow it!]

A: *It feels homey.* [You know how I feel; I know how you feel; it is homey. In this mo-ment, the analysis is a "safe place."]

L: *Yes, it is a beautiful day, and I am very happy. There are these two sides of me that cannot come together. I don't want to disappoint him, as if this feeling overtakes me. I hate that. I love Rambo, my new cat, but the memory of Ruby is there... it just doesn't go away. It is like re-experiencing old emotions... I don't like to think as all or nothing. There are these two sides of me... this dark side.* [Through Lisa the field signals that love and hate go together; certain degree of splitting is physiologic, and it enables order and discernment, but it can become excessive if it is not con-stantly integrated. Lisa's reply following the analyst's comment "it feels homey," may indicate that the couple is backing off a few steps, to avoid the madness and despair Rambo felt before he was brought home. But of course, at the unconscious level, who adopts you is also who previously abandoned you.]
     Pause

L: *It is uplifting to have Alex, but there's also this undercurrent doubtfulness. I always seem to lose someone when I start a new relationship. I lose contact with old friends, and everything revolves around the new relationship.* [It is interesting to think about the paradox that love brings more hate. The "old friends" that Lisa is afraid to lose, are not only concrete "real" connections, are also aspects of the other with whom she is in relationship. In short, the couple self-interprets the crucial affective ambivalence that is the fabric of our humanity. As we know, the integration of ambivalence requires some work of mourning.]

A: You *lose your old friends, find new ones, but you also lose a little bit of yourself, as if the boundaries became blurred.* [The analyst captures this aspect and refers to the risks of, as Loewald puts it, "oneness regained."]

L: *I sacrifice my own needs or somehow, my needs are being met through them. I'm hopeful this time. Alex made it clear that he really doesn't want to intrude on my life.* [The couple is negotiating the mutual distance when Alex becomes a character in the analytic field or better a function of reciprocity that does not compromise closeness.]

Pause

L: *Rambo is a fusty cat. My neighbor has a giant mastiff and … you know… he stands out in the doorway and waits for the mastiff to come up to him… yeah, he is super … super brave. That is why I named him Rambo.* [Along those lines, it takes courage to face the "giant mastiff" of her neighbor—let's not forget that Rambo "was lost wandering in the streets of my neighborhood." Also we know that Rambo is "huge."]

Pause

L: *Rambo seems happy he found a home … I don't know where he was before…his coat is really soft, he seems healthy. He is affectionate and purrs when I pet him. I woke up this morning, and he was right next to me, sleeping on the pillow. It is nice to have a little friend who follows me around all day.* [This is the latest micro-transformation. It informs us that the climate is absolutely positive and favorable to the creation of new links, to the extension not only of the semantic and conscious links, but also semiotic and unconscious. As Freud (1920) writes, after all, the dream allows one to transform the fright into anxiety; in this case from the fright that Rambo, although ultra-courageous, feels for the big dog, to a more manageable and useful sentiment of feline circumspection!]

A: (I think of Rambo as an affective hologram, representing violence, danger, passion, and animality. He is brave, strong, and aggressive. We are playing with the cat character who left, and it has been re-found; it is a hallucinosis. We are re-defining our relationship; it is a negotiation between the two of us). [The analyst chooses to be silent, but of course, this is another way of communicating. The analyst's receptiveness to the unconscious discourse will influence her deep emotional attitude that, naturally, will contribute to the emotional atmosphere shared by the couple.]

L: *He may be jealous of Alex, but I don't think it'll be a problem. Rambo likes attention from everyone…. My friend Lucy, she doesn't drink alcohol… she equates it to loss of control… someone taking advantage… men or women. She is terrified. Her aggressive and sexual impulses scare her. She presents as ultra-polite, ultra-conscientious… careful not to say any offensive things… kind of boring. She needs to loosen up. She is afraid of the dark side surfacing without any notice.* [Again, here the dark side of the link surfaces, jealousy is in the air. At a deeper level, the more Lisa gets closer to the analyst, the more she is exposed to the feeling of jealousy, and it is reciprocal. In fact, there are feelings that are hard to control in all of us and scare us when they come to light.]

Chemical Transmutation

Loewald powerfully relates sublimation to the moment of atonement, the reconciliation that keeps the tension alive between abandonment and reparation, between separateness and return to *one-ness*. Sublimation is the creation of a link, is the "oneness" that "stays alive as connection" (p. 13), is what is visibly actualized in the analytic field. In our clinical material, there is "reconciliation" (p. 33) in the form of the new and old cat—Rambo vs. Ruby. It is the work of sublimation, finding a common area, a transition from the old to the new—a new dimension or state—a transformation of restless and brave; together analyst/analysand were able to fight the neighbor's mastiff. Reconciliation is the pleasure of finding each other, a new appreciation, loosing contact and rediscovering each other again.

The post Bionian theory of the analytic field lends itself well to interpret and put to work Loewald's intuitions, even though they come from totally different traditions. In the vignette, the analyst focuses her attention on how the characters play out, but what she has in mind are the emotional transformations. The cat is neither *me* nor *her*, neither the analyst nor the patient, it is an affective hologram (Bezoari and Ferro, 1989). As a couple, they were able to fight a giant mastiff. Lisa lets the analyst know that Rambo is now calm and comfortable. She mentions emotions such as jealousy, love, anger. It is an idyllic reconciliation-with reservations about what will happen to them.

Interpretation is less what the analyst tells Lisa and more the analyst's receptivity to the unconscious as the shared medium that as a couple allows them to give meaning to their ongoing proto-emotional experience and transform it—in jargon, from beta elements to alpha elements. A pivotal therapeutic moment is when the analyst is able to move away from the relational angle of the split between *you/me*, which inevitably leads to an attitude of suspicion, to a place where at the center is the *we*, and consequently, to a basic trust in the capacity of the dyad to represent their dramas on the analytical stage. So, sublimation is the creation of a link, like in a chemical reaction, a new state of being. *At-one-ment* is not as much a transmission of information, it is an emotional syntonization. An analytic hour is like a play at the theater. The cat character is created in the field. It does not matter who wrote the play. The narrative is not about what is yours and what is mine. It is a reflection of the chemical transmutation of the atmospheric medium of the session.

We realize the essential gain we make when we listen from the perspective of the analytic field: there is no unconscious emotion that is not veridically felt by both patient and analyst; and for which even the latter should not take responsibility. If A tells the analyst that he has become his ex-girlfriend's stalker, the analyst cannot help but wonder if they are both actually functioning in a "stalking" mode. And, it might be, for example, that the analyst will insist on confronting the patient about his behavior instead of trying to resonate with the emotions that the stories he brings to the session reflect.

Of course, reconciliation can occur through different theoretical models that look at the analytic happenings and discern the main factors of the therapeutic action. We believe that this new reading from the viewpoint of the analytic field—as Ferro (2009) writes, in terms of the session as a dream—provides information that allows us to "measure" more accurately the level of attunement (we can say here "the capacity of sublimation") of the couple during the session: for example, following the development of the narrative (not only words, but feelings, emotions, reveries, actions, etc.), tuning with what has just been said on a temporal axis that can range from seconds to months.

One last clarification: the comments of the session in parenthesis are only an exercise aimed to elucidate our theoretical model. In no way, could they give a realistic idea of what happens when the analyst has not only internalized this method of listening, but also is able to relinquish it, according to the Bionian principle of negative capability (Civitarese, 2019b), meaning to renounce zealously wanting to understand and cure.

Epistemological Revolution

In summary, Loewald's theory of sublimation is of amazing interest and certainly anticipates our (Civitarese, 2016) recent reformulation of such a fundamental psychoanalytic concept. Paraphrasing a famous quote from *The Leopard* (Tomasi di Lampedusa, 1958, p. 28) "if we want things to stay as they are, things will have to change," we could say of Loewald "if we want things to change, things will have to stay as they are." Of course, we are referring to the Freudian metapsychology. Keeping things the same, does not come without risks. To some, Loewald could appear incendiary, too much of an instigator, to others too old style. Although many have tried "to assess the extent of Loewald's radicalism versus his conservatism [...] his thinking defies an either/or opposition" (Whitebook, 2004, p. 98). It is incredible how Loewald can use the Freudian lexicon and formulate such groundbreaking concepts within the frame of classical metapsychology. However, putting new ideas using established language could create confusion. For example, his use of the term "primary narcissism" intended as an undifferentiated state of self and other that creates a basis for human relatedness and self-individuation, adds to the complicated contradictions of the Freudian use of the term "primary narcissism"—either as an autoerotic state of the child in his writings of the period 1910–1915, or within the structural theory, as an undifferentiated state of mother-child, which is exemplified by the life in the womb.

So, Loewald's formulations run the risks of being outdated for the contemporary and too innovative for the classical. To give examples of radical theorists but not conservative, we can think of Melanie Klein who distances herself from Freud, already in the forties, Winnicott (1967; Girard, 2010) who rejects the Freudian metapsychology, or Bion who moves away initially from Freud and then even from Klein. In Chapter 4 of *Transformations* Bion makes a list of all the psychoanalytic theories available in his toolbox, his "theoretical equipment" (p. 51); it is 1965! and none of these theories is connected directly to Freud. It is easy to realize that the problematic loyalty of Loewald to Freud, as an attempt to reconcile Ego Psychology principles with relational psychoanalysis, represents for him a kind of ballast. Even when he introduces us to the most cutting-edge concepts, we are not always clear that its meanings are really new.

For example, Loewald's theory of sublimation is based on the concept of internalization. As Fogel (1991, p. 253) clearly explains

> Loewald states that 'the universal road to sublimation is [...] internalization' [...] and that sublimation is a high form of internalization, in which man may be 'reconciled' to separation and distinctions and original unity regained in the form of a new 'differentiated unity'.

Now, many find the concept of internalization original and of great value; others do not think it is sufficiently clear and different from the concepts of identification, introjection, introjective identification, etc. It is not a surprise if someone, for example Mann, in a pungent style, comments on Loewald's theory:

> here is a sense that he does not go far enough ... The reader is left wondering if sublimation is a mixture of reconciliation, defence and symbolic expression [...] Loewald's argument seems to imply that sublimation is such a generalised, catch-all term that it is almost meaningless as a specific description. [...] In effect, by showing that sublimation consists of a number of different processes, the status of sublimation is even more enigmatic at the end than at the beginning of the book. Far from clarifying Freud's confusion, Loewald, by expanding the concept of sub-limation, has made the confusion even greater. [...] I was left thinking how much deeper and further the British school goes and how much sooner the British ar-rived at their conclusions. For example, sublimation as reconciliation is old news in Kleinian theory [...] My only real criticism of this otherwise stimulating book is its lack of illustrative examples.
>
> (1992, pp. 107–108)

There is no doubt that the scarcity of clinical vignettes in Loewald's writings makes it more arduous to apply Loewald's theory of sublimation in a practice of innovative cure. We cannot say whether Loewald's vision, which is undoubtedly innovative for its time, is converted into tools of psychoanalytic technique as innovative as his the-oretical formulations. In one way, we agree with Modell (1991) who credits Loewald of having carried out an epistemological revolution, on the other side, we recognize that, prior to Loewald, there have been already extensive innovations (at least with Klein, Winnicott, Bion, etc.), in regard to the Freudian metapsychology, even though not within the Ego Psychology framework. Sometimes you may have the impression that Loewald omits relevant contributions of other authors; although he acknowledges ([1973] 1980) that his conceptions of internalization and internal objects were already discussed by Klein and Fairbairn.

This said, according to Chodorow (2007, p. 1141), Loewald

> seems to render Kleinian and Fairbairnian concepts in ego psychological terms, but he would also claim, as I have indicated, that the initiating processes of de-fensive projection and introjection postulated by Klein and Fairbairn cannot oc-cur from the beginning, because these assume a primary ego. In a later paper, Loewald (1973a) further clarifies that, although he is in similar territory to that traversed by Klein and Fairbairn, he is looking at structures and identifications, not at an intrapsychic map of an unconscious, internal, ego-object world.

Loewald also does not discuss the Kleinian concept of reparation, which we believe is one of the greatest psychoanalytic conceptions of aesthetic experience; or the work of Paula Heimann, who, already in 1942, talked about internalization and sublimation. For example, in the following passage (Heimann, 1942) we already find a significant departure from the Freudian naturalistic-instinctual theory of sublimation, and a step forward, an affective dialectic of love and hate. Internalization is already in the title, and "restoration," very similar to "reconciliation," is in the text:

Life is bound up with the dynamic processes set up by aggression, guilt, anxiety and grief about the internal objects, and by the impulses of love and *restoration*; Love and Hate are urging the subject to strive for sublimation. The internal freedom to which I refer is a relative, not an absolute fact; it does not abolish conflicts, but it enables the subject to enlarge and unfold his ego in his sublimation.

(Heimann, 1942, pp. 15–17)

It is true, however, that if read carefully, to the concept of internalization Loewald assigns the task, which similar concepts do not perform to the same degree, of conveying his conception of the radically intersubjective nature of the psyche (Balsam, 2018, p. 214).

What we assuredly do not find in the Loewald's theorization of sublimation is a specific, rigorous analysis of the essence of the aesthetic experience, that is the enigma-miracle of the form. Nowadays, it is exactly this type of connection with the sensoriality that urges us to reexamine the concept of sublimation, for example introducing the concept of intercorporeality and trying to capture the intuition that is enclosed. Otherwise symbolization would be sufficient. It is the same theoretical consideration that makes us say that at the heart of the analytic process is the relation mother-infant, not mother-child, in brief the secret of the intersubjective and aesthetic constitution of the individual.

Reconciliation

Aside from these few critical remarks, Loewald's idea that *reconciliation* leads to a re-constitution of a unity, though differentiated and intrinsically dialectic, resonates with Bion's concept of *at-one-ment* and authoritatively supports our own interpretation of a process that locates *sublimation* at the basis of therapeutic action. Furthermore, the idea of reconciliation helps us to theorize the paradoxical nature of human subjectivity, at the same time both singular and plural, individual and "groupal." Loewald's differentiated unity requires a metapsychological framework of shared unconscious, a psychoanalytic function of the group of two, deputized to the metabolization of the protoemotional experience.

The concept of sublimation as a reconciliation and restoration of the mother-child primary unit ("oneness regained," p. 81) coinciding with the process of symbolization, is central. It is not a unity without remainders, meaning completely undifferentiated. In fact, Loewald wonders if sublimation could be "both a mourning of lost original oneness and a celebration of oneness regained" (p. 81), and this way he lets us envision a much more sophisticated facet of this process that is not only the unity that needs to be regained but, each time, also a loss to be accepted, just like in our vignette Lisa expresses her fears of what it will mean to live with Alex.

Loewald, before moving to Winnicott, touches upon the thesis of Hartman and Kris, who view sublimation as reuniting what has been separated by the individuation and by sexual differentiation, leading back to the original mother-infant matrix (p. 24). But we know that individuation is also a re-union. What Hartman and Kris view as a separate process with distinct phases is in reality a one single and dialectic process. This is Loewald's thesis. Following Winnicott, Loewald adopts a very different vision of the mother-child matrix, of "a separation that it is not such, but it is a type of union," "reconciliation of polarities," "differentiation in a unitary field," "differentiated unity" (p. 24).

In fact, we do not think it is correct to say that mother and child constitute an undifferentiated unity. The mother is well aware of being an individual, separate from the child, although she is at one with the baby in the state of primary maternal preoccupation. It is the child, if anything, that lacking self-awareness experiences itself as undifferentiated from both her mother and her environment. It is more correct to say that both when the child is still an *infant*, i.e. without language, and thus only endowed with a pre-subjective or pre-personal individuality, and when it begins to be properly a subject, in both cases there is always a side to its being a subject, as well as to the mother's being a subject, which is given by a transcendental or indistinct or undifferentiated field, destined to last a lifetime. It is an intrinsic component of being a subject. In Heidegger's jargon, it is the concept of Being that is embodied in the individual *Being-there*. Those distinctions are indispensable to elaborate a more articulate concept of the essence of the subjectivity and the process of psychic development.

In this sense, sometimes Loewald's language could be misleading. The subject *always* consists of a dialectic of unity and difference–even before becoming a subject. There is nothing to repair, unless the links that constitute the area of intersubjectivity are broken. The task of expanding this area to maximize one's human potential in order to become oneself is *always* present. Furthermore, there is also an intersubjective area that is purely instinctual or animal. A perfectly homogenous unity could never occur. In the field or the unity there will be always a play of identity and difference, maybe pre-personal and pre-linguistic. The point is not to stay in the dichotomic logic of differentiated/undifferentiated. Rather, the question is at what respective levels we can talk of differentiation or undifferentiation. The child, although non-subject, is differentiated as a body, already as a fetus in the uterus. In regard to the mere matter, even a rock is differentiated. It is not without a meaning that as human beings we can empathize with animals, though less than with our fellow human beings, but it is much harder to empathize with things.

If, as Loewald writes, the field is permeated by waves, the points of the field are never in the same state. Then where is the unity that continuously has to be regained? We think it is in the molecular process of the act of thinking. It is the *at-one-ment* of Bion, meaning that the thought could originate only from a tolerable rhythm of encounter and separation with the object. The moment in which the link (symbol) is formed, the possibility that the trace of experience of satisfaction persists long enough in mind.

It is with the string that Ernst pulls back and retrieves the wooden reel after throwing it, that is, he recovers the object in the symbol (Freud, 1920). What we mean is that the concept of primary undifferentiated unity could veil the fact that in reality we are describing an ubiquitarian dynamic essential for the process of subjectivation. Rather, it is important to reiterate Bion's principle by studying the dynamic of groups (Civitarese, 2021b), and Winnicott's ([1952] 1975, p. 99) concept that there is no child without a mother, that is, no object can be understood in its development if it is not included in a vision of system, field, group, etc. We could say that the experience of loss of the object is recovered at first not as a concrete undifferentiation, but as an undifferentiation at a higher level–precisely symbolic. This way, we establish a dialectic between identity and difference: we have two types of undifferentiation, one concrete, the other symbolic, and the process can never stop: it is the "ascending spiral" of sublimation, as Loewald puts it, an image extremely suggestive, that not without a reason, we have anticipated in exergue.

In summary, we hope to have shown that some concepts of Loewald's theory of sublimation anticipate some aspects of Bion's and post-Bionian psychoanalysis. In particular, the post-Bionian theory of the analytic field examines Loewald's thought on this exciting topic and mutually allows itself to be examined. The fruitfulness of this dialogue demonstrates the relevance of Loewald's theories for contemporary psychoanalysis.

Notes

1 In this case "intersubjective" and "relational" do not refer to the interaction of separate subjects, but rather to the shared instinctual and symbolic area that we need to postulate in order to explain how a subject has access to another subject (Civitarese, 2021a).
2 From now on, when we do not mention the year, the page number always refers to this essay.
3 See Meltzer (1975, p. 12): "We are suggesting, then, the existence of some capacity (whose mechanism we will attempt to investigate later) for suspending attention, which allows the senses to wander, each to its most attractive object of the moment. This scattering seems, to bring about the dismantling of the self as a mental apparatus, but in a very passive, falling-to-bits way. There are toys which represent a dog (say), made of wooden beads and, held together by strings which pass through holes in a board and are fastened to a ring. A child holding the little board with his finger in the ring can make the dog stand up by exerting a tension on the ring or allow him to collapse into a reclining posture by relaxing the tension; and we are envisaging attention as the strings which hold the senses together in consensuality."

References

Balsam, R. H. (2018). Internalization, after Loewald: A powerful and clinically useful concept for psychodynamics. *Psychoanalytic Study of the Child* 71:208–216.

Baranger, M. & Baranger, W. (1961–1962). The analytic situation as a dynamic field. *International Journal of Psychoanalysis* 89:795–826, 2008.

Bezoari, M. & Ferro, A. (1989). Listening, interpretations and transformative functions in the analytical dialogue. *Rivista di Psicoanalisi* 35:1014–1050.

Bion, W. R. (1961). *Experiences in Groups: And Other Papers*. London: Tavistock.

Bion, W. R. (1962a). The psycho-analytic study of thinking. *International Journal of Psychoanalysis* 43:306–310. Reprinted as 'A theory of thinking' in *Second thoughts: Selected Papers on Psycho-Analysis*, pp. 110–119. London: Heinemann, 1967.

Bion, W. R. (1962b). *Learning from Experience*. London: Karnac.

Bion, W. R. (1965). *Transformations*. London: Routledge, 1984.

Chodorow, N. J. (2007). Reflections on Loewald's "Internalization, separation, mourning, and the superego." *Psychoanalytic Quarterly* 76:1135.

Civitarese, G. (2014). Bion and the sublime: Roots of an aesthetic paradigm. *International Journal of Psychoanalysis* 95:1059–1086.

Civitarese, G. (2016). On sublimation. *International Journal of Psychoanalysis* 97:1369–1392.

Civitarese, G. (2018). *Sublime Subjects: Aesthetic Experience and Intersubjectivity in Psychoanalysis*. London: Routledge.

Civitarese, G. (2019a). The concept of time in Bion's "A theory of thinking". *International Journal of Psychoanalysis* 100:182–205.

Civitarese, G. (2019b) On Bion's concepts of negative capability and faith. *Psychoanalytic Quarterly* 88:751–783.

Civitarese, G. (2020). *L'ora della nascita. Psicoanalisi del sublime e arte contemporanea* [*The Hour of Birth. Psychoanalysis of the Sublime and Contemporary Art*]. Milan: Jaca Book.

Civitarese, G. (2021a). Intersubjectivity and the analytic field. *Journal of the American Psychoanalytic Association* 69:853–894.

Civitarese, G. (2021b). Experiences in Groups as a key to 'Late' Bion. *International Journal of Psychoanalysis* 6:1071–1096.

Civitarese, G. (2022a). The identity of the terrible and happiness: On the sublime in art and psychoanalysis. *Fort Da* 27:7–31.

Civitarese, G. (2022b). Blackness of Red: Anish Kapoor and the sublimation of the flesh. In: T Dibbits, ed., *Anish Kapoor*. Venezia: Marsilio, pp. 43–61.

Civitarese, G. (2023) Invisible-visual hallucinations in Bion's "Attacks on Linking". *International Journal of Psychoanalysis* 104:197–222.

Civitarese, G. & Boffito, S. (2023) Greek chorus and the tactful therapist. *Psychoanalytic Inquiry* 43:526–538.

Deleuze, G. (1968). *The Fold: Leibniz and the Baroque*. New York: Continuum, 2006.

Ferro, A. (2009). Transformations in dreaming and characters in the psychoanalytic field. *International Journal of Psychoanalysis* 90:209–230.

Fogel, G. I. (1991) Book review: Sublimation: Inquiries into theoretical psychoanalysis, by Hans W. Loewald. *Journal of the American Psychoanalytic Association* 39:250–257.

Freud, S. (1920). Beyond the pleasure principle. *The Standard Edition of the Complete Psychological Works of Sigmund Freud* 18:1–64.

Girard, M. (2010). Winnicott's foundation for the basic concepts of Freud's metapsychology? *International Journal of Psychoanalysis* 91:305–324.

Green, A. (2002). A dual conception of narcissism: Positive and negative organizations. *Psychoanalytic Quarterly* 71:631–649.

Grotstein, J. S. (2004). The seventh servant: The implications of a truth drive in Bion's theory of 'O'. *International Journal of Psychoanalysis* 85:1081–1101.

Hardimon, M. O. (1994). *Hegel's Social Philosophy: The Project of Reconciliation*. Cambridge: Cambridge University Press.

Heimann, P. (1942). A contribution to the problem of sublimation and its relation to processes of internalization. *International Journal of Psychoanalysis* 23:8–17.

Klein, M. (1940). Mourning and its relation to manic depressive states. In: *Love, Guilt and Reparation and Other Works-1921–1945*. New York: Free Press, 1975, pp. 344–369.

Lafont, C. (2005). Hermeneutics. In: H. L. Dreyfus & M. A. Wrathall, eds., *A Companion to Heidegger*. Oxford: Blackwell, pp. 265–284.

Laplanche, J. & Pontalis, J-B. (1967). *The Language of Psycho-Analysis*. London: Karnac, 1988.

Lear, J. (2012) The thought of Hans W. Loewald. *International Journal of Psychoanalysis* 93:167–179.

Loewald, H. W. (1952). The problem of defence and the neurotic interpretation of reality. *International Journal of Psychoanalysis* 33:444–449.

Loewald, H. W. (1960). On the therapeutic action of psycho-analysis. *International Journal of Psychoanalysis* 41:16–33.

Loewald, H. W. (1973). On internalization. In: *Papers on Psychoanalysis*. New Haven, CT: Yale University Press, 1980, pp. 69–86.

Loewald, H. W. (1978). Psychoanalysis and the history of the individual. In *Papers on Psychoanalysis*. New Haven, CT: Yale University Press, 1980, pp. 529–579.

Loewald, H. W. (1988). *Sublimation: Inquiries into Theoretical Psychoanalysis*. New Haven, CT: Yale University Press, 1988, pp. x–89.

Mann, D. (1992). Sublimation: Inquiries into theoretical psychoanalysis by Hans W Loewald. Published by Yale University Press, 1988; 89 pp.; £12.50. *British Journal of Psychotherapy* 9:106–108.

Meltzer, D. (1975). *Explorations in Autism: A Psycho-Analytic Study.* Perthshire: Clunie Press.

Meltzer, D. & Harris Williams, M. (1988). *The Apprehension of Beauty: The Role of Aesthetic Conflict in Development, Art and Violence.* London: Karnac, 2008.

Merleau-Ponty, M. (1964). *The Visible and the Invisible.* Transl. by A Lingis. Evanston: Northwestern University Press, 1968.

Modell, A. H. (1991). *Sublimation. Inquiries into Theoretical Psychoanalysis.* By Hans W. Loewald, M.D. New Haven, CT/London: Yale University Press, 1988. 89 pp. *Psychoanalytic Quarterly* 60:467–470.

Ogden, T. H. (2019). Ontological psychoanalysis or "what do you want to be when you grow up?". *Psychoanalytic Quarterly* 88:661–684.

Tomasi di Lampedusa, G. (1958). *The Leopard.* Archibald Colquhoun (translator). New York: Pantheon, [1960], pp. 1–320.

Whitebook, J. (2004). Hans Loewald: A radical conservative. *International Journal of Psychoanalysis* 85:97–115.

Williams, D. (2017). *Language and Being: Heidegger's Linguistics.* New York: Bloomsbury.

Winnicott, D. W. (1945). Primitive Emotional Development. *International Journal of Psychoanalysis* 26:137–143.

Winnicott, D. W. (1951). Chapter XVIII. *Transitional Objects and Transitional Phenomena through Paediatrics to Psycho-Analysis* 1975, 100:229–242.

Winnicott, D. W. (1952). Chapter VIII. *Anxiety Associated with Insecurity. Through Paediatrics to Psycho-Analysis* 1975, 100:97–100.

Winnicott, D. W. (1953). Transitional objects and transitional phenomena—A study of the first not-me possession. *International Journal of Psychoanalysis* 34:89–97.

Winnicott, D. W. (1958). The capacity to be alone. *International Journal of Psychoanalysis* 39:416–420.

Winnicott, D. W. (1967). The location of cultural experience. *International Journal of Psychoanalysis* 48:368–372.

Chapter 3

Creative Innovators

Loewald and Laplanche

Doris K. Silverman

We owe Schopenhauer and especially Nietzsche the idea of the dynamic unconscious (Weinberger & Stoycheva 2021). They described a system of drives that can conflict with each other. The drives can be confused, contradictory, oppositional, complementary, untamed, brutal, and primitive stemming from one's early existence.[1] Freud (1926) developed these ideas into a complex system of mind and even spoke of the main focus of psychoanalysis as on the unconscious. Since Freud's death, there developed rich and multi-determined models of psychoanalysis. These models offer different motivational theories of mind and behavior. Nonetheless, the existence of unconscious processes is a major feature of these models. In writing about the unconscious Weinberger and Stoycheva (2021), point to two major features they have in common. They included the existence of unconscious processes and they all demonstrate a view of these processes as "affectively charged, non-rational, poorly integrated into the personality, and formed under the crucial impact of early experiences" (p. 2). When Freud wrote about early mainly unconscious experiences, he emphasized the body, the pre-symbolic, and the infantile, and their continued role these play in our sexual lives.

In this communication, I want to discuss two theoreticians who sustained and affirmed Freud's oeuvre: Loewald and Laplanche. In choosing to address the thinking of these two men, I am underscoring their emphasis on sexuality. This focus is relevant because currently there is a de-emphasis in our psychoanalytic literature on various aspects of our sexuality (Fonagy 2008; Silverman 2015).

In addressing these aspects, they both recognized and appreciated the complex and sophisticated theory Freud advanced and they have engaged in a scholarly analysis of his model and premises. They both rely on abstract theoretical conceptualizations, that is, neither man provided clinical examples, or even minimal case material to illuminate his theoretical views. Both were immersed in Continental philosophy which shaded their views in important ways. These two theorists enlarged and expanded our general psychoanalytic thinking but did it in a divergent manner. Whereas both have retained a major commitment to an array of Freud's ideas, nonetheless, each introduced significant changes in Freud's theory each in his own unique way. Loewald often used Freud's language and then with subtlety opened up Freud's ideas in innovative ways, providing increased nuance and density creating difference and added complexity. Laplanche pointed to aporias which he then described at great length. He labeled them Freud's "going astray" (2011, p. 35) a term that might point to minimal change, but in fact was a significant change in Freud's theory and clinical approach. Both in theory and technique, the two men diverge in their thinking about the psychoanalytic

DOI: 10.4324/9781032685151-4

process and its goals which will be amplified later in this chapter. Whereas I will be illuminating some similarities between the two theorists, the paper primarily addresses the tension between their two approaches.

I begin with the concept of the unconscious for these two scholars. Both theorists recognize the importance of patients experiencing and addressing the psychodynamic significance of early primitive impelling, daemonic fantasies, and their meanings. Both men acknowledge that drives are not endogenously generated. They both maintain that new understandings, new translations of meaning and their integration, are relevant for growth and vitality in our lives. Accessibility to early infantile sexuality, what is typically called primary process thinking, is vital for a creative, non-restrictive psychic life. Each theorist includes the caregivers, family, and community, that is, the larger environmental input as germane in shaping interactions and influencing fantasy life. These areas of agreement do not portray how each has arrived at his position.

In viewing the unconscious, here is one of Loewald's (1978a) many commentaries on this issue. Instincts do not impinge on an existing psychic apparatus, but rather drives "emerge in the early organizing mother-infant interactions" (p. 208). Here, Loewald is using instinct and drive interchangeably as Freud often did. However, for Loewald, the infant's fantasy life develops as a feature of inner life but as being shaped by the interactional experiences of the mother and child. Thus, sexual desire is within the child and the child's interaction with early mothering shape the nature of the child's fantasy life.

In contrast, Laplanche distinguishes between instincts and drives and he maintains less of a focus on instincts. Laplanche comments, "Instincts are innate, atavistic, and endogenous," "drives are acquired, yet anchored in the body" (Laplanche 2011, p. 11). Here Laplanche is amplifying an important distinction. He sees the infant having survival needs, for example, milk from the breasts, and he then proposes that sexuality leans on such vital needs. These survival needs are the instincts. What Laplanche is underscoring are not the vital needs necessary for survival, but the drives stemming from the erogenous zones. He recognizes the infants' need for a vital self-preservative life, but it is the sexual drives of psychic life that govern significant mother-infant interaction. For him, it is the unbound energies of the drive that push the ego to respond, to try to translate, to make meanings which bind energies.

For Laplanche, the drives are organized initially around mother's sexual breasts and the mother's fantasies about her exciting, stimulating breasts as communicated in the form of enigmatic messages to her newborn. The important point for Laplanche is the parent's primal seduction of her newborn, that is, her unconscious sexual desires stir primal scene fantasies which are transmitted to her passive infant. These enigmatic messages are not understood by the child and the child needs to make meaningful attempts at translation. Thus, by contrast with Loewald's position, it is the enigmatic external stimulation from the other; the other, that excites the infant and pushes for some decoding of the messages.

Loewald is a careful reader of Freud's texts. For Freud, the sexual instinct and the object were independent of each other. Loewald struggled to be true to Freud in the infant's initial objectless experience, while also beginning to push in a new direction. Early in his work (1951) he commented on the powerful stimulation of the breast for the infant "and that it is not always available. In this way for the first time something like an "object" becomes constituted... [The object is the] most primitive beginnings of the later structure." It is the experience of the early separation from the breast that stirs the recognition of an other. There is for Loewald a primitive bodily sense of the primary object. Mother's stimulating presence leads the child's ego to have a connection with her, and thereby to become aware of external reality. In this form commented Loewald, it makes the id pliable to the world and the world responsive to the id (Loewald 1951).

One of my favorite passages from Loewald (1980) is his description of the earthy, corporeal sexuality rooted in the body:

> The life of the body, of bodily needs and habits and functions, kisses and excrements and intercourse, tastes and smells and sights, body noises and sensations, caresses and punishments, tics and gait, and movements, facial expressions, the penis and the vagina and the tongue and arms and hands and feet and legs and hair, pain and pleasure, physical excitement and lassitude violence and bliss—all this is the body in the context of human life. The body is not primarily the organism with its organs and physiological functions' anatomical structures, nerve pathways, and chemical processes.
>
> (1971, p. 125)

Although typically abstract in his writing, in an unusual passage, Loewald wanted to undo sexuality from its abstraction, from scientific jargon to the immediacy of the body and its role in characterizing psychic life. The confused and contradictory images that are evoked through smells and sensations, body parts, movements, vague, strange, undecipherable somatic feelings exist and are stirred. It is clear that kisses and excrement are ambiguous somatic sensory experiences, so too are pain and pleasure, violence and bliss mixed together. They are often conjoined in a varied and confounding manner, certainly undecipherable and needing translation. Both men are communicating their own understanding of archaic infantile sexuality.

Laplanche, writing in a later era, was much more knowledgeable about early empirical findings about infant development. He maintained that mother and infant are relationally connected; all interactions between the two are intersubjectively organized. Since Laplanche maintained that messages are communicated by an other to a helpless, dependent baby, his idea can appear initially to be uni-directional rather than what's typically considered intersubjective, and bi-directional, however Laplanche commented, "Very quickly reciprocity will emerge" (Danon & Lauru 2015). Thus, Laplanche maintains an intersubjective position as well but based on different premises.

As I have reported, for Laplanche, the mother's sexual enticements are mysterious and puzzling for her infant The infant does not have a code to understand its meaning. Thus, the infant is forced to make sense of what is being experienced. Making sense out of these communications is in Laplanche's (2016) language to translate them (p. 126). Translations are not necessarily only about words. Laplanche, emphasizes the communicative and corporal aspects of the parent's transmissions, that is, the nonverbal, the gestures, the facial responses, body language that the child perceives. Laplanche refers to these messages as the "inter-semiotic translation" (Laplanche 2015, p. 249). In this way, the parent communicates the drive fantasies, the sexual perversities, which inhere in all of us. As Laplanche makes clear, he is addressing the normal pathologies of Freud's Three Essays. He remarks, "Human sexuality is by itself perverse" (1992, p. 62).

Laplanche is concerned with bound and unbound energy processes. What the child cannot comprehend or translate, the residue, becomes repressed and remains as unbound energy. In turn, when there is translation, although it helps to bind, there is inevitably unbound energy in repression because messages are never fully translated. What is untranslated, acts like an alien feeling. For Laplanche, this alien experience is like a splinter under the flesh. This leads to an increased feeling of drive propulsion from within which initiates the need for further translation both in childhood and lifelong.

Loewald, as well, addresses unbound primary and bound secondary processes in infancy and onward. His main concern though is with how the ego in interaction with the id and reality develop increased differentiation and complexity. Thus, Loewald's (1980) emphasis is on increasing ego expansion and consolidation.

For Laplanche, on the other hand, the key question is what are these bodily derived unconscious fantasies that continue to exert pressure on us? What does the body want from us? I now offer a clinical example. Primal fantasies can develop and coalesce around particular anxieties of a sexual nature according to both men. The clinical material to be presented is as narrated by the patient. The interpretation of this narrative is mine influenced by my understanding of Loewald and Laplanche's positions. It also reflects my style of working analytically. I find Laplanche's theoretical ideas about unconscious, infantile fantasies very helpful and useful; however, my typical way of working clinically is not along Laplanchian lines. I am too active for that. My aim was to help the patient synthesize the various wishes and fears he struggled with. My analytic approach is more in keeping with Loewald's ideas.

An analysand, a successful businessman who came from the Midwest, remembered that his father regularly gave him enemas in his childhood. It wasn't quite clear to the patient whether they were necessary. Sometimes he did have intestinal discomfort, and so, he wondered, whether his father had an idea that regular enemas were desirable for cleansing his internal body, purifying it so to speak. The boy's experience of these procedures was that it was an "external penetration." He thought of it as an "alien body that had penetrated him." It had "contaminated him and so he wanted to get rid of this external body." The enemas were a dreadful, painful experience for him, and led to the fantasy that sex can be hurtful and violent and that the fluids that emerge in sex are potentially polluting and dirtying. One way he thought to eliminate this feeling of toxicity was to engage in lots of exercise until he was fatigued. This he believed purified his body and therefore it was important to exercise lengthily and regularly.

I pause here in my case presentation to mention a couple of points. The patient reported fragmented events in his early life. The patient neither looked for nor sought further meanings beyond what he was communicating. He focused on his purifying methods.

The frequent enema experience should be understood differently by Loewald and Laplanche. It is reasonable that Loewald might consider the enema experience as a repeated traumatic invasion into the child's body, which stirred particular infantile fantasies. The structure of this enema fantasy might well be understood as perverse reflecting sado-masochism and anality. Sex is stimulating, painfully penetrating, dirty, and violent.

For Laplanche, the father's enemas intrusions into the child's body are not the trauma for the child. What is important for him, is the "effraction" – "the breaking in" of the father's seductive unconscious communication installed within the child's body. It is the unbound sexual unconscious of the father that is being implanted in his child. It is an implantation which the child will struggle to decipher, and thus to bind.

For Laplanche, the only possible understanding of what fantasies are stirred within, is to listen to the associative material of the patient. However, I now speculate about sexual fantasy, attempting it from a Laplanchian perspective. Following Laplanche, I would suggest that the father has implanted a primal scene fantasy of a sadistic parental coupling. The beginning Oedipal fantasy might be that of a violent castrating father. Although the enemas have occurred at a later stage in the boy's development, it is the father's unconscious fantasy that may be thought of as an initial traumatic implantation into the child. The later fantasy reoccurring around the enemas he received from the parent was an apres'-coup, that is, the enemas restirred the originary fantasy. This experience intensified his Oedipal feelings and associated sexual anxieties and led to significant inhibition in his adolescent and adult sexuality (1970, p. 34).

The patient was conscious of his considerable anxiety and shame about his sexuality. What was unconscious was the patient's lack of understanding and integration of his unconscious infantile sexuality. The analytic process made attempts to facilitate translation and symbolization.

We also addressed a second fantasy I viewed as linked to the first in that they both dealt with his wish and deadly fear of penetration. When he was a young boy, his family took him to a Chinese restaurant where he was served sliced bamboo shoots for the first time. It is not clear why this delicacy was both enticing and forbidden for him. He remembered that it made him feel uncomfortable to think of the bamboo inside of him. A fantasy developed around the idea that a small, external bamboo sprout that was consumed could take root and grow and continue to develop within his body. It could expand rapidly within him like the rapid growth of bamboo trees.

Once again, a secondary external penetration from without could grow in strength and length within his body. For Loewald, what would count is the oral and anal eroticism that is alive within the young boy (Freud 1908). For Laplanche, this fantasy formation is a manifestation of the originary implantation from the sexual unconscious of the father that continues to "excite" (Laplanche, 1915, p. 26). The originary meaning of the bamboo and its growth within him is in need of translation, of increasing symbolization. The child's fantasy of being sadistically attacked was overwhelming and consuming him.

As I listened my associations were about Freud's (1908) primal fantasies of childhood. How does one have a child? Something is taken within the body in this instance both mouth and anus are involved. Once within the body something develops and grows. I thought of it as a cloacal pregnancy fantasy involving both the oral and anal orifices (Freud 1908). It might also include a passive-masochistic homoerotic fantasy wish involving the father who demonstrated a more emotional connection, albeit sado-masochistic, with the young boy than did his mother. The Laplanchian yield of this fantasy might be, my father loves me best of all. Together we create a love child (Freud 1919). Akin to Freud's (1919) thesis in his paper, A Child is Being Beaten, the patient appears to have internalized the sado-masochistic primal scene of violence and masochistically turned it against himself in the unconsciously gratifying originary fantasy scenario of I am being beaten by my father (Laplanche 1976). "Loving for me is being beaten."

When I suggested that this was a pregnancy fantasy, the patient said I was wrong. For him, the growth was occurring in the lower part of his body. He was growing a penis and an erection, a counter to castration anxiety. In this error of mine you can see my own countertransference shaped by my early Oedipal wishes about my fecundity. The transference-countertransference matrix illustrates what Laplanche underscores as problematic. It occurs when analysts employ their own interpretations. Both the patient and analyst can be unconsciously stimulated by their early infantile wishes and of course they can be quite different for each.

At another time in treatment, this patient described how, when emotionally feeling hurt, isolated and alone, he often had recourse to sexual fantasies. To feel sexual for the patient was to counter deadened feelings. Sexual feelings typically stirred strong physical sensations in his genitals which he felt as very disturbing. Consciously, he believed he needed the fantasies as a soothing experience of connection with a valued other, unconsciously, we might speculate, the stirring and exciting feelings were from his originary psychic implantation. These heightened sexual ideas were often felt as intense, overwhelming, and unmanageable. He could not contain the feeling that he was being controlled by his sexual thoughts. Once again, he thought that a foreign body had invaded him. These sexual fantasies were so devastating and consuming that at times he fantasied about castrating himself. Along with Laplanche we might understand that the originary traumatic fantasy, manifests as an alien feeling stirring from within, the throbbing splinter within his flesh. What has not been integrated within his sexuality is his thorough-going chaotic, disequilibrium. What is important for Laplanche, on the one hand, is that his violent sexuality impels excitement which is assertive and transgressive and loosens super-ego restrictions. On the other hand, it challenges a taboo which signals sexual discharge which is viewed as dirty, shameful and sinful (Bataille 1986).

What I am underlining, along with these two theorists, are the polymorphous perverse fantasies of childhood. They reflect what is unbound, that is, the significant role of perverse fantasies of childhood in our lives. When primary processes are temporarily in ascendency, they dissolve integrations and at the same time potentially offer innovative understandings and enrichment of our psychic lives. When this occurs, it allows for sublimations. What both theorists understand as relevant is the increasing utilization of sublimation, that is, the integration of perverse elements from our archaic early life into symbolization-translation (Laplanche 2011, p. 296; Loewald 1978, p. 37). This phase of the paper deals with the interplay between the external environment and the internal world of archaic infantilism and their potential syntheses which can enhance growth and development.

Both Loewald and Laplanche employ the concept of identification in their understanding of how the external world becomes internal. Freud uses the term incorporation (from Ferenczi) and identification interchangeably. Loewald focused on identification, whereas Laplanche often used incorporation, as a more vivid bodily function.

Loewald's concept of identification is very general. In a late paper, he understands identification as a waystation on the road to internalization (Loewald 1973, p. 84). A much more relevant construct for Loewald is internalization. It includes incorporation, introjection and identification. He understood psychic structure is formed through the internalization process. Thus, there is "destruction of relationships and structures into their elements and an internal restructuring of these elements within a different organized setting, so that novel but in some ways related structures evolve" (Loewald 1973, pp. 75–76).

Loewald suggests that the ego develops and changes from a lower level of more primitive organization to a higher more developed psychological organization. Loewald holds that there is always an ongoing interaction between the boundaryless, chaotic, daemonic id of the primary process, in interchange with the ego, our secondary process, our more rational considerations (Loewald 1978a, 1978b). For him, our more primitive, pre-oedipal level of organization can be seen more directly, for example, when one is in an elevated, orgiastic state or a highly stressed one. In Loewald's view, our primitive organization never disappears. What is clear for him is the increased development of structure and the increased role of the ego and its many functions.

For Laplanche manifestations of unconscious sexuality with its primary process qualities are not limited to such rare, elevated states. We are inevitably being pressed by the residues of the enigmatic messages from the adult other because there are always only partial translations.

In Loewald's theorizing about the significance of the ego, he was responding to Freud's second typography challenge in 1920 and 1923. The challenge marked Freud focus on the ego. More generally this period can be considered an important turning point in traditional psychoanalysis. However, what Loewald set out to expand in his focus was eschewed by Laplanche. As a senior analyst as well as long-term mentee and supervisee of Laplanche's reported (Maya Monique Evard, personal communication 2022) "Laplanche's theory never related to ego psychology but always concerned the unconscious" (see also Laplanche 1976, p. 9). Their distinctive positions mark a significant difference between the two men.

Laplanche (2011) might dismiss Loewald's views as "Anglo-Saxon" (p. 35) and respond especially negatively to Loewald's engagement with the further development of the concept of the synthesizing ego.

Laplanche's interest and emphasis were consistent with Freud's early position as illustrated by the editorial comment in the preface to Freud's 1923 paper, "that after the Project (1895) Freud's work concentrated on his investigation of the unconscious and its [drives], particularly the sexual ones…" (p. 8). This is core to Laplanche's position. Psychic life is marked by the constant splinter under the skin and strange alien feelings which push for translation. Such internalized pressure allows for increasing openness and integration into one's neurotic character.

Laplanche's focus is on otherness, the intersubjective feature of the child, and the other rather than selfhood, or on complex ego functions that are key. Of course, even for Laplanche, the self changes but it emerges via a dramatically different route.

Scarfone challenged and changed Freud's well-known aphorism, "where id is there shall ego be" to "where id was the other will always and ever be" (Scarfone 2015, p. 65), to reflect how he(Scarfone) understood La Planche's thought.

The last section of this paper deals with the psychoanalytic process and its goals for these two men. Whereas, once again, there are similarities in their view about the analytic setting and ambience, however, there are substantial gaps in their views of analytic technique. Of course, both are aware that analysis is a joint endeavor, that there is a need to provide a welcoming environment – reasonable objectivity, openness, flexibility, interest and curiosity, empathic listening and seeing. These views have their origins in the ideal mother-child interaction. Both present the analytic invitation to the patient as evoking the mother-child interaction and it shapes the transference in a unique way. Free association is essential for both, although Laplanche would alter this idiom to his preferred term of "association-dissociation" (Laplanche 2011, p. 281). They both rely on the importance of what the term analysis means highlighting that it is a loosening, a separating and breaking apart of the whole into its constituent elements with an examination of these parts and their interrelationships.

Loewald envisioned the analyst as a new object, a mature object "who is stable and capable of controlled regression and who is optimally in communication with both his own and the patient's unconscious" (Loewald 1960, p. 252) and who recognizes the growth potential of his patient.

For Laplanche, "the analytic situation repeats the originary situation of primal seduction" (1999, p. 47). The Laplanchian question for the analysand is "What does this analyst want of me?" Laplanche is certainly not invested in the concept of a mature analyst who has knowledge of his and the patient's unconscious. The key element in Laplanche's thinking is the reopening in analysis of the enigmatic communication of the analyst and her infantile sexuality, the communication of which she is unaware. The analytic situation restirs the originary primal seduction of the mother-child intersubjective interaction.

Loewald recognizes the core of the patient as he or she is likely to become. Thus, he envisions that the patient's core self will emerge with the evolution in treatment. Although there is an asymmetry between the patient and the analyst, there is also an openness, and a recognition that each possesses his and her own psychic internalization. The analyst is also a co-creator and although offering a different level of psychic organization, the analyst is aware of the level of organization of the patient and offers timely interventions,

> structuring and articulating the material and productions presented by the patient…Analysts organize for the patient what was previously less organized… and thus gives him distance from himself that enables him to understand, to see, to put into words and to "handle what was previously not visible, understandable, speakable, tangible. A higher stage of organization is thus reached by the patient.
> (Loewald 1960, pp. 238–239)

The timely intervention should make unconscious-more primary process material available to the patient for integration on a new level of organization.

Laplanche by contrast is opaque to the future development of his analysand. He is not interested in organizing or synthesizing or offering interpretations for the patient. He believes patients, at times, have incorporated various cultural-social narratives that allow them to repeat defensive positions of sealing off, resisting disassociations which allow for increased defensive symbolizations. For example, he describes various "rules, myths ideologies and ideals that" help the ego to bind and thus defend against "the destructive tendencies of the drives" (Laplanche 2011, pp. 87–88). Laplanche is more careful and observant of the ways patients defensively elude their harsh unconscious, perverse fantasy life. Thus, more work on analytic dissociations need to take place.

Laplanche's primary concentration is on unbinding, destructuring, deconstructing, which allows for unusual elements to occur in the patient's "associations-dissociations" (Laplanche 2011, p. 281). For Laplanche, the entire analytic movement is against synthesis. "It is the dissolution of synthesis that has previously been accepted by the [patient]" (Laplanche 2011, p. 88). Of course, some syntheses are better at integrating the repressed, however, overall, they are defensive. "There will always be something of the repressed unconscious of the internal other that is the residue of the external other" (p. 88).

Laplanche insists on "refusement" (Laplanche 2016, p. 180) refusing to deal with conscious narratives, supportive interventions, knowledge, constructions, advice, or excuses. The analyst must refuse to know about possible meanings and the analyst "must refuse to believe that he knows" (Laplanche 2016, p. 182). The analyst may point out an unusual hidden element that he noted, or an atypical fragment that the patient presented, a slip of the tongue, or a patient's use of a homophone that could lead to the associative-dissociative network. All of the analytic work is the domain of the patient. Because these obscure elements can lead to painful associations, the analyst must be ever-present in his attending and holding of the patient. This I assume is of particular importance to Laplanche because what he illuminates when he intervenes is painful, disruptive, even aggressively hurtful interventions "when fissures or lines of cleavage can show themselves" (Laplanche 2016, p. 185). For Laplanche, learning about oneself is a devastating as well as a meaningful experience. Learning about one's unconscious polymorphous perverse fantasy life does not come readily, or acceptably. Working in this way for Laplanche is to engage in a spiral in which the patient returns again and again to deconstruct fragments and is relaunched again on a repetitive spiral but of potential new associative understanding.

One of the most dramatic differences is how both understand the effect of the analytic process on the patient and its goal. For Loewald, the source of the patient's conflicts stems from within. Acquiring knowledge about one's troubling unconscious archaic fantasies for Loewald is freeing and can provide a sense of mastery and resolution of the internal conflict.

The road is never-ending for Laplanche. We spiral back and again to our originary primal fantasy life with increasing new translations. The essence of the enigma is that there is always residue that needs further addressing. even when treatment ends, repression and its exigency is always with us. An experience with an other, after analysis, can surprise us, grip us, suddenly. It can inspire us and open us to new associations that come close to the repressed. We continue to be curious about the enigmatic other and thus sexuality is always with us allowing for inspiration.

In the unusual situation of an author presenting a paper, Laplanche holds the idea that the audience can be experienced as other. In this way, the audience can offer surprise and new associations-dissociations for the presenter. This suggests to me that you in the audience can have a potentially similar experience. As you the audience listen, you may be restirred by the Laplanchian thought, "What does this author of this paper want for me"? Yes, sublimated intellectual work and curiosity is relevant to the listener and both Loewald and Laplanche discuss the value of sublimation because of effective cognition. However, for Laplanche, we can speculate, as a listening audience, you too can be open to a surprise experience from the presenter, allowing disassociations to emerge for you leading to new translations. In recognition of the enigmatic other, inspiration is possible for the paper's author and the audience. Potential creativity is always ascendent.

When writing about the psychoanalytic process, Loewald's focus is on the relationship between the analyst and the patient. He is effulgent when describing their interactions. Warmth and caring shine through his narrative. To the extent that the analysand's defenses are flexible enough and close enough to his/her infantilism, that one's emancipation from early parental figures have developed and external reality has become integrated, "new depth and new dimensions" as a result of "reorganization" "of one's psyche can take place (Loewald 2000, p. 550). It is apparent that there is a deep commitment to his work; it is so much the case that he can genuinely write about love of his patient.

Here we have two gifted theoreticians who are thoroughly immersed in Freud's ideas. They both acknowledge and engage with his enormous theoretical contributions. Both advocated for the analysand's pursuit of her own desires, not of the analyst's nor of the culturally mandated ones. A major consideration for both was enabling the analysand to know, and experience the pleasures of their bodied sexuality, yet also recognizing the harsh, destructive, lustful underbelly of psychic life. In recognizing the dangerous abyss of unconscious sexuality for patients, each theorist is mindful of the attentiveness and care the analysand requires. They both consider psychoanalysis as providing a sense of agency and personal development for the analysand, an expansiveness of self- awareness and freedom that characterizes the endpoint of difficult analytic work. While there are some similarities, the larger issue is that each has adopted a different path to achieve psychoanalytic exploration and growth.

Note

1 Even the idea of the unconscious possessing psychic energy which needs discharge was presented (Weinberger, 2020).

References

Bataille, G. (1986). *Erotism: Death and Sensuality.* San Francisco, CA: City Lights Book.
Danon, G. & Lauru, D. (2015). Interview with Jean Laplanche. *The Psychoanalytic Review* 102: 709–719.
Fonagy, P. (2008). A genuinely developmental theory of sexual enjoyment and its implications for psychoanalytic technique. *Journal of the American Psychoanalytic Association* 56:11–36.
Freud, S. (1895). Project for a scientific psychology. *Standard Edition, Standard Edition* 1:281–397.
Freud, S. (1908). On the sexual theories of children. *Standard Edition* 9:205–226.
Freud, S. (1919). A child is being beaten. *Standard Edition* 17:175–204.
Freud, S. (1920). Beyond the pleasure principle. *Standard Edition* 18:3–64.
Freud, S. (1923). The ego and the id. *Standard Edition* 19:3–66.
Freud, S. (1926). Inhibition, symptoms, and anxiety. *Standard Edition* 20:87–172.
Laplanche, J. (1976). *Life and Death in Psychoanalysis*, transl. J. Mehlman. Baltimore, MD: The Johns Hopkins Press.
Laplanche, J. (1992). *Jean Laplanche: Séduction, Translation and the Drives: A Dossier*, ed. J. Fletcher & M. Stanton. London: Institute of Contemporary Arts.
Laplanche, J. (1999). *Essays on Otherness*, ed. J. Fletcher, transl. L. Thurston. London & New York: Routledge.
Laplanche, J. (2011). *Freud and the Sexual: Essays 2000–2006*, ed. N. Ray & J. Fletcher, transl. J. House. New York: International Universities Press.

Laplanche, J. (2015). *Between Seduction and Inspiration: Man*, transl. J. Mehlman. New York: The Unconscious in Translation.

Laplanche, J. (2016). *New Foundations in Psychoanalysis*, transl. J. House. New York: The Unconscious in Translation.

Loewald, H.W. (1951). Ego and reality. In *Papers on Psychoanalysis*. New Haven, CT: Yale University Press, 1980.

Loewald, H.W. (1960). On the therapeutic action of psychoanalysis. In *Papers on Psychoanalysis*. New Haven, CT: Yale University Press, 1980.

Loewald, H.W. (1971). On motivation and instinct theory. In *Papers on Psychoanalysis*. New Haven, CT: Yale University Press, 1980.

Loewald, H.W. (1973). On internalization. In *Papers on Psychoanalysis*. New Haven, CT: Yale University Press, 1980.

Loewald, H.W. (1978a). Instinct theory, object relations, and psychic structure formation. In *Papers on Psychoanalysis*. New Haven, CT: Yale University Press, 1980.

Loewald, H.W. (1978b). *Psychoanalysis and the History of the Individual*. New Haven, CT: Yale University Press.

Loewald, H.W. (1980). *Papers on Psychoanalysis*. New Haven, CT: Yale University Press.

Loewald, H.W. (2000). Sublimation: Inquires into theoretical psychoanalysis. In *The Essential Loewald. Collected Papers and Monographs*. Hagerstown, MD: University Publishing Group Inc.

Scarfone, D. (2015). *Laplanche*. New York: The Unconscious in Translation.

Silverman, D.K. (2015). An essay on Freud and the sexual: Essays 2000–2006. By J. Laplanche. *Psychoanalytic Psychology* 32:678–683.

Weinberger, J. & Stoycheva, V. (2021). *The Unconscious*. New York: Guilford Press.

Chapter 4

Theory of Language as Clinical Theory

Jeanine M. Vivona

A poem doesn't tell you how to live. It invites you to feel what living can be like. So it is with Hans Loewald's writing, which contains little clinical material and few comments about technique, as many have observed. Yet Loewald's uses of language afford his readers a sense of how to be as an analyst who thinks as he does.

The heart of Loewald's clinical theory is his view of the symbol and its quintessence, the word. For Loewald, the word is not merely a pointer to something of a different nature than itself but a portal to a world, including the interpersonal world. Consequently, language participates in meaning and relating from the beginning of life and, conversely, personal patterns of relating are written into language. Loewald's inspired and inspiring theory of the nature and development of symbolization and language undergirds his conceptualization of therapeutic action and offers psychoanalysis new ways to understand our familiar activities of speaking and listening.

Language: A Binding Power

In psychoanalysis today, we often find language conceptualized narrowly, particularly equated with abstract thinking and semantic content, and distinctly separate from the realm of lived experience. Other language functions, in which words play different roles, such as evoking feelings or conveying interpersonal action, are conceived as outside language, even when those functions are realized through speech (e.g., Reis 2021).

This is not Loewald's view of language, or of symbolism more generally. Quite the contrary. For Loewald, words are rooted in lived experience; more precisely, words grow out of experience yet remain connected to it. Thus, words function as bridges to lived experience; in fact, bridging is their purpose.

For Loewald, symbolism is at the heart of psychoanalysis. "It is the capacity for symbolization that clinical psychoanalysis promotes, usually by progressively leading the patient from repressed symbolism to actualizing and verifying live symbolic connections between hitherto disparate items of experience and thought" (Loewald 1987, p. 494). This therapeutic process, as we shall see, takes place in language, through particular uses of words, primarily the analyst's but also the patient's, which foster or recover symbolic connections between "experience and thought" that are *actualized and alive*.

In *Sublimation*, Loewald (1987) underscores that symbolism characterizes the nature of the *connection* between two things, not the nature of the things themselves. Something is operating as a symbol for someone when that person understands the symbol to be both connected to and distinct from the thing it represents.

DOI: 10.4324/9781032685151-5

For Loewald, symbolization is an act of imagination and thus subjective. "An item extant in reality becomes a symbol only when our imagination casts it to represent or stand for something else that it is not" (Loewald 1987, p. 483). This imaginative casting occurs, among other times, as infants come to understand that some of the vocal sounds they hear people utter are *words* with particular meanings. Perhaps paradoxically, Loewald understands symbols to be personal, products of one's own mind and often also the mind of one who came before, as is the case with most words. Loewald puts it this way: "Symbolism, more closely in touch with primary process, is seen as subjective in contrast to the objective world of secondary process" (1987, p. 503).

Because symbolism requires both connection and distinction of two entities or representations, symbolism is disabled if either the connection or the distinction is absent. When symbolism is disabled, its capacities are thwarted; the person does not have full access to the meanings, and to the kinds of mature and creative thinking, that symbolism affords. On the one hand, when the *connection* between two representations is disrupted, as happens with repression, the person cannot use the symbolic meaning; for instance, the person cannot know that the wish to be loved by the analyst represents the wish to be loved by the parent. On the other hand, when the *distinction* between the representations is disrupted, as happens with regression and in forms of thinking Loewald terms *protosymbolic or archaic*, the person experiences the symbol as the actual thing, as if there is no difference between the analyst's love and the parent's. Protosymbolic thinking, in which the symbol is taken for the thing itself, may occur normatively in early development and in psychotic states as well as in moments of reverie and creativity, for instance.

Crucially, language alone performs the therapeutic function of promoting symbolization.

> It is the prime function and intention of words to provide, to *be*, bridges between items of experience other than themselves and to bring out connections between them. … As symbolizing bridges they articulate differences and in that function, may be characterized as joints (the word *articulate* derives from the Latin *artus*, "joint"): they indicate differences and separateness while in the same act pointing at junction, relatedness.
>
> (Loewald 1987, p. 494)

Similarly, the words of interpersonal communication are joints, allowing separate individuals to connect and relate; words offer the possibility of relationships between separate individuals. Other types of symbolic and nonsymbolic representations (e.g., the analyst as symbol for the parent, tears as a sign of sadness) can be symbolized through articulation in thought and speech but cannot themselves create higher organization. That is the purview of language alone.

In his brilliant *Primary Process, Secondary Process, and Language*, Loewald (1978) summarizes succinctly the dual nature of language that drives therapeutic action:

> We may say that language, being a vehicle for secondary process or conscient mentation, being a medium of hypercathexis that creates higher organization, in its most genuine and autonomous function is a binding power. It ties together human beings and self and object world, and it binds abstract thought with the

bodily concreteness and power of life. In the word primary process and secondary process are reconciled.

(p. 204)

Importantly, the connecting or reconnecting of word and thing is itself an *experience*, both originally when one learns a word and subsequently when one uses words. This connecting is "a novel mental act" with "the nature of a perception" (Loewald 1978, pp. 182–183). For instance, when the analyst interprets the patient's wish for the analyst's love as representing a wish for maternal love, the patient may, if the words are mutative, have "a new experience," effected by the rejoining of the two representations, that has "the freshness and poignancy" of the original experience and is accompanied by "refreshed, modified memorial activity" (p. 183). Insight is new sight. In this way, words not only denote things other than themselves, as all symbols do. Words, in thought, speech, and writing, may signal the experience of the symbolizing activity, like a smile may signal the experience of joy.

Crucially, the word can bridge thought and experience, can be a binding power, because it is originally embedded in experience and emerges from it. Loewald (1978) describes in great depth the ways in which the words of language are embedded in and grow out of personal lived experiences, beginning with, and thus originally, the intimate experiences of infancy. Word and thing begin as one and become differentiated over development; variation in the degree of differentiation between word and thing supports the diverse functions of language. The use of words in a poem, for instance, may evoke the sensations of living because their connections to lived experiences, to memories of how things feel, are strong; the distance between word and thing is short. By contrast, words as used in technical language are more weakly or distantly connected to the things of experience, affording such words the autonomy required to convey such thoughts.

Nevertheless, although the distance between word and thing varies with particular uses of language, words are never fully autonomous from lived experience except when defenses render them so, resulting in "deadening insulation from the unconscious where human life and language are no longer vibrant and warmed by its fire" (Loewald 1978, p. 198). Indeed, the often-assumed abstractness of language is one of its functions, not its nature. "Words, including concepts used in science, are living and enlivening entities" (Loewald 1978, p. 193). Language in Loewald's view, and in his hands, is the natural habitat of a variety of types of thought with varying resonances with the things of experiencing.

Next I explore two related themes in Loewald's work that reflect his particular vision of both language and infancy (see also Mitchell 1998). The first is his idea that words are by nature enlivening entities, and that language offers the potential to know and use one's lived experiencing. The second, in the spirit of Loewald's vision, if not fully articulated in his writing, is the idea that language is originally, and thus potentially ever after, a mode of relatedness. Both ideas are consistent with current knowledge of infant development as well as unique within and generative for psychoanalysis.

The Thing with a Name

The first important theme in Loewald's work related to language is that words are, by their very nature, both alive and enlivening entities. First, it is a primary function of words to access lived experiencing; "This power of words is intimately related to their being physical, sensory-motor events or acts" (Loewald 1978, p. 200). Words are *lived action*. Second, words originate in lived experiences throughout life, and these origins involve a new experience: "The word is not simply added to the thing, but the thing itself becomes first defined or delimited as an alive circumscribed entity (hyper-cathexis)" (Loewald 1978, p. 197).

The thing with a name is suddenly not the same as the thing without one; the act of naming transforms the things of experience as it highlights and defines them. More-over, on both learning and remembering, the process of connecting word and experi-ence is itself an enlivening experience, "akin to perception," that builds or rebuilds a bridge to experience that can then serve as a foundation of living.

Importantly, other theorists, including those who have attended carefully to infant development, have drawn opposite conclusions from the recognition that knowing words changes experiencing. Notably and famously, Daniel Stern (1985, 2004) founded his theory of development and therapeutic action on the idea that language disrupts rather than expands our ability to know and use our lived experiencing as a mode of living; for Stern, language has a deadening rather than an enlivening effect.

Loewald and Stern present divergent views of the relevance and function of lan-guage in infancy (see also Vivona 2006, 2012). For Stern, language is a latecomer to development, relevant only after crucial foundations of self and relatedness have been laid. Prior to the age of eighteen months or later, the semantic meanings of oth-ers' speech are beyond the infant's grasp; subsequently, language becomes a verbal layer of experience that is and remains separate from the prior experiential layers. For Loewald, language is present in the infant's world from the beginning and inherently integrated with other aspects of experiencing; development involves not new layers of meaning but differentiation of meanings that involve various admixtures of word and thing.

Neither Loewald nor Stern could know the extent to which infants have the capac-ity to use the semantic meanings and structures of language. Current knowledge of infants supports the idea that infants can and do make use of words as words from very early life and long before they are speaking themselves. Specifically, infants in the first year of life use words to supplement their senses and to relate more complexly to the objects words denote, such that words enable infants to see and know their lived experiences more clearly, as is also true for adults.

Infants begin to recognize the semantic connection between spoken words and things in the world at around six months of age (Swingley 2009; Bergelson & Swingley 2012) and soon after, knowing word meanings affects infants' processing and understanding of their world, whether or not they hear the words being spoken. For instance, studies of brain activity demonstrate that nine- to ten-month-old infants sustain their visual processing on familiar objects whose names they know (Gliga, Volein, & Csibra 2010) and that seeing such objects activates brain regions associated with both the sound and the referential meaning of the word, enabling the infant to detect whether the use of the spoken word matches the expected meaning (Junge, Cutler, & Hagoort 2012). Moreover, infants can track the movements of such objects more accurately (Rivera & Zawaydeh 2007). For instance, ten-month-olds can keep track of a ball and a dog moving in and out of view if they know the meanings of the words *ball* and *dog,* even when those words are not spoken; when they don't know both words, infants of this age can track only one object at a time. Thus, in these ways, knowing word meanings facilitates infants' understanding of the happenings of their worlds.

Importantly, infants can discern and use the conceptual information conveyed by words to supplement the knowledge they gain from their senses, even when they do not already know the meanings of the words. For example, ten-month-old infants expect that similarly named objects share features that are not reflected in their appearance (Dewar & Xu 2009). That is, when infants are shown that a novel object labeled "wug" makes a sound when shaken, they will expect a new wug to do the same, even when the wugs differ in appearance and when the infant is not previously familiar with either the object or the word. Thus, infants form expectations about things in the world based on the words connected to those things; words offer a unique source of information about objects and events in the world, even to infants in the first year of life.

The importance of such conceptual information is related to the process of a thing becoming, in Loewald's words, "defined or delimited as an alive circumscribed entity" when it is connected to a word. Specifically, this delineation involves categorization. Decades of infant research by Sandra Waxman and her colleagues (1995, 2009) demonstrates the profound impact of spoken words on infant's creation of categories (see details in Vivona 2006). As early as six months of age, infants create categories in response to others' spoken words in particular. That is, when adults use the same word to refer to an array of objects, infants consider the objects to be the same kind of thing, even when the objects differ in appearance; conversely, infants do not categorize similar-appearing objects when they are labeled differently. Thus, even infants in the first year of life integrate information from words with information from perception when creating categories. Waxman summarizes her research thus: "Words serve as *invitations* to form categories" (Waxman 2009, p. 103).

These and other studies (see Vivona 2019) demonstrate that words, both known and new, whether heard or only remembered, affect how infants process and understand the world around them. Words provide information to infants that is otherwise unavailable and highlight features of the world they might otherwise overlook. In these ways, as Loewald knew and in ways he did not, a thing with a name is different from a thing without one, even to an infant, who is just beginning the process of learning and using language.

More generally, the research is consistent with Loewald's vision of the process of language development, in which words emerge from yet remain connected to lived experiencing, as well as facilitate a more nuanced understanding of that experiencing. By contrast, the research is not consistent with views, such as Stern's, that language is irrelevant to the infant or disconnected from lived experience.

The Personal Relational Origins of Language

The second theme that infuses Loewald's theory of language, although it is less articulated than the first, is that language is shaped by the interpersonal contexts within which words are learned. In this way, language is a mode of relatedness that develops in concert with other modes of relating; as such, language both memorializes and enacts the meanings and messages of one's personal relational history.

It is certainly true that some people, including some psychoanalysts, do not conceptualize or experience language as deeply or inherently connected to lived experience, and relational experiences in particular. Such differences confirm rather than contradict Loewald's theory, however. That is because, for Loewald, language is a legacy of one's development and thus personal despite also being shared. Writing about the interpersonal origins of language in infancy, Loewald puts it succinctly: "The emotional relationship to the person from whom the word is learned plays a significant, in fact crucial, part in how alive the link between thing and word turns out to be" (Loewald 1978, p. 197). I interpret Loewald to mean not only the aliveness of bridges that are one's particular words, but the pattern of aliveness and perhaps deadness that characterizes uses and meanings of language for a person.

We all learn what language is and what it can do from particular other people and through particular experiences. Following Loewald, we can appreciate that learning language begins in experiencing the ways language is used for relating, learning the things language can and cannot do, interpersonally and experientially. Both the contexts and outcomes of this learning are relational. The experiences words connect to and the quality of those connections are a legacy of one's personal relational history. These experiences are moments of being with another person, prototypically the mother (and also, of course, the analyst), who uses speech along with all the other actions of relating and communicating – looking, touching, smiling or crying, moving closer or farther away. Thus, the mother Loewald envisions for us is one who speaks to and for her infant. Correspondingly, the infant hears and is affected by her words. Maternal speech breathes life into language for infants.

Beatrice Beebe and her colleagues document a compelling manifestation of Loewald's idea that infants' relational experiences animate language in particular ways. The researchers analyze mother-infant interactions during face-to-face play, videorecording mothers and their four-month-old infants as they engage with and respond to each other using gaze, facial expressions, voice, and touch. Strikingly different patterns of behavioral (Beebe & Lachmann 2017) and verbal (Kaminer et al. 2007) interaction are associated with two maternal personality characteristics: *interpersonal dependency* and *self-criticism* (Blatt 2004). These interactional patterns illustrate that mothers have particular ways of using and integrating behavioral and verbal modes of relating with their infants, and that infants adopt complementary practices in their own ways of relating. Consistent with Loewald's view of language development, infants internalize and may later emulate the particular relational meanings and functions of language that they experience in their early intimate relationships.

People high on interpersonal dependency define their value in terms of interpersonal connection, strive for emotional closeness, and tend to avoid conflict with others (Blatt 2004). Correspondingly, interpersonally-dependent mothers and their infants are highly coordinated with each other in the realms of gaze, facial expressions of emotion, and touch (Beebe & Lachmann 2017). Such mothers closely match their gaze focus with their infant's gaze focus and their facial expressions with their infant's facial and vocal expressions of emotion, a kind of visual and emotional hovering. Similarly, the content of these mothers' speech is focused on the infant's current attention, action, or experience to a greater degree than the speech of other mothers (Kaminer et al. 2007). Infants mirror their mothers' attentional vigilance with high degrees of facial responding to their mothers' facial expressions, such that emotional states, both positive and negative, are mutually amplified. Importantly, interpersonally-dependent mothers are uniquely likely to respond to their infants' visual disengagement with verbal expressions of concern, often involving the infant's autonomous action. For example, when her infant looked away from her, one mother repeatedly asked, "What are you looking at?" in a worried tone (Kaminer et al. 2007). Conversely, interpersonally-dependent mothers comment less on their infants' actions while their infants are looking at them, compared to other mothers.

Thus, interpersonally-dependent mothers use speech as they use eye gaze and facial mirroring, to achieve tight interpersonal coordination with their infants. When infants visually disengage, these mothers use a particular kind of speech to reengage their infants, vocally and verbally enacting with the infant the interpersonal consequences of disconnection. Thus, the connecting and coordinating functions and meanings of words are particularly animated for these infants, especially compared to independent and autonomy-related functions and meanings. The infant lives in a world in which a primary function of language is to maintain interpersonal connection.

By contrast, people high on self-criticism value autonomy; they tend to be self-sufficient, interpersonally distant, and wary of others' needs of them (Blatt 2004). Consistent with these tendencies, self-critical mothers and their infants are relatively unresponsive to each other, compared to other mother-infant pairs (Beebe and Lachmann 2017). Self-critical mothers tend not to maintain mutual gaze with their infants or follow their infants' gaze when their infants look away from them, and they are less likely to respond to their infant's vocal affect with corresponding facial expressions (e.g., less likely to smile in response to their infant's happy cooing). Interestingly, self-critical mothers are more responsive than other mothers in the realm of touch; that is, they are more likely to respond to their infants' touches with more affectionate touches of their own. However, their infants are less likely than other infants to respond to their mother's affectionate touches with vocal expressions of pleasure. Thus, like their mothers, these infants tend not to respond to the other's bids for connection.

Verbally, self-critical mothers utter more negative and fewer positive expressions than other mothers (Kaminer et al. 2007). They are more likely to correct or criticize their infants (e.g., "Oh no, that's not a smile.") and less likely to use compliments and terms of endearment. Like interpersonally-dependent mothers, self-critical mothers verbally express discomfort when their infants visually disengage from them. However, their expressions more often take the form of criticisms, warnings, and redirections (e.g., "You're gonna sit up? No. Why don't you sit back?"). The tenor and timing of such comments suggest these mothers may feel injured when their infants look away, as though infant disengagement signals personal failure in mothering to self-critical mothers (Kaminer et al. 2007).

Thus, the speech of self-critical mothers is notable for conveying more negative and fewer positive judgments of infants' actions. By contrast, their behavioral and affective modes of relating are characterized not by overt contradiction and correction but by reticence and disengagement. Only in the realm of touch do these mothers convey their tenderness; not surprisingly, their infants do not appear to know what to make of it, as suggested by their lack of emotional response. In the context of their mothers' contradictory ways of relating, language may become a particular site for experiences of negativity and rejection for these infants.

These two mother-infant interaction patterns evince both distinct maternal uses of speech and contrasting relationships between speech and other modes of relatedness; these are the kinds of relational particularities Loewald understood to leave their mark in everyone's language, to render language inherently personal. Specifically, the speech of interpersonally-dependent mothers mirrors and likely amplifies the interpersonal coordination such mothers also effect through gaze and facial matching, such that all modes of relatedness convey a consistent message about the importance of interpersonal attentiveness and responsiveness. In contrast to this coherent multi-modal communication, the relatedness of self-critical mothers conveys contradictory messages across modes of communicating and relating, manifesting disconnect not only between verbal and behavioral modes, but among behavioral modes as well. Among these mixed messages, maternal speech is distinct for conveying negative judgments that are not overt in other modes.

As Loewald envisioned, mothers differ in terms of the ways they use speech in the context of other modes of relatedness and communication; maternal speech enlivens the connection between word and thing particularly. Infants experience and internalize maternal uses of speech, writing those lessons into a language of their own. In these ways, early developments of self and relatedness are connected to and lived through language, potentially if not invariably.

An Analyst Who Thinks Like Loewald

Loewald's theoretical innovations have been overlooked for many reasons, his use of Freud's language among them. Mitchell (1998) speculated that Loewald used Freud's terminology so faithfully in part because of the deep connection to Freud that lived in those words for Loewald. Yet Loewald infused those words, as living and enlivening entities, with new meanings. Mitchell puts it this way: "In his quiet, undramatic fashion, Loewald has transformed the basic values guiding the analytic process, substituting meaning for rationality, imagination for objectivity, vitalization for control. The central ameliorative impact lies in relinking" (p. 850).

This relinking, and the transformed values guiding the analytic process more generally, are centered in Loewald's theory of language, which is the heart of his clinical theory. Indeed, although Loewald offers us little clinical material and few comments on technique (Chodorow 2009), his writing both describes and enacts the potentials of language that fuel therapeutic action. Many authors comment on the poetic and musical qualities of Loewald's writing (e.g., Lang 2009), his evocative multilayered metaphors, the glorious "ghosts to ancestors" (Loewald 1960) being perhaps the most well-known. At other times, his writing is highly technical and dense, giving the reader the sense of a difficult problem being worked out. In these ways, Loewald shows us the various potentials of language and entreats us to use them all.

The transformative relinking that is therapeutic action for Loewald is enacted and achieved through the familiar actions of speaking and listening; nothing more. His clinical innovations are within language, not outside of it. Yet in envisioning language as inherently infused with lived experiencing, in inspiring a vision of language as a mode of living and in particular a mode of relatedness, Loewald potentiates these familiar activities of the analytic dyad, and offers new ways to think about and to be in the clinical encounter.

Loewald makes clear that speaking and listening have therapeutic potential because words are acts and bridges. People's actions and bodily states are not merely experiences in need of conversion to verbalization or linkage to words; such experiences embody words that may not have been spoken, but can be, when we know to listen for them. Moreover, the linking that is the word is itself a new experience that we can recognize in words – Aha! Now I see. That makes sense. I never thought about it that way before.

This linking is the integration or re-integration of thought and feeling, word and experience, primary process and secondary process, insight and relationship; it is the reunification of elements of being that Loewald conceptualizes as naturally integrated, rather than naturally separated. It yields the ability to see, accept, and use different elements of experiencing, being, and thinking, such that those elements are truly understood as mutually-constituting. It is a kind of "binocular vision," as Loewald once put it, that transcends dichotomies and expands the possibilities of being.

To be useful in this way, the analyst must think like Loewald, which is to say must have in mind and heart the potentials of words to connect to lived experiencing in a meaningful and enlivening way. Moreover, the analyst must be open to hearing the patient's language as a legacy of personal relational history, to noticing where the words are alive and where they are dead, to understanding the patient's hopes and fears about language as hopes and fears about relatedness. And the analyst must believe that speaking and listening more fully can lead to living more fully, that the lessons written into language in the past can be re-written through the relationship with the analyst.

In a manner both precise and inspired, both technical and moving, Loewald explains how speaking with a stranger can change a life.

Conclusion

In *The Therapeutic Action of Psychoanalysis*, Loewald (1960) famously claims that the analyst holds a vision of who the patient can become, ideally "a more articulate and integrated version of the core of his being" (p. 229). The analyst speaks to the patient with this image in mind, and this way of thinking and relating makes it possible for the patient to internalize and move toward this version of self, in Loewald's words "leading to a new way of relating to objects and of being oneself."

If we think of psychoanalysis as the patient, we can imagine Loewald writing his theory with our future selves in mind, envisioning for us a more articulate and integrated version of psychoanalysis in which we relate in new ways to the objects of our theories and to each other, and inhabit new ways of being ourselves as psychoanalysts. This is a future in which we may integrate and thus transcend the familiar theoretical oppositions that currently divide us. Perhaps these oppositions reflect our current stage of development or our preferred mechanisms of defense. Yet they do not reflect the totality of the mind or the potentials of living or the full promise of psychoanalysis.

Loewald envisions and embodies a psychoanalysis in which we attend to the simultaneity of both primary process and secondary process, both conflict and relatedness, both intrapsychic and interpersonal experiencing, both symbolized and enacted meanings, both insight and relationship, both "verbal" and "nonverbal" modes of being and knowing. Indeed, it is the purpose and purview of psychoanalysis to encompass both.

And just as language is both site and medium of the patient's transformation, so language might be both site and medium of the transformation of psychoanalysis. Loewald's theory of language breaks down by bridging over the dichotomies around which psychoanalytic camps have tended to coalesce. Most centrally, it helps us to reconcile these dichotomies by siting experience *within* language. In this way, Loewald offers psychoanalysis an understanding of language, including the speech that is our therapeutic method, that bridges over our disagreements and invites us to move forward toward a more integrated and whole version of our field.

References

Beebe, B., & Lachmann, F. (2017). Maternal self-critical and dependent personality styles and mother-infant communication. *Journal of the American Psychoanalytic Association* 65: pp. 491–508.

Bergelson, E., & Swingley, D. (2012). At 6–9 months, human infants know the meanings of many common nouns. *Proceedings of the National Academy of Sciences* 109: pp. 3253–3258.

Blatt, S. J. (2004). *Experiences of Depression: Theoretical, Clinical, and Research Perspectives.* Washington, DC: American Psychological Association.

Chodorow, N. J. (2009). A different universe: Reading Loewald through "On the therapeutic action of psychoanalysis." *The Psychoanalytic Quarterly* 78: pp. 983–1011.

Dewar, K., & Xu, F. (2009). Do early nouns refer to kinds or distinct shapes? Evidence from 10- month-old infants. *Psychological Science* 20: pp. 252–257.

Gliga, T., Volein, A., & Csibra, G. (2010). Verbal labels modulate perceptual object processing in 1-year-old children. *Journal of Cognitive Neuroscience* 22: pp. 2781–2789.

Junge, C., Cutler, A., & Hagoort, P. (2012). Electrophysiological evidence of early word learning. *Neuropsychologia* 50: pp. 3702–3712.

Kaminer, T., Beebe, B., Jaffe, J., Kelly, K., & Marquette, L. (2007). Mothers' dependent and self-critical depressive experience is related to speech content with infants. *Journal of Early Childhood and Infant Psychology* 3: pp. 163–185.

Lang, F. (2009). Hans Loewald and the transformation of passion. *The Psychoanalytic Study of the Child* 64: pp. 3–13.

Loewald, H. W. (1960). On the therapeutic action of psychoanalysis. In *Papers on Psychoanalysis.* New Haven, CT: Yale University Press, 1980, pp. 221–256.

Loewald, H. W. (1978). Primary process, secondary process, and language. In *Papers on Psychoanalysis.* New Haven, CT: Yale University Press, 1980, pp. 178–206.

Loewald, H. W. (1987). Sublimation. In *Sublimation: Inquiries into Theoretical Psychoanalysis.* Hagerstown, MD: University Publishing Group, 2000, pp. 483–501.

Mitchell, S. A. (1998). From ghosts to ancestors: The psychoanalytic vision of Hans Loewald. *Psychoanalytic Dialogues* 8: pp. 825–855.

Reis, B. (2021). The analyst's listening: For, to, with. *The International Journal of Psychoanalysis* 102: pp. 219–235.

Rivera, S. M., & Zawaydeh, A. N. (2007). Word comprehension facilitates object individuation in 10-and 11-month-old infants. *Brain Research* 1146: pp. 146–157.

Stern, D. N. (1985). *The Interpersonal World of the Infant.* New York: Basic Books.

Stern, D. N. (2004). *The Present Moment in Psychotherapy and Everyday Life.* New York: Norton.

Swingley, D. (2009). Contributions of infant word learning to language development. *Philosophical Transactions of the Royal Society B: Biological Sciences* 364: pp. 3617–3632.

Vivona, J. M. (2006). From developmental metaphor to developmental model: The shrinking role of language in the talking cure. *Journal of the American Psychoanalytic Association* 54: pp. 877–902.

Vivona, J. M. (2012). Is there a nonverbal period of development? *Journal of the American Psychoanalytic Association* 60: pp. 231–265.

Vivona, J. M. (2019). The interpersonal words of the infant: Implications of current infant language research for psychoanalytic theories of infant development, language, and therapeutic action. *The Psychoanalytic Quarterly* 88: pp. 685–725.

Waxman, S. R. (2009). How infants discover distinct word types and map them to distinct meanings. In *Infant Pathways to Language: Methods, Models, and Research Directions*, ed. J. Colombo, P. McCardle, and L. Freund. New York: Psychology Press, pp. 99–118.

Waxman, S. R., & Markow, D. B. (1995). Words as invitations to form categories: Evidence from 12- to 13-month infants. *Cognitive Psychology* 29: pp. 257–302.

Chapter 5

A Missing Link
Hans Loewald and Marion Milner

Nancy Olson

It is not uncommon for readers of Loewald to be moved by his narrative voice.[1] Fluent in philosophy and poetry, sometimes he evokes being read to, as we once used to be in the mother-child field. Of course we listen for his parental authority, his higher levels of organization, to reveal the secrets of psychoanalysis, at least whichever versions we are seeking. Our reading may be thought of as a dive into his "mind, that ocean where each kind does straight its own resemblance find."[2] In this spirit, I find my Loewald in conversation with Marion Milner. Their voices are distinct yet harmonious. Like artists, they sometimes cover their tracks to protect their opportunities to view things independently. Their creativity sets them apart, along with synthetic habits of mind, and often beautiful writing that resists paraphrase. They play well together, as if at my tea set or the same dinner party. I am struck by a coincidence of essays: Winnicott's "Primitive Emotional Development" (1945), Milner's *On Not Being Able to Paint* (1950) and "The Role of Illusion in Symbol Formation" (1952), Loewald's "Ego and Reality" (1951) and "Psychoanalysis as an Art and the Fantasy Character of the Psychoanalytic Situation" (1975). These were "Banquet Years" for psychoanalytic writing, with Winnicott's paper as *apéritif*, and Loewald's later paper, *digestif.*

Both Milner (1900–1998) and Loewald (1906–1993) were Europeans whose identities as analysts were informed by American experience—by fellowship and immigration, respectively. A Loewald biography remains to be written. He lived and worked in Colmar, Berlin, Marburg, Freiburg (where he read philosophy with Heidegger), Rome (where he took his medical degree in 1934), Padua, and Paris. In 1939, after trying unsuccessfully to become a citizen of France, he brought his family to the United States, soon to practice in the adult and child psychiatric clinics at the University of Maryland School of Medicine and the Baltimore-Washington Institute for Psychoanalysis. "Ego and Reality," from the Baltimore years, was his first psychoanalytic paper, a brilliant reimagining of development and Oedipal dynamics from the perspective of the oceanic feeling and the contribution of early, undifferentiated states. In 1955, he moved to New Haven, joining the faculties of Yale University and the recently founded Western New England Institute for Psychoanalysis.

I will say more about Milner as she may be less familiar to readers. If Loewald's first love was philosophy, hers was natural science. At age 11, she began keeping a diary of her observations and sketches of nature. This practice became what she would call "the roots of the tree" (1987b, p. 1). Her first job, at 18, was tutoring a seven-year-old boy. She discovered Montessori and was taken with the creative relation between work and play. After Montessori College, she studied psychology and physiology at University

DOI: 10.4324/9781032685151-6

College, London. Her brother, Patrick Blackett, gave her Freud's *Introductory Lectures on Psychoanalysis*. More "enchanted by physiology," Milner was drawn to a "brilliant" course by the psychoanalyst, J. C. Flügel (1884–1955), who "drew a parallel between the integrative functions of the nervous system as described by Sherrington and the principles of unconscious functioning as described by Freud" (1969, p. xli).

After taking her degree Milner worked with Cyril Burt in the vocational guidance service of the National Institute of Industrial Psychology, observing his interviews with juvenile delinquents. Searching, she enrolled in a mental training course at the Pelman Institute in London. The Pelman method promised to cure problems such as "grasshopper mind," forgetfulness, depression, phobia, procrastination, and "Lack of System." In 1926, she resumed diary-keeping, "this time studying the habits, not of the beasts and the birds, but my own ways of thinking" (1987b, p. 2). At 27 she married Dennis Milner, a writer and inventor. In 1927, they left for Boston, where Marion had a fellowship to study with Elton Mayo at the Harvard Business School. Mayo's work helped to establish the human relations movement. He emphasized that within the formal organization of a workplace, there exists an informal organizational structure. His ideas on group relations were advanced in *The Human Problems of an Industrial Civilization.* "We studied Pierre Janet on the neuroses, the early works of Freud, and Piaget's *Language and Thought of the Child* [1926]," Milner recalled; "As far as I remember we never used Freud's words 'primary and secondary processes' but talked instead in terms of 'directed and undirected thinking'. The former, according to Mayo, aims at establishing truths, the latter at establishing relationships" (1987b, p. 3).

In 1929, the Milners returned to London, where they entered treatment with Theodore Faithfull, whose *Bisexuality: An Essay on Extraversion and Introversion* explained neurosis in terms of conflict between masculine and feminine aspects of the personality. Dennis had developed asthma and proved unable to work. Their son, John, was born in 1932. Marion supported them in part by writing books for a general audience, based on her diary keeping, published under the pseudonym Joanna Field. "Joanna," as the feminine of John, suggests what Milner calls "our dual nature, the male and female aspects of the psyche" (1987b, p. 178). "Field" evokes Milner at play in the field of her mind, as well as the mother-child field, a vision shared with Winnicott and Loewald.

In *A Life of One's Own* (1934) Milner/Field shares with the reader her evolving practice of self-observation.[3] Not autobiography in the usual sense, the text is personal in the way of analytic hours, the details creating a context in which certain themes come to life. Assuming few persons have access to psychoanalysis, Milner uses herself to illustrate "a method by which an ordinary person can seek to become aware of some of the processes of life that are going on inside himself" (1937, pp. xlv–xlvi). Her appeal to the reader is democratic and empowering. *A Life of One's Own* met with critical acclaim (including from poets W. H. Auden and Stephen Spender) and inspired many readers. It was followed by *An Experiment in Leisure* (1937) and *Eternity's Sunrise* (1987a). The trilogy follows her path of accepting "the *x*, the unknown factor, the [unconscious] force by which one is lived" (1937, p. 146).

In 1933 Milner began conducting research for the Girls Public Day School Trust, using various concepts (Mayo's directed/undirected thinking, Jung's extroverted/introverted personality types) and methods to assess the capacity of teenage girls to be receptive to the inner life. For example, she asked the girls to record their daydreams and responses to paintings, adapting techniques she had used on herself. Her findings appeared in 1938 as *The Human Problem in Schools* (edited by the analyst Susan Isaacs, its title alluding to Mayo's *The Human Problems of an Industrial Civilization*).

1940 saw the beginning of her analytic training, supervised by Melanie Klein, Joan Riviere, and Ella Sharpe. During this decade, Milner wrote another book analyzing her doodles and sketches, *On Not Being Able to Paint*. A point of departure was *The Human Problem in Schools*: "I thought that by exploring an activity in which I had failed to learn what I wanted to learn [painting], I might find out something of what I felt was being left out of the school system" (1987b, p. 7). The book also reflects her analytic education in conversation with Klein, Winnicott and others. The first edition appeared in 1950, by Joanna Field, while the second appeared under her own name in 1957, with a foreword by Anna Freud.

Our Primary Madness

On Not Being Able to Paint begins with the idea that painting is concerned with the feelings conveyed by space. In line and color, Milner finds a painterly analogy to feeling states of separation and merger. She considers painting's ways of expressing distance, separation, transition, immersion: objects defined by outlines, the fading of light into darkness, the "plunge into color." She follows our developmental unfolding from an original unity or wholeness to the lifelong flux between positions of relative merger and differentiation. We are born not knowing the difference between thoughts and things, subjective and objective, wishes and reality. She notes that

> our inner dream and outer perception both spring from a common source or primary phase of experience in which the two are not distinguished, a primary 'madness' we have all lived through and to which at times we can return
>
> (1950, p. 33)

She travels in the wake of Winnicott's comment: "Through artistic expression we can hope to keep in touch with our primitive selves. It is from here that our most intense feelings and even fearfully acute sensations derive, and we are poor indeed if we are only sane" (1945, p. 140, fn. 3).

Milner describes our original state as narcissism, noting:

> Whereas narcissism, as usually understood, contains the idea of a withdrawal from reality, it is now becoming connected with the idea of oneness with the universe and a fundamental relatedness to reality, a state in which the libidinal cathexis of the body (body ego) may become the source, reservoir, for a new cathexis of the external world.
>
> (1969, p. 308, fn. 4)

She goes on: "Sublimation then begins by a reactivation of narcissism, which somehow overflows and extends to objects" (1969, p. 308, fn. 4).[4] To bestow the world with our cathexis (one might say, the stamp or signature of our desire) is a perceptive—and creative—act. "Outer reality is never permanently the same as our dreams, yet such moments are the vital illusions by which we live" (1950, p. 35).

For Milner, our human predicament has to do with the primitive hating resulting from disappointment, from the discrepancy between our dreams and what reality offers. "'The lunatic, the lover, and the poet' (or painter) try to transcend this hate and either succeed or fail" (1950, p. 80). From this point of view, painting may be considered the restoration of what one had loved and internally hurt or destroyed. She retains Klein's concept of the depressive position and the need to make reparation. But for Milner, creativity as reparation is secondary to the original creative gesture—overflow—in which we make the world according to our dreams. We are forever seeking to return to the original feeling of being at one with the world. At first an illusion, it becomes a reconciliation, a bringing together of what had become separate, creating something new. We are close to the role given to the oceanic feeling in Loewald's "Ego and Reality." Milner imagines a circular process: our dreams transform reality; reality, in turn, transforms our dreams.

Controlled Exuberance

Milner finds her "good" drawings involve something other than conscious effort, something having to do with what she calls "a deep impulse to rhythmic repetition inherent in our being" (1950, p. 113). This leads her to distinguish two kinds of order, the willed or imposed and the non-willed or inherent. The non-willed order is rather like the patterns that emerge in free association. She believes we may be wary of, but need this kind of order, which is given by the unconscious. "Along with this internal sense of rhythm," she continues, "there are external rhythms and rules imposed by authority and the clock... something alien imposed from above, the submission to which might seem to involve the loss of one's whole spontaneous life" (1950, p. 113). Here she approaches the superego and Winnicott's false self (1960a). The two orders are in dynamic tension. Milner concludes: "Fearful subservience to an imposed authority either inside or out, or complete abandonment of all controls, neither of these was the solution"; better "a controlled exuberance," lest without these external rules of order, "the free movement of feeling threatens to become an overwhelming sea" (1950, p. 56). We are reminded of Loewald on the ecstasies and terrors of the oceanic feeling (akin to the sublime) and our ambivalent relationship to the—life-enhancing—unconscious.

Thus, we find Milner and Loewald, in their respective ways, concerned with the maternal-infant field before differentiation, watching the emergence of the psyche from a circular and developmental perspective that may describe and be resumed in psychoanalytic treatment.[5]

American and British Independents

In *The Psychoanalytic Ear and the Sociological Eye* (2020) Nancy Chodorow describes Loewald's "doubled vision," his integration of ego psychology with object relations, creating a hybrid she chooses to call intersubjective ego psychology. American analysts of this persuasion sought to combine the perspectives of Hartmann and Sullivan, much as the British Middle School of independents saw themselves between, and putting together, Anna Freud and Melanie Klein. Milner was part of this Middle group. *A Life of One's Own* (1934) and *On Not Being Able to Paint* (1950) are studies in coming to grips with Freud and Klein, respectively.

Chodorow sees the American independent tradition reaching beyond close personal relationships and identifications to include social and cultural determinants and expressions of the intrapsychic domain. Here, Erik Erikson (1902–1994) is her exemplar. Room is made for the formative nature/effects of internalized relationships (individual objects), and for contributions to the inner life from groups dynamics and the cultural surround.

As a sociologist and psychoanalyst, Chodorow sees connections yet to be explored between the fields. She further suggests

> the American independent tradition grew from the beginning, much as did interpersonal psychoanalysis, partly from connections to and collaboration with social science and from an attention to history, culture, and the social in both psychic life and the clinical process.
>
> (2020, p xvi)

Like Freud, who "brought consistent attention to the sociocultural in relation to the psyche... Loewald too was deeply interested in the social" (2020, p. xvi). Chodorow notes especially his Freud Lectures, *Psychoanalysis and the History of the Individual* (1978), and his invitation to sociologist Talcott Parsons to participate in a conference on internalization (Chodorow, 2020, p. xvii). In "Psychoanalysis as an Art and the Fantasy Character of the Psychoanalytic Situation," Loewald observes:

> Freud was conscious of attempting to do more than heal neuroses of individuals. In fact, this latter purpose of psychoanalysis seemed more and more to take second place in his interests. That he and his friends spoke of psychoanalysis, not only as a science and as a form of psychotherapy, but as the psychoanalytic *movement*, that they were concerned with anthropology, mythology, and civilization and its discontents—all this shows that they had larger aims and vistas, namely to influence and change the outlook and behavior of a whole era in regard to the relationship and balance between rational and instinctual life and between fantasy and objective reality.
>
> (1975, p. 364)

In his last published essay, "Psychoanalysis in Search of Nature: Thoughts on Metapsychology, 'Metaphysics,' Projection" (1988), Loewald considers how as humans we evolve and relate, not only to the social field but to nature and the cosmos, as if he anticipates our current crisis in relation to the climate and our planet (Downey, 2015, p. 993). His imaginative grasp of our responsiveness to spaces, scale, emptiness, fullness, infinity, and related qualia was already present in "Ego and Reality" (1951).

For her part, Milner agrees that the

> isolation of psychoanalysis, by its terminology, from related fields, may not have been a disadvantage in the early days of the struggle to establish analytic concepts in their own right, but now such isolation can, I think, lead to an impoverishment of our own thinking.
>
> (Milner, 1952, p. 105)

Her social science *bona fides* were hands-on: Montessori College, the National Institute of Industrial Psychology, the Harvard Business School, the Girl's Public Day School Trust. Looking back, these institutions and their research appear more "psychoanalytic" in her time than today (Elton Mayo studied reverie in monotonous work, for example, and the worker's need for a meaningful role in the group). It was another Zeitgeist, ready to apply Freud's ideas, and open to the study of relationships.

Creative Experience

Near the end of *On Not Being Able to Paint* Milner writes:

> The prose quotations given here as chapter headings are from a book published in the United States in 1930. The book is concerned with the implications of scientific studies of creative experience between people and groups of people, whether in industrial, social or political relationships.... I had first read the book before making this study, even though, when choosing these chapter headings, it had seemed that I was reading them for the first time.
>
> (Milner, 1950, p. 159)

The book was *Creative Experience* by Mary Parker Follett (1868–1933), American social worker, management consultant, and pioneer (some say prophet) in the field of organizational theory and behavior. *Creative Experience* first appeared in 1924. We do not know how Milner found it—perhaps through Mayo, who knew them both at Harvard, or in London, where Follett was embraced by British management circles.

Imagine working social science, philosophy, poetry, and psychoanalysis into a book ostensibly about not painting! In Milner's pages, Follett mingles synergistically with Santayana and Blake. In Follett's pages, we find a critique and corrective to ego (one-person) psychology, *avant la lettre*. Reading Follett, at times it is hard to believe that Loewald hasn't read her too.[6] If Milner and Loewald took an American road trip, Follett could be their sidecar.

Follett was born in 1868 in Quincy, Massachusetts. Her father died when she was in her teens, leaving her responsible for her frail mother and younger brother. A gifted student, she was the youngest pupil admitted to Thayer Academy, where she flourished. She went on to attend the "Harvard Annex," chartered as Radcliffe College during her time there. In 1890, she had a formative year abroad at Newnham College, Cambridge, where she read political theory with Henry Sidgwick. Her undergraduate thesis, *The Speaker of the House of Representatives*, was praised by Theodore Roosevelt, and listed by *The New York Times* as one of "The Fifty Best Books of 1896."

Living Democracy

After graduation Follett became a social worker, pioneering the use of Boston school buildings after hours for community recreation, study, and vocational placement. These endeavors were very successful and copied elsewhere. (Europe, in a similar spirit, saw the founding of psychoanalytic free clinics.) Follett describes what she learned about group process in her second book, *The New State: Group Organization, the Solution of Popular Government* (1918). "The potentialities of the individual remain potentialities until they are released by group life" (2017, p. 69). "Thus, the essence of democracy is creating. The technique of democracy is group organization" (2017, p. 103). Her advice became sought by business and industry; leading to further ideas and *Creative Experience*, the book on which Milner relied. Although little known to psychoanalysts after Milner, Follett has been studied (and forgotten, and rediscovered) in the international world of business management, where there even exist Follett groups, which bring to mind the Balint groups in which physicians discuss the psychodynamics of patient care in a format of peer supervision.[7]

No Development Without Others

Before the relational or interpersonal schools of psychoanalysis, the ongoing process that Follett calls *living democracy* expresses what Steven Mitchell would call a social theory of mind. We develop in response to others. Without others, why bother?—there is neither need nor nutriment to do so. Or as Winnicott puts it: "There is no growth because there is no enrichment from external reality" (1945, p. 142). Follett's stance is optimistic, politically and therapeutically.[8] She aims for "power with" not "power over" others, a difference corresponding to Chodorow's distinction between analysts who listen *to* the patient and those who listen *for* what corresponds to a preferred theory or technique.

From Reflex Arc to Integration

Follett takes her working metaphors from psychology and physiology: integration, the circular response, the Gestalt or relationship of parts to the whole, and the total or evolving situation. Integration and the circular response are drawn from Charles Scott Sherrington, the neurophysiologist, known also to Milner, who "gave us his view of mental life as the progressive creation of new and higher functions through integrative processes" (Follett, 1924, pp. 114–115). Sherrington discovered the synapse (1887). His *The Integrative Action of the Nervous System* appeared in 1906. Prior to his work, reflexes were thought of as isolated pathways (the reflex arc). Sherrington showed that reflexes involve integrated activation and the reciprocal innervation of muscles (Sherrington's Law). With Edgar Adrian, he received the Nobel Prize in Physiology and Medicine in 1932.

Already in 1906, neuroscience was moving away from considering the brain as a closed system. Instead, we have development, an evolving system integrating with itself and its environment, inscribing new structures at higher levels of organization. Where neuron was, there shall become synapses. Some saw a parallel to the psyche: Where mind was, there shall be relationships, in reciprocity.

Integration becomes Follett's term for conflict resolution. Conflict is found wherever there is difference, say between one person and another. She toggles between physiology and social science: "Integration, the most suggestive word of contemporary psychology, is, I believe, the active principle of human intercourse scientifically lived. When differing interests meet, they need not oppose, but only confront, each other." Milner pairs this with another pithy Follett: "Our 'opponents' are our co-creators, for they have something to give which we have not" (1950, p. 90). Like Loewald, Follett, and her beloved Blake ("Without contraries there is no progression"), Milner thinks in terms of integration (1950, p. 87).

Follett prefers integration to the notion of compromise formation. The latter implies conflict or difference has been minimized or kept from awareness. Whereas with integration, meaning is enlarged by allowing connections and associative absorption, as it will be for Milner and Loewald in their understanding and use of the concept, transference.

The Circular Response and Total Situation

Follett's definition of integration as creating something new from constituent, perhaps opposing, elements, leads her to consider psychical states and processes whose evolving properties differ from those of their so-called parts. The relationship between wholes and parts is a circular one of reciprocal influence. We exist in a field of relationships in continuous feedback: what Follett calls the total and evolving situation.[9] Winnicott gave us a famous example: "There is no such thing as an infant, meaning, of course, that whenever one finds an infant one finds maternal care, and without maternal care there would be no infant."[10] Similarly, Loewald uses the term recognition to describes the mother's empathic interventions and reflection of the baby's feeling states, which organize its sensations into rudimentary instincts taking shape in relation to an object. Through our circular responses we recreate each other all the time. "The process is continuous," notes Follett (1924, p. 103), "the making of wholes and the breaking of wholes are equally important." Like a psychoanalyst, she has in mind a lifelong process of fragmentations and linkings, separations and reconciliations.

Only Connect

Milner and Loewald share a generous view of transference, its extent and effects. Whether from old object to new one, from ego to object, or from unconscious to preconscious, transference is everywhere and life-enhancing. Both are drawn to fire to describe it. Here is Milner on the transference from thing- to word-presentation, and the resulting hypercathexis:

> In particular I was struck by the effect of writing things down. It was as if I were trying to catch something and the written word provided a net which for a moment entangled a shadowy form which was other than the meaning of the words. Sometimes it seemed that the act of writing was fuel on glowing embers, making flames leap up and throw light on the surrounding gloom, giving me fitful gleams of what was before unguessed at.
>
> (Milner, 1934, p. 47)

Compare Loewald, "Primary Process, Secondary Process, and Language," in which he speaks of (re)establishing links between words and the primary process, in search of "a viable compromise between too intimate and intense closeness to the unconscious, with its threatening creative-destructive potentialities, and deadening insulation from the unconscious where human life is no longer vibrant and warmed by its fire" (1978, p. 189).[11]

Chodorow notes it does not escape Loewald's close reading that Freud used the term transference in three ways, to mean: (1) the transfer of relations with infantile objects onto later objects, (2) the transfer of libido from ego onto objects and (3) the transfer of intensity from unconscious ideas onto preconscious or conscious ones, as in dreams, where unconscious ideas may "surface" when connected to day residues. She notes:

> For Loewald, transference in all three senses is normal and desirable, but it is the third meaning, the least object–related or interpersonal meaning, that most concerns him.... The transfer of intensity from unconscious to conscious... gives conscious life its depth, texture, and richness.
>
> (Chodorow, 2020, p. 104)[12]

For Loewald, the integration of ego and reality consists in and depends on transference. Neither a resistance to reality nor a sign of immaturity, transference is the recurring process whereby id becomes ego, reality is integrated, and maturity is attained. "Without such transference, or to the extent to which such transference miscarries, human life become sterile and an empty shell" (Loewald, 1960, p. 250).

If We Are Only Sane

Freud and Follett, it would seem, had little use for oceanic feelings. Here Milner and Loewald part company with them, insisting, as Milner would have it:

> there are such moments in which subject and object do seem to become one. And the mistake we make is surely not in believing such moments exist, but in not realizing their subjective quality, in not recognizing them as illusions, even though vital illusions.
>
> (Milner, 1950, p. 160)

Similarly, Loewald critiques Freud's failure to consider early integrative processes, such as hypnoid states, which exist prior to defenses but may later be employed defensively. Perhaps nowhere are they closer than in their respective essays, "The Role of Illusion in Symbol Formation" and "Psychoanalysis as an Art and the Fantasy Character of the Psychoanalytic Situation," which bring together the oceanic feeling and the analytic process.

Milner opens with our original situation. We start life in an objectless state, of self and object not experienced as separate. Winnicott says "there's union but no *idea* of union" (Milner, 1952, p. 112, fn. 13). Milner cites Fenichel:

> There always remain certain traces of the original objectless condition, or at least a longing for it ("oceanic feeling"). Introjection is an attempt to make parts of the external world flow into the ego. Projection, by putting unpleasant sensations into the external world, also attempts to reverse the separation of ego from non-ego.
>
> (Milner, 1952, p. 100)

Here projection both rids and connects.
  She continues:

The idea that these states of illusion of oneness are perhaps a recurrently necessary phase in the continued growth of the sense of twoness leads to a further question: What happens when they are prevented from occurring with sufficient frequency or at the right moments?

(1952, p. 100)

She answers that

if, through the pressure of unsatisfied need, the child has to become aware of his separate identity too soon or too continually, then either the illusion of union can be what Scott calls catastrophic chaos rather than cosmic bliss, or the illusion is given up and premature ego-development may occur; then separateness and the demands of necessity may be apparently accepted, but necessity becomes a cage rather than something to be co-operated with for the freeing of further powers.

(1952, p. 101)

Here again we seem close to Winnicott's idea of the false self.

For Milner, oceanic feelings are "an essential recurrent phase in the development of a creative relation to the world" (1952, p. 104). From the ebb and flow of introjection and projection we develop, under good-enough conditions, the capacity to endow the world with meaning, to identify one object with another, to find familiar in the unfamiliar, and to use symbols and metaphor (from *metapherein*, to transfer). The original/primary fusion of self and object recurs in fusions between new objects and previous ones.

Our relationship to the world is like that to a person. If the world is unresponsive, if it fails to mirror us (Winnicott's term), or to recognize us (Loewald's term), we cannot develop and are left in despair. For the artist, Milner suggests, the medium is an "other," more malleable than another person, with which to experiment and play, a bit of the outside world willing to go along with our dreams.

Milner describes her analysis of a boy called Simon, whose life had been disrupted by the Second World War. He was oppositional, having trouble in school, dismissive of his "nonsensical" dreams, and maintained he was "no good at art." He frequently took a bullying tone with Milner, which relaxed when he played with the things in her office. She recalls:

at times there was a quality in his play which I can only describe as beautiful.... He would close the shutters of the room and insist that it be lit only by candle light, sometimes a dozen candles arranged in patterns, or all grouped together in a solid block. And then he would make what he called furnaces... And often there had to be a sacrifice... this type of play had a dramatic ritual quality comparable to the fertility rites described by Frazer in primitive societies.

(1952, p. 96)

The fact that in this type of material the boy's play nearly became 'a play', in that there was a sense of pattern and dramatic form in what he produced, leads to many questions about the relation of a work of art to analytic work... he seemed

> to me to be trying to express the idea of integration, in a variety of different ways. Thus the fire seemed to be here not only a destructive fire but also the fire of Eros.
>
> (Milner, 1952, p. 96)

Here she seems close to Eros as Loewald uses the term, with connotations of binding together, reconciliation, *at-one-ment.*

In addition to our growing capacity to tolerate the difference between the feeling of oneness, of being united with everything, and the feeling of twoness, of self and object, Milner considers the environmental provision

> to foster this growth, by providing conditions in which a recurrent partial return to the feeling of being one is possible; and I suggest that the environment does this by the recurrent providing of a framed space and time and a pliable medium.
>
> (1952, p. 101)

Playing with candles and paper mâché gave Simon "a bit of the external world that was malleable; he had found that it was safe to treat it as a bit of himself, and so had let it serve as a bridge between inner and outer" (1952, p. 103).

Milner supposes that moments when the "poet" within us created the world, by finding the familiar in the unfamiliar, tend to be forgotten or guarded in memory.

> Perhaps, in ordinary life, it is good teachers who are most aware of these moments, from outside, since it is their job to provide the conditions under which they can occur, so to stage manage the situation that imagination catches fire and a whole subject or skill lights up with significance. But it is in the analytic situation that this process can be studied from inside and outside at the same time.
>
> (1952, p. 88)

"Like art, analysis provides a method, in adult life, for reproducing states that are part of everyday experience in healthy infancy" (Milner, 1952, p. 98). How well she anticipates Loewald on the analytic process and the analyst's role in the transference neurosis. In *Psychoanalysis as an Art*, Loewald reimagines the analysis of adults as a form of imaginary play, with a pliable medium, within a frame. As he sees it, "patient and analyst—each in his own way and on his own mental level—become both artist and medium for each other" (1975, p. 369).

> In the promotion and development of the transference neurosis, analyst and pa-tient conspire in the creation of an illusion, a play. The patient takes the lead in furnishing the material and the action of this fantasy creation, while the analyst takes the lead in coalescing, articulating, and explicating the action and in reveal-ing and highlighting it as an illusion (note that the word illusion derives from the Latin *ludere,* to play). The patient experiences and acts without knowing at first that he is creating a play. Gradually he becomes more of an author aware of being an author, by virtue of the analyst's interventions which reflect back to the patient what he does and says, and by transference interpretations which reveal the rela-tions between the play and the original action that the play imitates.
>
> (1975, p. 354)

Milner's account of premature ego development, entrapping the patient, finds a corresponding passage in Loewald I find always moving, given the rarity of clinical examples in his writing:

> I stated that the patient tends to be caught up in the poignant immediacy of the transference and the analyst recognizes and reveals its fantasy character. This is not always the case. An obsessive-compulsive patient may have so much distance from himself, may be such a compulsive self-observer or so obsessively entangled in psychoanalytic theory, that he remains or only too promptly reverts to being a detached spectator insisting on the unreality of the transference. It is the analyst who then must take the lead in accentuating and intensifying the patient's experience of the here-and-now immediacy of the transference.
>
> (1975, pp. 355–356)

Only Reconnect

Fantasy does not imply the transference neurosis is unreal or not taken seriously. Rather, both fantasy and present actuality become unreal or meaningless when they are kept apart. (As Follett liked to say, "Evil is non relation.") In the analytic process, by linking fantasies, memories, and the analytic situation, present and past can recover meaning and growth can resume. Like Milner, Loewald is concerned with the communication (transference) between unconscious fantasy life and so-called objective reality:

> If communication between them is disrupted we have each in its own corner: a conscious and/or unconscious fantasy life which proliferates on its own (a kind of malignant growth), and opposed to it what we call objective reality which tends to lose meaning as it seems to gain in objective rationality. This is a caricature of ego and id in irreconcilable opposition. In the healthier adult, communication and interplay between the world of fantasy and the world of objectivity, between imagination and rationality, remain alive.
>
> (1975, p. 363)[13]

Transcend the Common Ego

Milner's young analysand, who declared himself "no good at art," went on to discover he was good at art as well as science. He confessed "the delights he took in the colours of the various crystals he had studied in chemistry," chasing his pride with apology: "It's childish to like them so much" (1952, p. 97). Simon's evolving capacity to relax an ego that tried too hard to see crystals objectively, without emotional coloring, reminds Milner of Bernard Berenson's "aesthetic moment" (1952, p. 97). Milner supposes the artist and scientist are persons whose endowment or life experience has made them more aware of the shortcomings of "the common ego"[14] They seek to contribute something of their own perception or making to the social field of art or science and so lessen the discrepancy between the self and reality. She asks herself whether a patient's struggle "to make me see as they saw" is in essence any different from the artist's struggle to communicate his private vision. She recalls that a turning point in Simon's analysis came when his school agreed to host his photography club. Previous efforts to help by the school had not taken the form of accepting something he created. "Now the school, by being receptive, by being in-giving as well as out-giving, had shown itself capable of good mothering" (1952, p. 93). Milner goes on: "This... happened in response to the vividness of his belief in the validity of his own experience; a vividness which also had contributed to a refashioning in me of some of my analytic ideas."

Such receptive revision is indeed part of analytic technique.[15] As her ideas changed, influenced by her patient, Milner notices that "even though I knew that I was not succeeding in putting these ideas clearly into words in my interpretations, [his] aggression did begin to lessen and the continual battle over the time of the beginning of each session disappeared" (1952, pp. 102–103). Change may occur before or absent our interpretations, or despite their provisional nature. Rosemary Balsam says something compatible based on her experience as Loewald's supervisee:

> He did not think that the essence of psychoanalytic treatment lay in technical recommendations on its conduct.... Loewald was not caught up in the rights and wrongs of exactly what one said, but was interested instead in how one understood what one heard or saw. The care and purpose of communication, and the consideration of alternative communications, would follow from this.
>
> (Balsam, 2008, p. 1122)

Milner and Loewald see the individual in creative relation to the world. Of course, challenging accepted views (the common ego) and attempting to make others share one's vision carries danger—an obstacle for many (artist, scientist, teacher, pupil, analyst, patient, parent, and child) who would become creative people. To wage this battle might seduce the world to madness (Milner, 1952, p. 107), or be seen as aggressive, perhaps to be countered with "the stiletto of silence."[16] Despite these risks, the individual must impose his own vision if pre-existing ideas and symbols are to become, and remain, fully significant. Milner says, "Without our own contribution we see nothing" (1950, p. 33). Thus, Loewald's close reading of Freud gives us a new Loewald and newly meaningful Freud. We are grateful to Loewald and Milner for remaking our world so to include their experience.

> The mind, that ocean where each kind
> Does straight its own resemblance find;
> Yet it creates, transcending these,
> Far other worlds, and other seas;
> Annihilating all that's made
> to a green thought in a green shade.
>
> —Andrew Marvell, from *The Garden*, 1681

Notes

1 See for example T. Wayne Downey on his philosophic density and poetic lilt (1994, p. 840), and Nancy Chodorow on Braxton McKee's observation that Loewald's writing style evokes his living presence, much as Freud's writing had done for Loewald himself (Chodorow, 2020, p. 128).

2 From Andrew Marvell, quoted by Loewald in concluding "On Internalization" (1973).

3 For more on Milner's oeuvre see Olson (2013), "Marion Milner: Unventing Psychoanalysis."

4 Recall that Freud, in "On Narcissism," postulates a cathexis of the ego which can be given off to objects "much as the body of an amoeba is related to the pseudopodia which it puts out" (1914, p. 74).

5 Theirs would seem to be parallel play, although Loewald thought highly of Milner (T. Wayne Downey, 1994, and personal communication). As with Milner and Winnicott, it is hard to retrace when and how they came to know one another's other's ideas.

6 The Loewald family copy of *On Not Being Able to Paint* was the 1957 edition (Elizabeth Loewald, email communication).

7 Like Loewald, Follett inspires a "discovery" kinship with readers, given to ask one another other, "How did you meet Mary Parker Follett?" See *The Essential Mary Parker Follett: Ideas We Need Today* (2017, p. 1).

8 Chodorow notes the pragmatism and optimism of Loewald and Erikson, and of Americans analysts in general as compared to their European counterparts (2020, p. 15).

9 Melanie Klein, "The Origins of Transference" (1952), speaks in terms of total situations transferred from the past into the present. The choice of words is striking; one wonders if Klein knew Follett's ideas through Milner, her supervisee. Betty Joseph returns to Klein's idea in "Transference: The Total Situation" (1985).

10 Statement to a meeting of the British Psycho-analytical Society in 1940. See Winnicott, "The Theory of the Patent Infant Relationship" (1960b, p. 587, fn. 4).

11 One wonders if they knew Gaston Bachelard's *The Psychoanalysis of Fire* (1938). Bachelard (1884–1962) was a philosopher of science who also wrote *The Poetics of Space* (1958). Elizabeth Loewald wrote a paper using Bachelard's concepts, "Therapeutic Play in Space and Time" (1987). Her clinical work with children and its influence on Hans Loewald remain to be explored.

12 Chodorow has expressed reservations about our current shift in attention and technique from the external world to the detailed unfolding of process in the clinical hour, and to what we reify as "the" transference, often first observed through "the" countertransference (2020, pp. 58). Focusing on what Chodorow calls the microdynamics of minds in the consulting room is something Loewald might do sparingly, lest the patient feel "It may be us they wish to [treat] but it's themselves they want to talk about." (I paraphrase Cyril Connolly, as chosen by Nicholson Baker (1991) for the epigraph to *U and I: A True Story*, evoking his transference to John Updike.)

13 Here Loewald thinks of Winnicott: "I am here, I believe, in the neighborhood of Winnicott's 'third area, that of play which expands into creative living and into the whole cultural life of man' [1967]" (1975, pp. 369–370).

14 Milner adopts the term, the common ego, from Christopher Caudwell, *Illusion and Reality* (1937).

15 Elsewhere, Milner makes a remarkable statement: "Since as someone has aptly said, the child's external world is the mother's inner world, it is therefore true that it is the analyst's own inner struggles with the world of theoretical concepts—testing them, doubting them, refining them, rejecting them, using them—that must determine what one does with what the patient gives and therefore what goes on in the analysis; it is this that is really the patient's external world during sessions" (1969, p. 266). This seems akin to Loewald's views on maternal identification of— and with—the child's experience and needs as the fulcrum of development and prototype of analytic treatment.

16 Downey (2015, p. 994) uses the term to describe the initial response of psychoanalysts to Loewald's work.

References

Bachelard, G. (1938). *The Psychoanalysis of Fire*. Boston, MA: Beacon, 1968.

Bachelard, G. (1958). *The Poetics of Space*. Boston, MA: Beacon, 1969.

Baker, N. (1991). *U and I: A True Story*. New York: Random House.

Balsam, R. (2008). The Essence of Hans Loewald. *Journal of the American Psychoanalytic Association*, 56: 1117–1128.

Caudwell, C. (1937). *Illusion and Reality*. London: Lawrence & Wishart.

Chodorow, N. (2020). *The Psychoanalytic Ear and the Sociological Eye*. London and New York: Routledge.

Downey, T. W. (1994). Hans W. Loewald, M.D. (1906–1993). *International Journal of Psychoanalysis*, 75: 839–842.

Downey, T. W. (2015). Hans Loewald's *Psychoanalysis and the History of the Individual. Journal of the American Psychoanalytic Association*, 63: 993–1011.

Follett, M. P. (1924). *Creative Experience*. New York: Longmans, Green.

Follett, M. P. (1918). *The New State: Group Organization, the Solution of Popular Government*. New York: Longmans, Green.

Follett, M. P. (2017). *The Essential Mary Parker Follett: Ideas We Need Today*, 2nd edition. Heon, François; Davis, Albie; Jones-Patulli, Jennifer; Damart, Sebastién (eds). The MFP Group.

Freud, S. (1914). On narcissism: An introduction. *Standard Edition*, 14: 73–102.

Joseph, B. (1985). Transference: The total situation. *International Journal of Psychoanalysis*, 66: 447–454.

Klein, M. (1952). The origins of transference. *International Journal of Psychoanalysis*, 33: 433–438.

Loewald, E. (1987). Therapeutic play in space and time. *The Psychoanalytic Study of the Child*, 42: 173–192.

Loewald, H. (1951). Ego and reality. In *Papers on Psychoanalysis* (pp. 3–20). New Haven, CT: Yale University Press, 1980.

Loewald, H. (1960). On the therapeutic action of psychoanalysis. In *Papers on Psychoanalysis* (pp. 221–256). New Haven, CT: Yale University Press, 1980.

Loewald, H. (1973). On internalization. In *Papers on Psychoanalysis* (pp. 69–86). New Haven, CT: Yale University Press, 1980.

Loewald, H. (1975). Psychoanalysis as an art and the fantasy character of the psychoanalytic situation (pp. 352–371). In *Papers on Psychoanalysis*. New Haven, CT: Yale University Press, 1980,

Loewald, H. (1978). Primary process, secondary process, and language. In *Papers on Psychoanalysis* (pp. 178–206). New Haven, CT: Yale University Press, 1980.

Loewald, H. (1988). Psychoanalysis in search of nature: Thoughts on metapsychology, "metaphysics," projection. *Annual of Psychoanalysis* 16: 49–54.

Milner, M. (1934). *A Life of One's Own*. London and New York: Routledge, 2011.

Milner, M. (1937). *An Experiment in Leisure*. London and New York: Routledge, 2011.

Milner, M. (1938). *The Human Problem in Schools*, ed. S. Isaacs. London and New York: Routledge, 2018.

Milner, M. (1950). *On Not Being Able to Paint*. London and New York: Routledge, 2010.

Milner, M. (1952). The role of illusion in symbol formation. In *The Suppressed Madness of Sane Men: Forty-Four Years of Exploring Psychoanalysis* (pp. 83–113). London: Tavistock, 1987.

Milner, M. (1969). *The Hands of the Living God: An Account of a Psycho-Analytic Treatment*. London and New York: Routledge, 2010.

Milner, M. (1987a). *Eternity's Sunrise*. London and New York: Routledge, 2011.

Milner, M. (1987b). *The Suppressed Madness of Sane Men: Forty-Four Years of Exploring Psychoanalysis*. London: Tavistock.

Olson, N. (2013). Marion Milner: Unventing psychoanalysis. *Journal of the American Psychoanalytic Association*, 61: 1003–1022.

Winnicott, D. W. (1945). Primitive emotional development. *International Journal of Psychoanalysis*, 26: 137–143.

Winnicott, D. W. (1960a). Ego distortion in terms of true and false self. *International Psycho-Analytical Library* (1965), 64: 140–152.

Winnicott, D. W. (1960b). The theory of the parent-infant relationship. *International Journal of Psychoanalysis*, 41: 585–595.

Chapter 6

Musical and Sacred Resonances in Loewald's Writing

Recapitulative Journeys, Celebrations of Oneness Regained

Jenifer Nields

Introduction

Two decades ago, I began working on a paper exploring potential religious correlates of Hans Loewald's developmental theory: on the themes of separation and reunion, alienation and atonement and the processes of mourning and internalization central to both Loewald's work and the religious traditions with which I was familiar. Sometimes when I would mention to a colleague that I was working on a paper to do with Loewald's work, I could see that their interest was sparked. When I mentioned that the paper had to do with religion, however, I would see their eyes glaze over.

Then 9/11 hit and suddenly lots of people—most strikingly, among my patients—were talking about religion, not only about its destructive potential, but also its value, especially at such times of communal need. Some were saying, in effect, "You *see*?! This is just one more proof of how pig-headed and destructive religion is. Think about how many horrific things have been done in the name of religion!" and others were saying, in effect, "You see?! *Now* people are flocking to synagogues, mosques and churches." The Monday after 9/11, the New York Times ran excerpts from sermons given at churches, synagogues, mosques and Buddhist monasteries all over the city and beyond. People have a natural need to gather at such times, to seek meaning and solace. To understand better the potential for both destructive and life-enhancing forms of religious expression became a compelling task, now of general interest. What general characteristics define these disparate forms of religious experience and expression?

Loewald's understanding of ego development seemed to me to help with this. I saw in it a model for the process of maturation in relation to a religious tradition or other, non-religious "ultimate concern." It offered a way to understand the development of religious life when it is proceeding in a healthy and generative fashion, in contrast to the failures of such development that seem to underlie, for example, some forms of religious fundamentalism. It offered a developmental framework from which to understand the religious life of a given individual and the process of maturation—or pathological fixation—in religious experience, with its consequent generative—or disastrous—effects.

Nowadays, we face a new wave of destructive polarizations in our nation and world. Discourse between political, ideological and racial groups has become as hate-filled—and deadly—as religious oppositions have been in the past, and Loewald's work seems

DOI: 10.4324/9781032685151-7

as important as ever to bear in mind as we attempt to speak to one another across these cavernous divides.

This chapter will be divided into three parts. The first will provide an overview of Loewald's developmental theory, including emergence from a primal unity through progressive stages of separation and reunion, alienation and atonement, presented alongside some religious correlates from Judeo-Christian and Islamic traditions. The second section contrasts Loewald's trajectory of healthy development with some of its distortions, the derailments into (or fixations at), for example, the paranoid-schizoid position and how these derailments relate to extremes of religious fundamentalism and political and racial divisiveness. In this section, I will discuss excerpts from Yossi Halevi's autobiographical *Memoirs of a Jewish Extremist* that serve to illustrate both the mindset of a religious extremist and the process of one's development toward a more inclusive and mature religious faith. This case example provides a segue into the third section which offers further reflections on the dynamics of mature faith as understood in light of Loewald's developmental theory. The third section explores Loewald's later writings on sublimation, timelessness and metaphysics in which he circles back to his early interest in religion and, perhaps, to his early roots as a fatherless child bathed in the sound of his grieving mother's playing of Beethoven's piano music (Jones 2001, Lang 2009, Mitchell 1998).

It was only in reading once more through Loewald's collected work that I realized that an interest in religion and in transcendent, mystical or unitive human experience has "bookended" his work. Among Loewald's first published papers following his arrival in the United States was one in the *Journal of Pastoral Care* in 1953 entitled "Psychoanalysis and Modern Views on Human Existence and Religious Experience," and among his last were his lectures on *Psychoanalysis and the History of the Individual*, his book on *Sublimation* and his 1987 paper, "Psychoanalysis in Search of Nature: Thoughts on Metapsychology, 'Metaphysics,' Projection." Peppered in between are references to religion and to the 'sacred' that are suggestive, if not often expansively so, of how these kindred domains relate to his more explicit psychoanalytic formulations.

I shall briefly sketch out some of the points made in my earlier paper (Nields 2003), and then expand on lines of thinking that were left out or not yet evident to me then, particularly having to do with the interweaving—the cyclical differentiations and reintegrations—not only of self and other, but also of the individual and culture, including the role of music and the arts in mediating an experience of transcendence and in providing models for reconciliation and healing. The Halevi case, and Loewald's work, point to an essential role for mourning in accomplishing such reconciliation, and in this regard, I shall also bring in recent work on mourning by Otto Kernberg and shall suggest that the societal transformations called for at the present time will require a process of mourning that is all too easily evaded by giddy adherence to extremist views or by rigid adherence to devitalized practices.

In speaking of religious experience and tradition, I shall be speaking mainly of the three "Abrahamic" and monotheistic traditions, Judaism, Christianity and Islam, because these are the traditions I know best, and because it is Judeo-Christian tradition to which Loewald makes explicit reference.

Section I: Ego Development and the Development of Faith: A Basic Framework

In the Beginning

Most religions offer an "origin story," concerning the creation of the world and of humankind. Similarly, as we shall see, Loewald's understanding of the individual psyche is predicated on a sort of psychological "origin story" that parallels, in important ways, that of our Western religious traditions.

Here is the opening of the Book of Genesis:

> In the beginning... the earth was without form and void, and darkness was upon the face of the deep.... And the Spirit of God moved upon the face of the waters....
>
> (Genesis 1:1–2)

and from the Qu'ran:

> The heavens and the earth were joined together as one unit, before We clove them asunder.
>
> (Qur'an 21:30)

For Loewald, ego and reality emerge in tandem through the process of identification and differentiation from a primary infant-mother matrix, a pre-objective, pre-subjective state. From this are set up the complementary pulls toward separateness and (re-)union that pervade life throughout and indeed provide the dialectical tension that drives psychic development. In this earliest phase, there is as yet no differentiation between ego and reality, baby and mother. There is, instead, an "all-embracing feeling of intimate connection or... unity with the environment" (Loewald [1951] 1980, p. 5).

He writes:

> [I]nner and outer,... past and present, here and there, physical and psychical, gradually evolve from a kind of unitary, global experience. This unitary experience perhaps may best be called *being*.
>
> (Loewald 1978, pp. 35–36)

Emergence and Return

Loewald writes:

> Mother and baby do not get together and develop a relationship, but the baby is born, becomes detached from the mother, and thus a relatedness between two parts that originally were one becomes possible.
>
> (Loewald [1951] 1980, p. 11)

In Loewald's view, as in the three Abrahamic religious traditions, there is an imagined—or postulated—sense of original unity, followed by a rift, or a Fall, an enforced separation, that is experienced as a loss. For the baby, this rift occurs physically in the event of birth and psychologically only gradually during the first year of life. In the Qu'ran, it is the deity who cleaves heaven and earth asunder; in Judeo-Christian tradition, it is humankind who fails to resist the temptation of the forbidden fruit—though it is God who places temptation into the midst of the garden. At the same time, this separation is necessary to the development of the individual in relation to the world around him or her, and of mankind in relation to God. Furthermore, relationship, interaction, even compassion depend upon—indeed are defined by—some degree of separation and distinction.

With this original emergence, a dialectical tension is set up between separation and reunion, between connectedness and autonomy or independence—from Mother, for example, or from God.

Whereas in Freud's view, the trajectory of healthy development is more or less unidirectional: from a state of dependency toward independence and autonomy, for Loewald, development occurs as it were in spiral form. The pull back toward oneness with the environment is ever-present, as is the pull toward differentiation and independence. The sense of unity with the environment remains as a life-giving foundation in psychological life, even as the need to make distinctions between inside and outside, self and other, fantasy and rational thought are likewise necessary components of individuation, creativity and human freedom. Emergence and return are perennial processes occurring at progressively higher levels of organization.

Triadic Relations: Mourning and the Depressive Position

The movement from dyadic to triadic relations in the oedipal phase provides both a crisis and an opportunity. Mourning the exclusiveness of the maternal-infant bond is accompanied by advances: perspective, symbolization, and mentalization.

In Loewald's view, as both a subjective world and a world of objects ("reality") distill out, via processes of introjection and projection, from a primary, mother-infant matrix, there are set up within the developing psyche both a profound desire to recapture something of the all-embracing original unity and a dread of being once more swallowed up in it. The spiraling course of separation and reunion is recapitulated in the oedipal phase, again in adolescence, and over and over in human development.

Loewald sees the role of the "third" in the nuclear family, traditionally the father, both as a source of identification for the growing child, and of protection from the threat of loss of the ego via merger with the mother, from "dread of the womb" (Loewald [1951] 1980, p. 13). On the other hand, the longing for reconciliation, atonement (at-oneness), a return to perfect union with another and with the world around him or her remains a powerful motivating force for the developing individual.

Internalization

Loewald recasts the relationship of ego and reality as essentially nutritive and mutually life-enhancing rather than reflexively or primarily defensive.

> Just as the biological organism grows and develops and becomes more and more independent of the mother organism through the incorporation, assimilation and metabolism of food, which is an active process of the infantile organism,

so does the psychological organization of the personality grow and develop through psychological incorporation, assimilation, and transformation of the moods, attitudes, general behavioral characteristics, and the abilities, interests, and feelings of those around the infant and child. They become changed, condensed, re-arranged, elaborated, magnified and minimized, altogether molten and molded into what materializes as the psychological structure of the newly evolving individual.

(Loewald 1953, p. 12)

The Oedipus complex "wanes" as aspects of parental functions are internalized. Loewald emphasizes that what is internalized is not, strictly speaking, an "object" (the parent or analyst) but an "interaction process" between mother and child, analyst and patient, an "integrative experience" (Loewald [1960] 1980).

Interactions with our parents are taken in, refined, and made our own. Some are repeated, more or less blindly, on an internal plane and carried forward to the next generation. In fuller, healthier ego development, such blind reproductions are reexamined, understood and refined. Rather than being introjected whole-hog, they are modified and changed, via catabolic and anabolic processes. Such internalizations become aspects of the child's own ego formation or, with lesser "degrees of internalization" (Loewald [1962] 1980, pp. 483–504) remain as aspects of a punitive superego or as unintegrated imitations or persecutory introjects.

Internalization plays a central role in religious life as well, both for the individual and for the collective in ways more fully developed in my prior paper (Nields 2003) and in the third section below.

"Maturity" in Psychological and Religious Development

Opening up pre-oedipal phases to psychoanalytic inquiry has contributed to a rapprochement between psychoanalysis and religion. Concepts such as Erikson's basic trust, Mahler's symbiotic phase and Kohut's self-object can serve to link religious experience to "bedrock psychic strengths" for which religion can provide a language and support (Wallwork & Wallwork 1990, p. 162).

Developments in theology, too have reinforced a rapprochement between psychoanalysis and religion. Tillich views faith as a synthetic activity born out of an interaction process between humankind and God, an individual and his/her "ultimate concern(s)" (Tillich 1957) much as for Loewald psychological development consists in the synthetic activity of the ego in mediating the relationship between the growing child and his/her environment, including the moods, attitudes, ideals, and moral injunctions of parents, teachers, and mentors. "Faith," for Tillich, consists in the evolution of a relationship, of the connection between the individual and his/her transcendent values and ultimate Ground of Being. It need not be—and often is not—explicitly religious nor tied to traditional theistic conceptualizations, but indeed can take many forms in human life. As the individual grows, so, too does his/her conception of God, truth, democracy, Love, marriage, parenthood, or of the Ultimate. Religious (or nonreligious) faith, like human love, occurs in many iterations throughout the lifespan. Its expressions change, informed by one's original environment and adjusting as frustrations, losses, contradictions, and challenges are encountered. Here is Loewald in 1953:

The omnipotent, blind power of unconscious drive and need, experienced first as omnipresent and timeless, changes gradually, through the integration with an environment of much higher organization, to become the more free, seeing relatedness of trusting interdependence and love, and its modifications of distrust and clinging. As the unconscious becomes transformed into ego-freedom—and this is a process which in healthy development continues throughout life—the images and concepts of this relatedness change to higher forms.

(Loewald 1953, p. 14)

He goes on to say,

The images and concepts of God and of the bond and the gap between God and man undergo similar transformations, in the history of civilization and in the history of the individual as a member of his civilization. The mature individual, being able to reach back into his deep origins and roots of being, finds in himself the oneness from where he stems, and understands this in his freedom as his bond of love with God. The concept of God itself seems to change from that of a blindly omnipotent power to that of the transformation and incarnation of such power in individual freedom and love.

(Loewald 1953, pp. 14–15)

A developmental understanding of faith has been elaborated by James Fowler, a late 20th-century theologian heavily influenced by Tillich's concept of faith as a dynamic activity rather than a static belief system and by the developmental psychological theories of Erikson, Piaget and Kohlberg. The developmental stages Fowler (1981) describes move from the preconventional to the conventional to the post conventional. The earliest, "undifferentiated" stage, where the infant's world is a blur of sensations and impressions, parallels "primary narcissism."

With each developmental step come changes not only in the child's sense of self, of an internal world, but also of others, of the world around him or her. Through various stages of differentiation and internalization, disintegration and reintegration, the individual's sense of relatedness to others, to reality and to the divine evolve. With the dawning of triadic relations, and, especially, in the re-working of oedipal conflicts in adolescence, comes a corresponding movement in the development of faith, from the "pre-conventional" to the "conventional" stages. This movement involves the capacity to imagine how another person perceives the world, to see oneself through the eyes of another and to see how one's relationship with that person exists within a network of other relationships outside the dyad. The movement from the "conventional" to the "postconventional" stages which occurs, if at all, in adulthood, involves the capacity to engage deeply with alternate views, to tolerate ambiguity and paradox, to balance dynamic tensions without collapsing them and to seek a reconciliation that encompasses, rather than disavows or splits off discordant aspects of reality. Thus the arc of development, for both Fowler and Loewald, moves through stages of separation and reunion, individualization and belonging, toward reconciliation and atonement.

For late 20th-century theoreticians and researchers such as Fowler (1981), Rizzuto (1978), Meissner (1986), and Tillich (1957), the development of faith, at least initially, parallels ego development. At the earliest, undifferentiated stage, as in primary narcissism, there exists no differentiation between self and other, ego and object-world, humankind and God, self and concerns outside of self. As the baby separates from the mother, and as one's inner life becomes distinguishable from an "objective," outer world, connectedness between the elements of an original unity must take increasingly complex forms. In similar fashion, as life-experience casts doubt on early concepts of the divine and as the faith traditions learned in childhood are seen anew through the eyes of adulthood, one's images of God and one's religious understanding undergo development and change. As the ego gains in richness and complexity, so, too must one's constructions and images of the divine or of ultimate meaning. Faith thus formulated is primarily synthetic and embracing rather than defensive and exclusionary, much as Loewald's theorizing emphasizes the creative and synthetic functions of the ego over the defensive ones.

Mature religious understanding, according to Fowler, grapples with paradox, does not give up on life nor on other individuals... involves objectivity... is dynamic in nature and open to change without denying or failing to integrate and come to terms with one's rootedness in the past. In similar fashion, Loewald's writing asserts, again and again in different ways, the need to hold oppositions in dialectical tension with one another: ego and reality, love and aggression, faith and doubt, primary and secondary process thinking. Without this lively tension, there is no growth, no development. In Loewald's view, the psyche is dynamic in nature, made up not of introjected objects or static structures, but rather the internalization of interaction processes between ego and reality, baby and mother, self and one's cultural surroundings.

Section 2: Derailments of Psychological and Religious Development: Fundamentalisms and the Paranoid-Schizoid Position

What happens when deprivation or trauma interferes with the developmental trajectory as described above, whether in terms of ego development or the development, in an individual or community, of religion, "faith," and/or relatedness to "ultimate concerns"?

Fundamentalisms, in the form of extremist movements, involve and depend upon unmitigated dualisms: us vs. them, right vs. wrong, power vs. weakness (Marty & Appleby 1991, p. 822). It is in this quality of dualism, simplification and projection that they call to mind the paranoid schizoid position. All goodness is felt to reside in the extremist group and evil is projected outside. "Thinking is concrete... the leading edge is paranoid and the pre-occupation is with the survival or the self" (Steiner 1997, p. 198) or the embattled group. The "third" position, so important for symbolic thought and for psychological development, is disavowed. Religious symbols are "stripped of their symbolic power to evoke a multiplicity of meanings" (Donald Swearer, quoted in Marty & Appleby 1991, p. 837). These are fear-driven religious movements, characterized by all-or-nothing thinking and the inability to grieve what is or threatens to be lost.

Marty and Appleby (1991) describe how fundamentalist movements have arisen, in the 20th century and beyond, in reaction to the growth of secularism and the rise of pluralist societies around them. They *come to prominence in times of crisis, actual or perceived*" (Marty & Appleby 1991, p. 822, italics in original). In this regard, fundamentalisms provide defense against loss, vulnerability, and change. It is not surprising, then, given massive societal changes, the growing interdependence of the global community and the threat of climate change, that nationalist and fundamentalist movements are now, in the early 21st century, on the rise (for a fuller and more nuanced discussion and of fundamentalisms, see Armstrong (2000), Jurgensmeyer 2001, Lawrence 1995, Marty & Appleby 1991 Nields 2003).

Nominally religious, extremist groups have given religion a bad name, and have diverted the life-enhancing, self-transcending potential of religious belief and spiritual practice toward political ends. These ideologies are magnetic and allow individuals to bypass the hard work of discernment and mourning so central to development as apprehended and described by Loewald. Nominally Christian movements such as White Christian Nationalism—earning the appellation "Imposter Christianity" (Blake 2022, Gorki & Perry 2020)—have been fashioned in the service of white supremacist and patriarchal aims that are a far cry from the "Jesus of the disinherited" (Thurman 1976) who preached universal love and respect for the poor and the marginalized and who posed a deep challenge to the existing centers of power. Similarly, secular, sociopolitical movements "disguised by religious discourse, rites and collective behaviors" have monopolized not only the news media, but also scholarly discussions on Islam. This "loud Islam" has been contrasted to the "silent Islam" of the majority of practitioners of the faith who "attach more importance to the.. relationship with... God than to the vehement demonstrations of political movements" (quoted in Frishkopf & Spinetti, foreword by Ali Asani, p. xiii). Often fundamentalisms, like other extremist movements, gain appeal and find fuel among action-oriented, idealistic youth seeking a path distinct from, yet in reaction to, their parents. For the young individual, extremist movements can protect against identity diffusion that has, arguably, become increasingly prevalent as society becomes more pluralistic and developmental tasks accordingly more complex.

Case Study: Yossi Klein Halevi Memoirs of a Jewish Extremist

In his 1995 book, *Memoirs of a Jewish Extremist,* Yossi Klein Halevi provides an example of how an individual may progress from the polarized world of a religious extremist (and activist) through a process of disillusionment, self-scrutiny and mourning, to a more mature and balanced view of the world and of himself and a more individualized, complex and life-enhancing religious understanding. It is suggestive, thereby, of extremism as a kind of fixation-point and illustrates some of the developmental processes, both spiritual and psychological, requisite for the movement beyond it.

Halevi begins with the story of the roots of his extremism in the education which his father, a Holocaust survivor, imparted to him. Halevi's father had succeeded in escaping the Nazis by hiding—alone—in a forest in Transylvania in a hole in the ground just big enough to accommodate his body. At night, he foraged for food. He had emerged from this "grave" (p. 4), as he called it, to find "a Jewish wasteland" (p. 3), and out of this devastation, had to reconstitute a life for himself. Halevi's father taught young Halevi that one could never be too wary, that it was "safer to live without exceptions" (p. 7), not to live like the "weak," trusting Jews. "Don't listen to what people say. 'People' are fools, victims. When they say left, go right; when they go to the cattle cars, go to the forest" (p. 4).

As a late adolescent in rebellion against his father, Halevi found a cause that enabled him to both imitate and outdo his father by adopting a more extreme form of Jewish separatism and mistrust of the world and then by translating that mistrust into violent action. He became a member of what he terms a "terrorist underground" whose young members dared each other to perform ever more outrageous acts and, over time, came to experience the world in increasingly polarized and paranoid ways. As he saw it, the group, given its devotion to a greater cause, was as it were above mundane morality: "There was nothing holier than a terrorist underground, I thought." (p. 113). The cause was everything, and service to that cause engendered in him and others a sense of grandiosity and elation and a kind of exemption from ordinary pain, grief and doubt. He described being in "an ecstasy of rage" (p. 83), living "as though addicted to intensity" (p. 180). Over time, the group lost its original focus on freeing the Soviet Jewry and took on a cultish tone. Its leader, Rabbi Meir Kahane, advocated, with growing vehemence, an extreme isolation from the dominant culture. His beliefs became, in Halevi's view, increasingly nihilistic and paranoid, and the group followed suit. Halevi and his fellow activists came to feel, to believe, and to feed on their belief that "the whole world is against us" (p. 165).

Over time, Halevi became disenchanted with the group, put off by the dehumanization and devaluation of individual life that he began, increasingly, to notice. As he came to view the world in a more complex way than that offered by the black-and-white perspectives of the group, he found himself distanced from (and at odds with) his activist friends. He describes one friend's reaction when Halevi decided to become a journalist:

> Krup feared the journalist's objectivity. He understood, better than I did, that my becoming a journalist would conflict with our shared passion. A good journalist empathized with opposing sides of a story; Krup rightly suspected that in knowing many truths, I would abandon our absolute judgements, betray the basis for our friendship.
>
> (p. 187)

As he faced the world, now stripped of his extremist focus, Halevi felt at first bewildered, then grief-stricken:

"I reread the Holocaust classics with stunned disbelief, as if only now discovering the camps. I felt poisoned by the intrusion of my father's knowledge into my life. I'd grown up with a vocabulary in which daily life and the demonic commingled: oven, gas, shower, train. Suddenly, the violation of innocent words enraged me."

> From the moment my father introduced me to the Holocaust, he taught me how to confront it: with Jewish resistance and solidarity. But now, no longer an activist, I faced its enormity without antidotes and felt, for the first time, inconsolable. I sat in my apartment and wept; I felt I could go to bed crying, wake up the next morning and find myself still weeping.
>
> (p. 188)

Facing the world as an individual, rather than as part of a collective, and stripped of his manic defenses, Halevi was stunned by a new awareness of his helplessness and mortality and by the unexpected feeling of solidarity not only with fellow Jews, but with everyone he encountered:

> And yet it wasn't the Holocaust I mourned for, but my own transience... Ironically, the Holocaust had made death abstract for me. By equating death with the murder of Jews, I submerged my fear of mortality into the collective experience of genocide. When death became murder, it was no longer an amorphous, unstoppable force but a tangible enemy one could resist and even defeat. I could save myself as a Jew, like my father outwitting the Nazis; but as a human being, confronted with a random vanishing, I was helpless... I walked the streets, watching passersby and thinking, 'They're all going to die, *we're* all going to die.' I felt a sudden, disorienting commonality with my fellow human beings, pathetic creatures marked for a mysterious disappearance, unable to resist or even understand.
>
> (pp. 188–189)

Following this crisis, and after his father's death, Halevi reclaimed his Jewish identity, his own relationship to the Holocaust and his religion, on new terms.

> I wasn't a practicing Jew. Borough Park's vision of religious intactness didn't tempt me: I saw myself as part of a generation for whom the tradition had ruptured and from whose brokenness would emerge new ways of being Jewish.
>
> But I believed in God, believed that behind its veil of chaos existed a purposeful universe. Ironically, I drew my faith in part from the Holocaust. The Final Solution seemed in essence an attempt by nihilism to defeat meaning.
>
> And yet Hitler's attempt to prove the absence of soul failed. It was defeated by all those who secretly blessed their food and marked sacred time in the ghettos and camps, who refused to be reduced to matter. Starving inmates fasted on Yom Kippur. A friend of my mother's, imprisoned in Auschwitz, picked out anything resembling meat from her soup, even though Judaism permits eating nonkosher food in life-threatening situations: She wanted to reaffirm humanity over animal need.
>
> (p. 195)

and to resist the dehumanization that Hitler intended to effect.

Halevi came to a more balanced, a more human understanding of his father, a deeper appreciation of him and a new form of identification with him—one could say... an atonement with him—a new kind of reconciliation with him, a return to feeling "at one" (cf. Loewald [1978] 1980, p. 390) with him, but in a new way, one that accompanied and encompassed a new understanding of Halevi's own motivations and beliefs. Halevi developed a tolerance for uncertainty, ambiguity, and paradox:

> ... I wanted to stop fearing the body's death, know that the soul endures and can't be violated except by one's own weakness. Like [my father], I wanted to know everything the cynic knows, penetrate the most brutal reality, and emerge praising life. I wanted to achieve what [my father] never became: a Jew who related to the world not with the grudges of a victim, but with the generosity of a survivor.
>
> (Halevi 1995, p. 197)

Case Discussion: Beginnings of Emergence—Parricide, Mourning, and Internalization

As Halevi abandons his extremist stance, he has to reorient himself to the world and find a new place for himself within it. In facing this challenge, he reaches back to what had shaped his worldview in the first place: his father's experience of the Holocaust. But what he finds in and creates from this reaching back is very different from what he had previously absorbed from his father. Indeed, he vehemently rejects much of what he had passively taken in in this regard. He rereads the Holocaust narratives "with stunned disbelief, as if only now discovering the camps" (p. 188) and becomes enraged by the intrusion of his father's experience into his own life, by the "violation of innocent words" (p. 188) that had become an integral part of his childhood. In this way, and in terms of Loewald's theory, he commits a form of parricide, necessary for him to take responsibility for his own life and to develop as an individual. In this act, he destroys within himself the as it were unmetabolized introjections of his father's beliefs and builds, out of the products of this destruction, a new identity, and a new religious understanding. He eschews his father's radical separatism but draws on his father's faith: in God, in a purposeful universe and in the human soul as in some way inviolable. This renewed faith constitutes his "atonement" for the crime of parricide, for going against his father's separatist beliefs, and effects a reconciliation with his father as well as with a broader range of other human beings.

Loewald observes that as the individual matures and as the ego gains in synthetic power, depth and complexity, one is able to engage more deeply and broadly with others. "It is this richer self-organization that can lead to novel ways of relating to objects while being enriched by their novelty" (Loewald [1979] 1980, p. 394).

Similarly, Halevi's transition away from the extremist group was marked by an increased sphere of compassion, an awareness of the universality of the mortal human condition and an embracing of paradox. In this way, Halevi reclaims (or claims for the first time), paradoxically, both his individuality as separate from a single-minded cause and his connectedness/commonality and solidarity with other human beings, regardless of ideology.

In "The Waning of the Oedipus Complex," Loewald writes,

> In an important sense, by evolving our own autonomy, our own superego, and by engaging in non-incestuous object relations, we are killing our parents. We are usurping their power, their competence, their responsibility for us, and we are abnegating, rejecting them as libidinal objects. In short, we destroy them in regard to some of their qualities hitherto most vital to us.
>
> ([1978] 1980, p. 390)

This "crime" is "atoned" for through processes of mourning and internalization whereby parental functions, ideals, and moral injunctions are modified, transmuted, changed and made more fully one's own. This internalized reconciliation paves the way for new modes of relating to one's parents (now seen and related to increasingly as the individuals that they are), greater freedom, and the capacity to engage more deeply with new objects.

In Loewald's view, the work of mourning comes about through processes of internalization and is more or less successfully accomplished to the extent that aspects of the relationship with the one who is lost are taken in as parts of oneself. Mourning

> comprises the relinquishment of intimate object relations and the reestablishment, in the internal arena, of elements of these object relations by identificatory processes... [A]n object relation is given up, involving pain and suffering, and is substituted by a restructuring of the internal world which is in consonance with the relinquished relationship.
>
> (1978, pp. 45–46)

Indeed, for Halevi, his further development was marked by both a deepening of his Jewish faith and a broadening of his appreciation, understanding and outreach to individuals of other faiths and traditions. In his subsequent book, *At the Entrance to the Garden of Eden*, following his marriage to a woman of Christian heritage and a move to Israel, he explores the interweaving of the three Abrahamic faiths in Jerusalem and comes to a place of caring and respect for a multiplicity of faith traditions. He observes,

> For me, the test of whether a religion is true is in its capacity to turn ordinary people into decent believers and extraordinary people into saints whose presence affirms the reality of God. By that measure, Christianity, Islam and Judaism—and Hinduism and Buddhism—are all true faiths, regardless of their conflicting theologies.
>
> (Halevi 2001, p. 2)

Section 3: Deepening Internalizations, Movements Toward Unity Regained

Mourning and Internalization: Further Psychoanalytic and Religious Reflections

In a 2010 paper, Kernberg writes movingly about the process and phenomenology of mourning in later life. Like Loewald, he affirms the centrality of internalization in the mourning process, as well as the ways the ego may thereby become further expanded and enriched. Based on his own experience as someone who has recently lost his wife of many decades, as well as in-depth interviews with others who have lost a spouse following a long and fulfilling relationship, he recasts mourning, not as a process that comes to an end with the gradual relinquishment of the lost object and the reinvestment in present-day life, but rather as one that may go on indefinitely in a way that does not constitute pathology. He writes:

> Mourning interminably may become part of the increased capacity for love and appreciation of life.
>
> (p. 614)

He goes on to say, furthermore,

Perhaps the most impressive aspect of the mourning process is the... moral or ethical injunction to carry on the aspirations of the now deceased person.

(Kernberg 2010, p. 616)

Kernberg describes a paradoxical intensification of loving feelings after the death of an intimate, as if the intrusion of quotidian demands detracted from full appreciation of the other person. He writes:

From a religious perspective, Rabbi Moshe Berger (personal communication) has formulated this development, stating that all human love relations are finite, while the absence that necessarily follows the death of one of a couple is infinite. The paradox, he goes on, is that only at the time of infinite absence can the time of finite presence be fully appreciated in all its potential luminosity....

(Kernberg 2010, p. 617)

Mourning and internalization are central themes in many religious traditions, and indeed it is in a paper on "Internalization, Separation, Mourning and the Superego" that Loewald makes one of his few explicit references to religion, in this instance, Christianity:

The death of a love object, or the more or less permanent separation from a love object, is the occasion for mourning and for internalization. The unconscious and conscious experiences of threats to one's own existence as an individual, heightened by the increasing awareness of one's own eventual death, are, I believe, intimately connected with the phenomenon of internalization. It seems significant that with the advent of Christianity, initiating the greatest intensification of internalization in Western civilization, the death of God as incarnated in Christ moves into the center of religious experience. Christ is not only the ultimate love object, which the believer loses as an external object and regains by identification with Him as an ego ideal. He is in His passion and sacrificial death, the exemplification of complete internalization and sublimation of all earthly relationships and needs.

(Loewald [1962] 1980, p. 260)

Taken from a historical perspective, central to the development of Christianity as a religion was the crisis Jesus' disciples faced when Jesus was crucified. Mourning the loss of their leader, they were challenged with the question: What does a community (or individual) do when its spiritual leader dies or, worse, is humiliated and killed? Is there any way forward other than despair? One of the responses to this conundrum in Christian tradition is this: that with the death of Jesus comes the gift of the Spirit, also called the "Comforter" (see, e.g., *The Holy Bible, KJV*, John 14:26) and representing, in some sense, the spiritual leader's binding love for the community, that person's own ideals and loving example as transmuted by each believer individually and by the community as a whole. Following the crucifixion, the Spirit comes to reside within and find expression through believers in an enduring way. It could be understood as a metaphor, or template, for internalization.

When the mourning process proceeds in a healthy way, this "taking in," transmuting and carrying forward into the future of the relationship with the lost object can be a source of energy and strength. Loewald writes,

> Whether separation from a love object is experienced as deprivation and loss or as emancipation and mastery will depend, in part, on the achievement of the work of internalization. Speaking in terms of affect, the road leads from depression through mourning to elation.
>
> (Loewald [1962] 1980, p. 263)

But Christianity is not the only religion in which mourning and internalization play a central, indeed foundational, role. Rabbinic Judaism, too, developed in the wake of a loss: the destruction of the Second Temple in Jerusalem. Because the Temple as the center of Jewish life and the locus of encounter with the divine was no longer there, Judaism became a religion of the Book, focusing on learning and scriptural interpretation; Temple prayers and rituals were recast as daily practices of individual and communal devotion, "Temple ritual in the heart." And prior to that, the Jewish people suffered exile from their native soil. It was in the context of this loss and displacement that Moses received the Ten Commandments and Torah became the central focus of the Jewish faith. The believer, even in displacement, could retain connectedness to God by aligning oneself with these moral injunctions and codes of behavior. Deuteronomy affirms: "The Lord himself will go before you. He will be with you. He will not fail you or forsake you (31:8)."

Central to Islam, too is a process of mourning the separation from Allah, and the longing for return. "That is why we weep tears of longing when we read the Qu'ran." Islamic worship includes a strong mystical tradition, supported by the arts such as Qu'ran recitation, the musicality of its language, the beauty of its script, the architectural spaces that have been set up for worship. Perhaps best known in the West among Islamic mystics is the poet Rumi whose "Song of the Reed" expresses and exemplifies the beauty that flows forth from the mourning process and its paradoxical nature. The reed has been separated from its origins, "Since I was cut from the reedbed,/I have made this crying sound" (Rumi/Keshavarz 2012). It is only by virtue of having been cut from the reedbed that the reed has been made into a flute, and yet its longing for return is what motivates its song. "The reed is hurt/and salve combining. Intimacy/ and longing for intimacy, one/song. A disastrous surrender/and a fine love, together." (Rumi/Keshavarz 2012). These are examples of the "silent Islam" so different from the "loud Islam" that has coopted both journalistic and academic representations of the religion.

Kernberg writes:

> The profound emotional conviction about the continued existence, in another realm of reality, of the soul or the spirit of the person who has died, of the immortality of the soul, in short, is an essential component of the mourning process. It dovetails with religious assumptions of the resurrection of the soul and of the body, and of re-encounter with the love object as an aspect of the final encounter with God...This emotional conviction of the continued presence of the lost

object points to an important psychological root of the religious impulse as a basic aspect of the human psyche.

(Kernberg 2010, p. 165)

There can be no mourning, no internalization, no arriving at something transcendent or new, without the initial acknowledgment of the loss, including the agony and depth and scope of that loss. At such a time of global unrest and societal change as we currently face, there is a temptation to deny the irrevocability of such losses as a pretechnological world, a globe not characterized by interdependence of nations and cultures, a climate unaffected by industrialization. Many of our current polarizations involve attempts to maintain a status quo, or to live only within the sphere of one's own political party, nation, religion, or race. The world we are faced with now is, in many ways, deeply unfamiliar. A recent New York Times guest essay by Gary Greenberg, psychotherapist and small-town first selectman, states it beautifully in an essay entitled "In Grief is How We Live Now:"

I am also bereft, heartsick over the incipient loss of a shared world so total that we can't even agree on what has been lost, let alone mourn it in unison. Or, for that matter, pick up the pieces and see if we can fashion something better out of them…[A]s the links in the supply chain of our familiar world weaken and snap, we may need to be reminded that behind the outrage and blame is bereavement, that we may be entering a long age of grief and we have no one to console us for our losses or to build something new with, except one another.

(Greenberg, NYT, May 7, 2022)

Music, Ritual and Sublimation: Reclaiming an "Early Magic"

In this concluding section, drawing from Loewald's later writings—his paper "Psychoanalysis in Search of Nature" and his book on *Sublimation*—I wish to explore some resonances in Loewald's writing to do with music and nature, moving beyond both psychoanalytic thought and organized religious language to circle back to his early interest in religious experience and his early exposure to music. These subjects, music, ritual, sublimation, contemplation of the natural world, have in common their capacity to reflect and to recreate an "early magic" (cf. Loewald 1988, p. 81).

Since ancient times, natural philosophers and cosmologists have sought knowledge about the deeper workings of the universe through linkages between music, mathematics, and the movements of the planets. Music, movement, and rhythm have been integral to religious ritual from long before the separation of music, dance, theology and doctrine into independent disciplines. Music is nonverbal, in one sense the most abstract of art forms, and yet also, perhaps, the most primal.

In his 1987 paper "Psychoanalysis in Search of Nature," Loewald refers to an "obscure recognition of the deep sameness of instinctual driving forces in the inner and external world" (Loewald 1987, p. 52) best apprehended, not by dispassionate study, but by what he calls "unison and reverberation with the rest of nature" (p. 50).

Music, a pattern of soundwaves that induces a corresponding movement of the human eardrum that, in turn, creates physiological, emotional, and even spiritual responsiveness in the listener, can perhaps offer one model for how such "driving forces" are transmuted into human experience and understanding. The "pattern" of soundwaves that becomes "music" is one that follows mathematical principles: ratios of frequencies wherein simple ratios (1:1, 1:2, 2:3) are experienced as "unison" or "consonance," and complex ones as "dissonant" (for a fascinating analysis of the features of music that lead to its emotional power, see Zuckerkandl 1969; for the vicissitudes of the relationships between music theory and cosmology, see Hicks 2017).

Music thus provides a readily accessible example of interpenetration of outer and inner worlds, of universal principles informing both metaphysics and metapsychology, both physics and physiology. Loewald rarely speaks of music directly in his writing—he speaks instead of rhythm and resonance (1988, p. 32), unison and reverberation (1987, p. 50)—and yet the formal aspects of his writing and his use of language are inherently, sometimes strikingly, musical (see Downey 1994, Lang 2009).

Hans Loewald grew up in a household suffused with the sound of classical music. His mother, grieving the loss of her husband, Hans' father, during pregnancy (Jones 2001, Lang 2009, Mitchell 1998) or shortly after Hans' birth (Downey 1994, p. 839), consoled herself by playing Beethoven on the piano (Jones, Lang, Mitchell). Thus baby Hans, in the crib next to his mother's piano, was bathed in a "primal dense unity" (Mitchell 1998, p. 827) of sound and feeling, of his mother's grief, her comforting presence and his own sensory experience.

Classical music, in particular late classical European music as typified by Beethoven's piano sonatas, quartets and symphonies, the music Hans's mother played on the piano, consists in a journey from consonance, through permutations of dissonance, leading tones, neighboring tones, back to consonance. It thus entails "recapitulative journeys" akin to those I have sketched out as characterizing religious and psychological development from an original unity, through cycles of alienation and atonement, concluding with some form of return. The return to an opening theme and/or tonic chord is made infinitely more meaningful by virtue of all that went before. And there is a comfort in this return, like a coming home. Music relates, furthermore, to human bodily rhythms: andante a "walking" tempo, vivace a faster, "livelier" one. We speak of "beats" in music, like beats of the heart, faster reflecting excitement, slower reflecting a calmer, more meditative state. Our first exposure to music, arguably, is in utero, with the beating of our mother's heart, the sound of her voice. We respond to music physiologically via fluctuations in our autonomic nervous system, in our breathing and pulse. Music can emerge from us as an expression, it can move us to tears, or to action... Trumpet calls and battle songs make use of this musical potential for courageous arousal, much as lullabies engage music and the mother's voice in the service of restful sleep.

These correspondences of the inner workings of our bodies and emotions with the structures and movements of the external world affect us in ways that defy verbal explication, that strike with an ineffable sense of familiarity, resonance, and immediacy.

Most of Loewald's writing seems deeply agnostic, aside from the one reference to Christianity mentioned above and certain statements in his Pastoral Care article. In this and other ways, he leaves the door wide open, cautioning against both simplistic theistic certainties that, for many, have become at best devitalized and at worst deeply destructive, and positivistic reductionism that fails to account for much that is (or can be) most creative in human nature and contributory to human flourishing, including religious and aesthetic experience as well as much that has been labeled "primitive." He leaves the way open for mystery, passion, immanence, and transcendence. Elsewhere he uses words such as "sacred" ([1978] 1980, p. 396), "magical" ([1951] 1980), and "magic" (1988, p. 81), in connection with both early infant experience and certain adult states of mind wherein the subject–object distinction is blurred or suspended. He links such experiences to intimations of "eternity," "timelessness," in contradistinction with "everlastingness," "sempiternity" ([1971] 1980, p. 141, 1978, pp. 59–72), measured time that goes on and on. He relates these to a kind of boundaryless feeling of unity with the environment, presumed to be the state of mind in infancy, an experience that can be recapitulated throughout human life in experiences in nature, lovemaking, religious experience, and in apprehending a work of art.

Music, like psychological structure, is dynamic, it moves through time, and it is built not out of discrete parts, but out of a relatedness between the parts: the intervals that make up a chord are based on proportions of frequencies, not on static properties or concrete entities. Music is an unfolding, more akin to *natura naturans*—nature as process—than *natura naturata*, nature as created forms (cf Hicks 2017, p. 43, Loewald 1988, p. 79); it is made up of "waves," not "particles." Listening to music is an immersive experience, a partaking in something beyond ourselves that at the same time speaks to our deepest core.

In his paper on the Waning of the Oedipus complex, Loewald observes,

> The more we understand about primitive mentality, which constitutes a deep layer of advanced mentality, the harder it becomes to escape the idea that its implicit sense of and quest for primitive nondifferentiation of subject and object *contains a truth of its own,* granted that this other truth fits badly with our rational world view and quest for objectivity.
>
> (Loewald 1977, p. 402, my italics)

He then goes on to say,

> In the psychosexual and social life of the present day 'archaic' currents are more in evidence, less repressed, I believe. They consequently make for different troubles, often closer to 'perversion' than 'neurosis'… Our hitherto normal form of organizing reality, aiming at a strict distinction between an internal, subjective and an external, objective world, is in question. I believe that our quest for individuation and individuality, and for an objective world view, is being modified by insights we are gaining from the 'psychic reality' of pre-oedipal life stages.
>
> (Loewald 1977, p. 403)

These insights have offered, too, a deeper psychoanalytic understanding of religious experience, aesthetic experience, and the interpenetration of individual life and culture. "Health" consists not of dominance of ego over id, secondary over primary process or science over religion, but a nuanced interweaving of the two modes. Winnicott ([1960] 1965) said "there is no such thing as an infant," only an infant-and-mother… We see more clearly now that "there is no such thing as an individual," only an individual-in-culture, a psyche-in-nature. And yet… there is no culture, no nature, without the individuals that form its parts, any more than there is harmony or counterpoint without the individual tones and musical lines. And it is as individuals that we have agency and can take responsibility for our own lives. So we are left with a dialectical tension, a toggling-back-and-forth, a "hovering between the poles of identification and object cathexis, between merging and individuality" (Loewald [1978] 1980). It is this dynamic, dialectical tension that constitutes human liveliness and creativity, that creates music.

Loewald sees in Freud's "last instinct theory," his conceptualization of Eros and Thanatos, love and strife, the dual instincts that inform not only the human dynamic unconscious, but also nature itself, (cf. Freud 1937, pp. 245–247, 1940, pp. 148–149) a movement toward transcendence (Loewald 1987, pp. 524–525). He writes, "if there is such a thing as a life instinct, its 'aim' would be satisfaction through the attainment of higher, more *differentiated unities*, in which tension is not eliminated, but 'bound'— satisfaction of a different kind" (1988, p. 27, my italics).

It is often through the arts that such differentiated unities can best be represented and thereby cultivated. Music has been called "the universal language." Often it is through the arts that seismic shifts in the social and psychological landscape are first apprehended and expressed. And the arts can offer experiential glimpses of what we might wish to be and to become. They are necessary, if not sufficient, for human development and flourishing.

Loewald concludes the final chapter of his final book with the following:

> Nowadays we seem to acknowledge and yield most readily to the magic of a great work of art. May we assume that this magic is connected with the achievement of a reconciliation—with the return, on a higher level of organization, to the early magic of thought, gesture, word, image, emotion, fantasy, as they become united again with what in ordinary nonmagical experience they only reflect, recollect, represent or symbolize? Could sublimation be both a mourning of lost original oneness and a celebration of oneness regained?
>
> (Loewald 1988, p. 81)

References

Armstrong, K. (2000). *The Battle for God*. New York, Ballantine Books.

Asani, A.S. (2018). Foreword. In *Music, Sound and Architecture in Islam*, M. Frishkopf & F. Spinetti, eds. Austin: University of Texas Press. pp. xiii–xviii.

Blake, J. (2022). An 'Imposter Christianity' is threatening American democracy. *CNN*. Sunday, July 24th. https://www.cnn.com/2022/07/24/us/white-christian-nationalism-blake-cec/index.html.

Downey, T.W. (1994). Hans W. Loewald, M.D. (1906–1993). *International Journal of Psychoanalysis* 75:839–842.

Fowler, J.W. (1981). *Stages of Faith: The Psychology of Human Development and the Quest for Meaning*. New York: HarperCollins.

Freud, S. (1937). Analysis terminable and interminable. *S.E.* 23:209–255.

Freud, S. (1940). *An outline of psychoanalysis. S.E.* 23:139–208.

Frishkoff, M. & Spinetti, F., eds. (2018). *Music, Sound and Architecture in Islam*. Austin: University of Texas Press.

Gorsky, P.S. & Perry, S. (2020). Practices of relation: Gorsky and Perry. *The Immanent Frame: Secularism, Religion and the Public Sphere*, April 2nd. North Tarrytown: Social Science Research Council. https://tif.ssrc.org/2020/04/02/gorski-and-perry/

Greenberg, G. (2022). Guest essay: in grief is how we live now. *The New York Times*, 5/7/2022.

Halevi, J.K. (1995). *Memoirs of a Jewish Extremist*. Boston, MA: Little, Brown & Co.

Halevi, J.K. (2001). *At the Entrance to the Garden of Eden.* New York: William Morrow & Co.

Hicks, A. (2017). *Composing the World: Harmony in the Medieval Platonic Cosmos.* Oxford: Oxford University Press.

The Holy Bible (1962). *Authorized King James Version* (1611). Oxford University Press, *The Oxford Self-Pronouncing Bible.*

The Jewish Publication Society (1985) *Tanakh, The Holy Scriptures, The New JPS Translation According to the Traditional Hebrew Text.* Philadelphia, PA: The Jewish Publication Society.

Jones, J.W. (2001). Hans Loewald: the psychoanalyst as mystic. *Psychoanalytic Review* 88:793–809.

Jurgensmeyer, M. (2001). *Terror in the Mind of God: The Global Rise of Religious Violence.* University of California Press, Berkeley and Los Angeles, CA.

Kernberg, O. (2010). Some observations on the process of mourning. *International Journal of Psychoanalysis* 91:601-619.

Lang, F. (2009). Hans Loewald and the transformation of passion. *Psychoanalytic Study of the Child* 64:3–13.

Lawrence, Bruce (1995). *Defenders of God: The Fundamentalist Revolt Against the Modern Age.* University of South Carolina Press.

Loewald, H.W. (1951). Ego and reality. In *Papers on Psychoanalysis.* New Haven, CT: Yale University Press, 1980, pp. 3–20.

Loewald, H.W. (1953). Psychoanalysis and modern views on human existence and religious experience. *The Journal of Pastoral Care* vii, 1:1–15.

Loewald, H.W. (1960). On the therapeutic action of psychoanalysis. In *Papers on Psychoanalysis.* New Haven, CT: Yale University Press, 1980, pp. 221–256.

Loewald, H.W. (1962). Internalization, separation, mourning and the superego. In *Papers on Psychoanalysis.* New Haven, CT: Yale University Press, 1980, pp. 257–276.

Loewald, H.W. (1977). Transference and countertransference: the roots of psychoanalysis (Book Review Essay on the Freud/Jung Letters). *Psychoanalytic Quarterly* 46:514–527.

Loewald, H.W. (1978a). *Psychoanalysis and the History of the Individual.* New Haven, CT: Yale University Press.

Loewald, H.W. (1978b). The waning of the Oedipus complex. In *Papers on Psychoanalysis.* New Haven, CT: Yale University Press, 1980, pp. 384–404.

Loewald, H.W. (1987). Psychoanalysis in search of nature: thoughts on metapsychology, 'metaphysics' and projection. *Annual of Psychoanalysis* 16:49–54.

Loewald, H.W. (1988). *Sublimation.* New Haven, CT: Yale University Press.

Marty, M.E. & Appleby, R.S. (1991). *Fundamentalisms Observed.* Chicago, IL: University of Chicago Press.

Meissner, W.W. (1986). Psychoanalysis and Religious Experience. New Haven: Yale University Press

Mitchell, S. (1998). From ghosts to ancestors: the psychoanalytic vision of Hans Loewald. *Psychoanalytic Dialogues* 8:825–855.

Nields, J.A. (2003). From unity to atonement: Some religious correlates of Hans Loewald's developmental theory. *International Journal of Psychoanalysis* 84:699-716.

Omar, A.R. & Omar, A.M., Trs. (2008). *The Holy Qur'an.* Hockessin, DE: Noor Foundation International, Inc.

Rizzuto, A-M. (1979). *The Birth of the Living God.* Chicago, IL: The University of Chicago Press.

Rumi, J. al-D. (Author), Keshavarz, F., Tr. (2012). 'Song of the Reed.' in "The Ecstatic Faith of Rumi" https://onbeing.org/poetry/song-of-the-reed/

Steiner, J. (1997). The interplay between pathological organizations and the paranoid-schizoid and depressive positions. In *The Contemporary Kleinians of London*, ed. R. Schafer, Madison, CT: International Universities Press, pp. 195–220.

Thurman, H. (1976). *Jesus and the Disinherited.* Boston, MA: Beacon Press.

Tillich, P. (1952). *The Courage to Be.* New Haven, CT: Yale University Press.

Tillich, P. (1957). *Dynamics of Faith.* New York: Harper & Row.

Wallwork, E. & Wallwork, A. (1990). Psychoanalysis and religion: current status of a historical antagonism. In *Psychoanalysis and Religion*, ed. J. Smith & S. Handelman, Baltimore, MD: Johns Hopkins University Press, pp. 160–173.

Winnicott, D.W. (1960). The theory of the Parent-infant relationship. In *The Maturational Processes and the Facilitating Environment*, ed. M. Masud R. Khan. London: Hogarth Press, 1965, pp. 37–55.

Zuckerkandl, V. (1969). *Sound and Symbol: Music and the External World.* Princeton, NJ: Bollingen Series.

Chapter 7

Hans W. Loewald
Thoughts About Religion

Lorraine D. Siggins

Introduction

Religion is not a topic frequently discussed in psychoanalytic circles. Certainly not when I began my psychoanalytic training in the mid-1960s at the Western New England Institute for Psychoanalysis (W.N.E.I.P.). The first thing I had to do was to find a training analyst from the list I was given. As I was browsing the list, I commented that I thought I knew someone on the list from church. A senior analyst in the vicinity responded, "Don't worry! we will soon get religion analyzed out of you. Then you will be fully analyzed." I was not surprised by the comment about religion, but I was concerned about the concept of being "fully analyzed."

As Roy Schafer later commented, "around 1960, psychoanalysts in the United States were ultraconservative Freudian theorists" (Schafer, 1991 in Fogel, 1991, p.81). I was concerned that "being fully analyzed" meant that I would turn into a narrow-minded, rigid, obsessive person. The choice of training analyst seemed very important to me at this point.

I knew the name Hans Loewald, but I had not met him personally. I decided arbitrarily to read one of Loewald's papers, "The Ego and Reality" (1951). When I got to the last paragraph, I was stunned. Here, I read the following:

> If we look closely at people, we can see that... stages of ego- reality integration... shift considerably from day-to-day, at different periods in their lives, in different moods and situations, from one such level to other levels. In fact, it would seem that the more alive people are (though not necessarily more stable), the broader their range of ego-reality levels is. Perhaps the so-called fully developed, mature ego is not one that has become fixated at presumably highest or latest stage of development, having left the others behind it, but is an ego that integrates its reality in such a way that the earlier and deeper levels of ego-reality integration remain alive as dynamic sources of higher organization.

So here was an analyst stating that the aim of the analysis was not that the analysand become fixated at the highest or latest stage of development, "fully analyzed" as I had imagined it! Loewald saw the mature ego "as one of higher organization that is open to the unconscious from which it derives life and energy from the earlier and deeper ego-reality levels of integration" (Loewald, 1951, p.20).

For Loewald, the end phase of development was not one of fixed, narrow rationality. As he said, we all know the madness that is "the madness of unbridled rationality"

DOI: 10.4324/9781032685151-8

(Loewald, 1978a, p.56). The aim of analysis was for the analysand to stay open to taking the analyst as a new object through the lifelong separation-fusion or internalization/projection dialectic process. With the oscillation from the unconscious to the conscious, the integrated power opened the ego to the wealth of the id's creativity.

Thus began a seven-year analysis. I knew Loewald for around thirty years—first as an analysand, then as a colleague, and then as a colleague and friend.

It was during my analysis that I first wondered about Loewald's views on religion. In general, I was surprised by the wide range of knowledge he had. For instance, he knew a great deal about the British Royal family. (Having been brought up in Australia at that time, the Royal Family was a presence in our lives.) In fact, he knew more about them than I did. There was one occasion when I made an association to Princess Margaret, and it turned out that he knew all about her and her "scandalous relationship" with Group Captain Townsend. He also knew why the Queen, as the Head of the Church of England, could not allow her to marry him. On another occasion, I was describing to him some part of the Italian film "La Dolce Vita," which I had erroneously assumed that he had not seen. He had not only seen it but pointed out to me how my account had left out a major part of the story of the film and in the discussion that followed, he pointed out how my omission was related to a childhood experience. I had not expected an interpretation to come out of "La Dolce Vita!"

During the course of the analysis, his intelligence, warmth, caring, and empathy were very clear. He also had a wonderful sense of humor, often ironic. His office was set up to encourage regression and to encourage transference to the analyst. His couch had a light blanket at the end of it, so, you could take off your shoes and get your legs under the blanket. He was a smoker, and the office was always full of smoke, which was very comforting to me as my father was a smoker. It certainly helped the transference. Loewald was also very straightforward. There were times when he would be irritated, and sometimes angry. One understood that the analyst was a real person. It was clear that the relationship between analyst and analysand was central and that it was a mutual undertaking. Toward the end of the analysis, I commented that the work that we had done over the last few years had been more collegial than it had at the beginning. I wondered in what ways I had changed. I did not expect a response, but he said, "We have both have changed. You have changed and I have changed."

It was in this context, during the analysis that I realized that Loewald knew a surprising amount about Christianity. I was puzzled where this knowledge came from. I understood he was agnostic and was not part of an active religious tradition. (Loewald E. 2022). However, he knew a great deal about the Anglican liturgy, and the place of the Eucharist in the service at the Episcopal Church I attend. At other times, he would remind me of a New Testament passage and though he did not know the reference, he would correctly know the gist of the passage.

Recently, I decided to explore Loewald's writings to see if I could find out what he thought about religion. I discovered that some of Loewald's published papers were not included in the "Collected Papers" (1980), nor in the "Essential Loewald" (2000). The titles of some of these left-out papers are Regression (1981), Transference/Countertransference (1986), Termination, Analyzable and Unanalyzable (1988a, 1988b), Psychoanalysis in Search of Nature: Thoughts on Metapsychology, "Metaphysics" and Projection (1988a, 1988b). Then there was a very early paper, "Psychoanalysis and Modern Views on Human Experience and Religious Experience," in The Journal of Pastoral Care, vol. VII Spring 1953 No.1. This paper was adapted from a lecture Loewald had given in Washington, D.C. in a four- lecture series entitled "Christianity and Modern Man." At that time he was Assistant Professor Psychiatry, University of Maryland Medical School, Baltimore. This paper was published two years after "Ego and Reality." As I reviewed the many papers Loewald had written in a thirty-year period, there was only one other section in a small monograph that had "Religious" in the title. That was "Comments on Religious Experience" in Loewald's monograph, "Psychoanalysis and the History of the Individual" (1978a) which contained his "Freud Lectures at Yale." So these two papers with "Religion" in the title, were at the beginning and the end respectively of his approximately thirty year writing period. In the many papers that he wrote during that time, there were several occasions when there was a paragraph or two containing a religious idea or observation. Many of them were followed by a statement such as, "I cannot go further with this at the present as it would take us too far afield."

In the Freud lectures at Yale, he also says,

> These lectures perhaps have turned out to be, in the end – far more than they should have been, tentative, philosophical reflections on psychoanalysis. Some of the things I have discussed, I have wanted to say for a long time. I am most grateful for the opportunity this series has provided, and for your interest .
>
> (1978a, p.77)

It may be that one of the reasons Loewald did not continue his discussion about religion in several of the other papers is that he was apprehensive about how it would be received, as well as the difficulty of the topic itself. He had said to some people after the lecture that it took courage to discuss religion. (Siggins, personal communication.)

At this point, I want to turn and look at the early paper published in the Journal of Pastoral Care. In what follows, I want to address what Loewald has actually written about religion. I shall quote him often, so we can get the actual words. I want to be clear about what he is saying. This will not be a critique of his ideas, but a clarification of what he is saying. A critique would be a different undertaking.

"Psychoanalysis and Modern Views on Human Experience and Religious Experience" (1953)

The first section of this paper is "Remarks on the Psychoanalytic Theory of Personality" (p.2). Loewald states that

> In our time failure and lack of faith (which includes pseudo-religiosity) are the modes of religious experience of many people in all walks of life. The philosopher Nietzsche, one of the fathers of existentialism as well as of psychoanalysis, expressed this modern lack of faith in the words "God is dead." Urgently he attempted to find a way to a living God, because he knew that God is dead insofar as he had fallen out of our experience and our existence. Nietzsche knew that it is our existence which we have to re-evaluate, that we have to find new ways of our own to the grounds, the limits, and the relations of our existence with God. The people who profess disinterest in or contempt for their religion have to deny their need

for faith and trust. Anxiety arises when man is confronted, in a conflict with the reality of freedom: that is that he has to choose, has to decide in order to realize one of his possibilities, in order to come to self-realization.

(p.3)

Loewald goes on to say that anxiety is not understood either by existentialism or by psychoanalysis (p.4). Loewald emphasizes that "the continuous evasion and avoidance of anxiety leads to crippling neurosis, a whole deadening of the personality. It needs to be confronted" (p.4).

Loewald goes on to describe psychoanalytic theory of development. "It involves various steps that leads eventually to what we see as an integrated personality. The child starts off close to and dependent on the mother but with continued growth there is increasing separation. The ultimate integrated personality is built on the more primitive processes of the oscillation between dependence on the mother and the increasing separation" (p.7). As Loewald emphasizes "the highest faculties and the highest achievements and feelings of human beings – are to be understood as developed from the lowest, most primitive organizational stage in the process of psychological integration" (p.7). Later on page 12 he elaborates that " the interaction between the mother and the infant is no longer based on biological processes alone but on behavior and activities, it's the dawning of that which we call psychological" (p.12).

Loewald makes a detour from the discussion of the psychoanalytic theory of development to look at Freud's view of religion and in what way Loewald found it wanting. Religion according to Freud, "originates in man's early feelings of helplessness; and his need for a powerful father, to whose demands he submits in order to enlist his help, which brings forth the idea of God" (p.9). Religion was considered by Freud as a phenomenon which represented a rather primitive stage of development of mankind; whereas Loewald considers religion, "in its mature form, no more primitive than love is, even though both have primitive beginnings and some of the early, old elements remain and persist within maturity" (p.9). Loewald comments that Freud's description "does not take into account the feeling of oneness, of trust, and of belonging which also enters into religious feeling" (p.9). Loewald points out that Freud like other scientists at that time believed that science was going to provide the rational answers to the major problems of mankind. "But while science was for a while very optimistic in its belief, science grew more skeptical in the face of world events which shattered all expectations of rational control and progress" (p.10). This then moved Loewald back to relying on the psychoanalytical description of development.

Just as the biological organism grows and develops and becomes more and more independent of the mother organism, so does the psychological organization of the personality grow and develop through psychological incorporation, assimilation and transformation of the moods, attitudes, general behavioral characteristics, and the abilities, interests, and feelings of those around the infant and child. As the individual grows, ...There is the need for warmth, care, closeness; and there is also the drive toward emancipation as a separate being, moving toward integration as a new individual unit of existence.

(p.13)

As the unconscious becomes transformed into ego-freedom ---and this is a process which in healthy development continues throughout life--- the images and concepts of this relatedness is the experience of relation to a Universal Being. The images and concepts of God and of the bond and the gap between God and man undergo similar transformations, in the history of a civilization and in the history of the individual. The mature individual being able to reach back into his deep origins and roots of being, finds in himself the oneness from where he stems, and understands this is his freedom as his bond of love with God. The concept of God itself seems to change from that of blindly omnipotent power to that of transformation and incarnation of such power in individual freedom and love.

(p.14)

Kierkegaard in his essay "Repetition" says that Repetition "is the modern life view."

When one says that life is a repetition one affirms that existence which has been, now becomes......Seen in this perspective, psychoanalytic treatment is a collaborative process of repetition. It is reworking, of life stages with which the patient has not come to terms.

(p.14)

"With the majority of patients, there is no danger of destroying or inhibiting their genuine religious feelings and beliefs. The problem is to help them to a stage in their development where they can begin to be spiritual beings, so that whatever their religious beliefs may be can become meaningful. Psychoanalysis can then let them go on their way. No psychoanalyst who understands anything about himself and his work would, no matter what his own beliefs may be, want to destroy or nip in their buds those early, and in the true sense liberating, childhood experiences any memories of which contain the germs of genuine religious experience. Psychoanalytic treatment, as an educator or re-educative process, implies and appeals consistently to the ego's potentiality for growth; that is, it appeals to the individual's freedom to repeat. This, in its highest form of awareness, is the freedom for faith and love" (p.14/15).

The final understanding that Loewald leaves us with at the end of this 1953 paper is that religious experience is a higher-level experience which is possible once the other developmental re-working of close care/ego dialectic has occurred.

That psychoanalytic treatment prepares the person to be free to be able to choose religious and spiritual experiences.

Writings between 1953 and 1988

I now want to give a few examples of the references to religion that are scattered through some of the thirty papers or so, written between the 1953 paper described previously, and the last one, in 1988.

In "Ego and Reality" (1951) Loewald describes Freud's understanding of religious experiences as outlined on page 9 of his paper "Civilizations and Its Discontents" (Freud, 1930). Freud says that religious feelings are part of the boy's turning to God as the father the boy needs for protection from the father's castration threat. Freud does not describe the mother as having any part in this. As Loewald describes,

The idea that religious feelings may contain elements having to do with the primary narcissistic relationship with the mother is rejected by Freud or else declared by him to be too obscure or unimportant. The boy also fears he will be engulfed by his mother womb and unable to continue his dialectical process of forming the ego and the reality. Between the danger of a loss of object relationships and the danger of a loss of ego- reality boundaries, the ego pursues its course of integrating reality. While the primary narcissistic identity with the mother forever constitutes the deepest unconscious origin and structural layer of ego and reality, and the motive force for the ego's 'remarkable striving toward unification, synthesis '---this primary identity is also the source of the deepest dread, which promotes, in identification with the father, the ego's progressive differentiation and structurization of reality.

(1951, p.16)

In the paper "Defense and Reality" (Loewald, 1952, p.30), Loewald continues his critique of Freud's attitude to religion. Freud sees religion as being similar to an obsessional neurosis. Loewald points out that Freud took into consideration only certain aspects, and not the most essential aspects of religion, and by doing that, what Freud was left with, was similar to an obsessional neurosis. Loewald states that "the meaning and function of religion is narrowed down to these magical-obsessive aspects and Freud took this to be what religion objectively is" (p.30).

Going ahead to the paper "Repetition and Repetition Compulsion" (Loewald, 1973), among several other things, Loewald points out that the repetitions occurring in life of the religious, contrary to Freud's assertions that they are the same as primitive man in his society, are not the same. "We moderns affirm, even thrive on duality, conflict, individuality, process in time; we affirm the direction of time as going onto the future. For us, the past is important insofar as it foreshadows present and future; it is the present that counts, as activity leading into the future, in contrast to the pre-modern present, which is meaningless unless it proves that what is now, has been and has not perished. The import of repetition in the modern life view lies in its aspect as active re-creation" (Kierkegaard, 1847, p.99). It is repetition with its face toward the future while aware of the past. The aspect of repetition that is stressed is the individual act of repeating in the present. "The dialectic of repetition, Kierkegaard says is easy; for what is repeated has been, otherwise it could not be repeated, but precisely the fact that it has been, gives to repetition the character of novelty" (p.99). As Loewald says, this is "diametrically opposed to the concept of repetition inherent in the life view of traditional archaic societies" (p.100). Loewald continues "...it perhaps points to a deep reason for Freud's bias against religion. Kierkegaard, a most religious man although no mystic in the usual sense, saw repetition very differently from primitive man" (p.100).

In speaking about the idea of a personal God, Loewald sees it as personally motivated "and is an interpretation that flows from a particular understanding of man implied in monotheism – the belief in a personal God as exemplified in Western Judaea – Christian religion and civilization." This he discusses in his paper "On motivation and Instinct Theory" (Loewald, 1971). He notes that "Freud's uncompromising strong stand against Judaea– Christian religion is certainly not incidental to his life-work, but I shall not go into these matters here" (1971, p.104). This is a typical way in which Loewald ends these incursions into more religious topics, that is to say, "I will not say more about this at this time." Or sometimes, "this will take us too far afield."

At this point, I want to make mention of two distinct words or phrases that Loewald uses infrequently but bear a great deal more attention. One is in the paper "Primary Process, Secondary Process, and Language" Loewald, 1978a). Here he uses the phrase "authentic religion" in the following paragraph:

> in most creative forms of language, such as in its authentic religion use, in oratory, poetry, and dramatic art, the primordial power of language comes again to the fore. In great poetry and creative prose...there is an interweaving of primary and secondary process, by virtue of which language functions as a transitional mode encompassing both. We may say that language, being a vehicle for secondary process or conscient mentation, being a medium of hyper cathexis that creates higher organization in its most genuine and autonomous function is a binding power. It ties together human beings and self and object world, and it binds abstract thought with the bodily concreteness and power of life. In the word primary and secondary process are reconciled.
>
> (1978a, pp.203–204)

The other word that deserves more thought is "love" in the psychoanalytic endeavor. Loewald addresses this in "Psychoanalytic Theory and the Psychoanalytic Process" (1970). Loewald points out that during an analysis, there are similarities with periods of the oedipal phase and adolescent thought and behavior. Much has gone into the analysis both from the analyst's and the patient's point of view, in terms of personal investment, than in strictly psychoanalytic work in the sense of detached, dispassionate research. He also says that love of truth is no less a passion because it desires truth rather than some less elevated end. He continues with

> scientific detachment in its genuine form far from excluding love, is based on it. In our work, it can be truly said that in our best moments of dispassionate and objective analyzing we love our object, the patient, more than at any other time and we are compassionate with his whole being. To discover truth about the patient is always discovering it with him and for him as well as for ourselves and about ourselves. And it is discovering truth between each other, as the truth of human beings is revealed in their interrelatedness. While this may sound unfamiliar and perhaps too fanciful, it is only an elaboration, in non-technical terms, of Freud's deepest thoughts about the transference neurosis and its significance in analysis.

(Loewald, 1970, p.297, and see also Jonathan Lear, 1998 in "The Introduction of Eros" in "Open Minded," Harvard U.P.)

In a 1962 paper "Internalization, Separation, Mourning and the Superego" (Loewald, 1962), Loewald turns his discussion of mourning and internalization toward analysis itself, focusing on the termination phase of the analysis. This is a very important phase as it involves working on the loss of the analyst but also the many transference situations that had been active during the analysis. Here Loewald emphasizes again the importance of the internalization of the analyst. Also, "there is an externalization of some of the already present internalizations. The process of internalization will continue and come to relative completion only after termination of the analysis" (p.260). The death of a love object or the more or less permanent separation from a love object is an occasion for mourning and internalization. For the bereaved person, it is also a reminder of their own mortality. Loewald then turns to Christianity and the death of Christ to illustrate some of his points. To quote from Loewald 1962: "It seems significant that with the advent of Christianity, initiating the greatest intensification of internalization in Western civilization, the death of God as incarnated in Christ moves into the center of religious experience. Christ is not only the ultimate love object, which the believer loses as an external object and regains by identification with Him as an ego ideal, He is, in His passion and sacrificial death, the exemplification of complete internalization and sublimation of all earthly relationships and needs" (p.260). Loewald also warns that it is important that a sharp distinction must be maintained between a relationship to fantasy objects and an internal relationship that is a constituent of ego structure. He ends this example with his usual sentence, "But to pursue these thoughts would lead us far afield into unexplored psychological country" (p.262).

In talking about symbolism in the small 1988 monograph on Sublimation, Loewald, quotes a passage from Winnicott on symbolism in the Eucharist, showing movement from symbolic equivalence and to the growth to symbolism proper as traced in his movement. In this context, he discusses the wafer of the Blessed Sacrament as a symbol of the body of Christ; for Roman Catholics, the wafer is the body, whereas for Protestants it is a substitute, a reminder but not the body itself (pp.59,72).

Now I will draw attention to Loewald's review essay on the Freud/Jung Letters (1977), looking specifically for any passages that might add to our knowledge of Loewald's views on religion. If one were to ask about the crux of the differences between Freud's and Jung's views, famously it was Freud's insistence on the centrality of sexuality. However, Loewald takes a different angle:

> Still what Jung labelled Freud's concretistic terminology and personalistic view of the unconscious manifests Freud's awareness that authentic transcendental experience and insights ("spirituality") are anchored in the individual's personal life history and its instinctual roots. Psychoanalysis, I believe, shares with modern existentialism the tenet that super personal and transcendental aspects of human existence and of unconscious and instinctual life (so much stressed by Jung) can be experienced and integrated convincingly – without escapist embellishments, otherworldly consolations and going off into the clouds-only in the concreteness of one's own personal life, including the ugliness, trivialities, and sham that go with it. It would seem that Jungian psychology and psychotherapy jump all too readily from the here-and-now of individual life, from concrete personal experience to the collective unconscious, myth, archetypes, religiosity, and "spirituality" – as refuge and healing visions to cling to, lending easily to evasions and hypocrisy instead of to genuine transcendence or, in psychoanalytic terminology, to sublimation and true ego expansion.
>
> (Loewald, 1977, p.416)

From this material, we can see why Loewald often speaks about "authentic religion," in trying to distinguish it from" escapist embellishments" and "going off into the clouds" that he sees in Jung's ideas. He thinks Jung's ideas may well lead to hypocrisy and shame instead of to genuine transcendence.

"Comments on Religious Experience" 1978a

I now want to consider "Comments on Religious Experience," a paper of Loewald's written around twenty-five years after the first paper with religion in its title. It is one of the three Freud Lectures delivered by Loewald at Yale University in 1974. They were collected together in a monograph entitled "Psychoanalysis and the History of the Individual" in 1978a. The first two lectures in the monograph are titled, "Man as Moral Agent and Transference and Love." This is the third, "Lecture III: Comments on Religious Experience."

Loewald begins by giving a brief summary of his theory of development. Toward the end of that account, Loewald especially emphasizes on page 56 that primary and secondary mentation need to be in constant contact with each other. We need our moorings in the unconscious and the unity and integration and identity that goes with it, instead of fragmentation. However, he warns,

> We know the madness that is the madness of unbridled rationality. Secondary process mentation is an achievement of the highest order, but it must be seen as a constant activity of the mind, not as a static state reached once and for all. If we do not evolve it again and again from the primary form of mentation and return to and evolve from the latter again, rational thought becomes sterile and destructive of life, as it denies and ignores its own living source.
>
> (pp.56–57)

Loewald then goes on to say that some aspects of religious experience are related to unconscious mental processes. He considers that other aspects can be approached by interpreting them in terms of dialectic between unconscious and conscient mentation, between the irrational and the rational. Loewald also made the comment about how he hoped that psychoanalysis could go a step beyond what psychoanalysis has contributed to the understanding—and misunderstanding—of religion, to go beyond Freud's view that religion was an illusion, and that the idea of "God" and eternal life are consolations or defenses to help man to cope with human life. Freud's friend, Romain Rolland, tried to interest Freud in "the oceanic feeling" but Freud said that he had never experienced it.

In developing his argument, Loewald then returns to his own papers written earlier, on "Time." They involved the concepts of "Eternity" and "Everlasting Time." (1972, 1978b, pp.66–69). "Eternity" is where there is no time, and "everlasting time" is where there is never-ending time. This is where there is a different state of mind. Another level of our mind has been touched, and the rational form of mentation has lost its weight. These are felt as religious experiences. Loewald comments that "the concept of everlasting time after death is closest that we come to eternity." (p.67). The fact that these experiences are timeless implies that they are structured or centered differently (p.68). They are transtemporal and there is no sense of duration. Psychoanalysts tend to consider the idea of eternity, religious experiences connected with it as useful defenses—mental sanctuaries to cope with fear of death, castration and the trials and tribulation of human life. Loewald says he does not doubt the truth in this view, but he does not think it is the whole truth (p.69). Loewald believes that "intimations of eternity" bring us in touch with levels of our being, forms of experiencing and of reality that themselves may be disturbing and anxiety provoking to the common sense rationality of everyday life.

> Conscious forms of mentation are primarily responsible for our success and achievement. Seen from this angle our unconscious forms of mentation are, in a non-metaphysical sense, unworldly. They evince another mode of reality. I am not speaking of a realm of Being beyond....
>
> (p.69)

Loewald raises the question as to whether his own age may bring these issues to his mind. But he also wonders if being older gives him greater freedom to voice ideas he has previously held, in public. (He had indicated after this lecture that speaking about religious ideas "takes courage." Siggins, Personal communication.) Loewald went on to say in this lecture, that

> the distinction between conscious – more precisely between preconscious or conscient—and unconscious mentation, rightly understood, places psychoanalytic psychology in the position of shedding new light on important aspects of religious experience. Under the dominating influence of Freud's views on religion, psychoanalysis has shied away from this task.
>
> (p.71)

Loewald went on to say that certain forms of religious experience are aspects of unconscious mentation. In modern civilization religious experiences are more deeply repressed than sexuality. Loewald thought this might be changing, because of the deep common source of sexual and religious life. He says that mystical writers and poets of differing religions have expressed or described their ecstatic experiences in language that is very close to language used to describe passionate sexual or intimate erotic experiences or fantasies (1978b, p.76). This led him to bring up the issue of sublimation which was "a large topic for another time" (Loewald did write a short monograph on "Sublimation" and it was published in 1988a, 1988b).

Loewald finishes this third Yale lecture on religious experience, with:

> I have attempted to juxtapose this historicity with an ahistorical, a timeless dimension of human life. The realm of religious life and thought of course is not limited to mystical and other timeless experiences; the dialectic of history or temporality, and eternity, is itself a central problem in all developed religions and in theology. In this perspective, what I discussed as morality, in terms of owning up, of responsiveness and responsibility, of mutual appropriation of unconscious and conscient modes of experience, can be seen as a religious concern. And the dialectic of id and ego/superego can be understood as paralleling the philosophical-theological or religious dialectic of eternity and temporality.
>
> (1978b, pp.74–76)

Loewald concludes: "Some of the things I have discussed I have wanted to say for a long time. I am most grateful for the opportunity this series has provided, and for your interest" (p.76).

It has been interesting to find that from 1953 to 1988 thoughts about religion have not been far from Loewald's mind. His conclusion in1953 was pragmatic in that he saw psychoanalytic treatment as preparing the person to be able to choose religious and spiritual experiences. In later writings among other issues, he addressed religion as being consonant with several of his philosophical reflections, such as Time and eternity; death, mourning and internalization and the central place of the Eucharist in Christianity. He also highlighted the difference between "authentic" religion and the "escapist religiosity" and discussed the topic of "love" in the psychoanalytic treatment. He cites Freud's negative ideas about religion as a reason that religion has not been discussed more in psychoanalytic theory. One regrets that he did not allow himself to develop some of these themes more than he did.

References

Fogel G.I. (1991) (Ed.) *The work of Hans Loewald: An introduction and commentary*. Northvale, NJ: Jason Aronson.

Freud, S. (1930). Civilization and its Discontents. The Standard Edition of the Complete Psychological Works of Sigmund Freud, Volume 21. *S.E.* 21: pp. 57–146.

Kierkegaard, S. (1847) *Repetition: An Essay in Experimental Psychology*, Princeton, NJ: Princeton University Press, 1946.

Lear J. (1998) *The Introduction of Eros: Reflections on the Work of Hans Loewald in Open Minded*, Cambridge: Harvard University Press, pp. 123–147.

Loewald, E. (2022) *The Tree Grows Standing Still., A Memoir*, Thomaston, ME: Maine Authors Publishing, p. 353.

Loewald, H.W. (1951) Ego and Reality. In *The Essential Loewald*, Hagerstown, MD: University Publishing Group, 2000, pp. 3–20.

Loewald, H.W. (1952) The Problem of Defense and the Neurotic Interpretation of Reality. In *The Essential Loewald*, Hagerstown, MD: University Publishing Group, 2000, pp. 21–32.

Loewald, H.W. (1953) Psychoanalysis and Modern Views on Human Existence and Religious Experience (Third of four lectures in Series Christianity and Psychoanalysis in Washington, DC. May 6, 1952). *Journal of Pastoral Care*, VII: pp. 2–15.

Loewald, H.W. (1962) Internalization, Separation, Mourning, and the Superego. In *The Essential Loewald*, Hagerstown, MD: University Publishing Group, 2000, pp. 257–276.

Loewald, H.W. (1970) Psychoanalytic Theory and the Psychoanalytic Process. In *The Essential Loewald*, Hagerstown, MD: University Publishing Group, 2000, pp. 277–301.

Loewald, H.W. (1971) On Motivation and Instinct Theory. In *The Essential Loewald*, Hagerstown, MD: University Publishing Group, 2000, pp. 102–137.

Loewald, H.W. (1972) The Experience of Time. In *The Essential Loewald*, Hagerstown, MD: University Publishing Group, 2000, pp. 138–147.

Loewald, H.W. (1973) Some Considerations on Repetition and Repetition Compulsion. In *The Essential Loewald*, Hagerstown, MD: University Publishing Group, 2000, pp. 87–101.

Loewald, H.W. (1977) *Book Review Essay on the Freud/Jung Letters in the Essential Loewald*, Hagerstown, MD: University Publishing Group, 2000, pp. 405–418.

Loewald, H.W. (1978a) Primary Process, Secondary Process and Language. In *The Essential Loewald*, Hagerstown, MD: University Publishing Group, 2000, pp. 178–206.

Loewald, H.W. (1978b) *Psychoanalysis and the History of the Individual*, New Haven, CT: Yale University Press.

Loewald, H.W. (1978c) Comments on Religious Experience. In *Psychoanalysis and the History of the Individual*, New Haven, CT: Yale University Press, pp. 55–77.

Loewald, H.W. (1981) Regression: Some General Considerations. *Psychoanalytic Quarterly*, pp. 22–43.

Loewald, H.W. (1986) Transference-Counter transference. *Journal American Psychoanalytic Association*, 34: pp. 275–286.

Loewald, H.W. (1988a) Termination Analyzable and Unanalyzable. *Psychoanalytic Study Child*, 43: pp. 155–166.

Loewald, H.W. (1988b) *Sublimation, Inquiries into Theoretical Psychoanalysis*, New Haven, CT: Yale University Press, pp. 59–75.

Schafer, R. (1991). Internalizing Loewald. In G. I. Fogel (Ed.), *The work of Hans Loewald: An introduction and commentary* (pp. 79–89). Northvale, NJ: Jason Aronson.

Chapter 8

Of Timelessness, Ineffability, and Unity

Hans Loewald, Psychoanalysis, and Our Psychedelic World

Gretchen Hermes

Introduction

In the most important way, the inspiration for this chapter came from work with a patient whom I see routinely in a methadone clinic, Sam, a forty-eight-year-old man who is a single parent to a ten-year-old boy. Sam works from time to time as a lawn care technician, but mostly he is at home with his son and elderly father, whom he also cares for. One day, in a conversation about the challenge he was facing in avoiding additional relapses on opioids, a discussion which also included his sadness over the overdose death of his nephew, Sam told me about an experience he had had several months before, one that he said he would never forget.

> One afternoon in July, I was resting on my bed. Out of nowhere, I felt as though my head was no longer on my pillow, but that my whole body was being held by two yellow/golden arms that enveloped me. I had the sensation that my head was no longer on my pillow. Tears began flowing from my eyes. It was a joyful cry. I knew that these gentle arms had no hateful or hurtful intent. I experienced complete loss of worry and anxiety. The entire experience lasted 5 minutes, but it felt like hours and that it was something I never wanted to end. No drug I have ever taken felt like this.

At the time Sam told me about his experience, I was co-teaching a course on the *Neurobiology of Addiction* in which we were reviewing research on psilocybin and looking closely at instruments used to measures the oceanic dimensions of those experiences. In a subsequent meeting, I asked Sam to recall his experience on that afternoon in July, and we analyzed the memory of his experience using the Mystical Experiences Questionnaire (MEQ). On the key dimensions of feelings of unity, timelessness, and ineffability, Sam's scores on the MEQ were the highest possible. In the weeks and months to follow, Sam became sober. He no longer tested positive for fentanyl on toxicology reports in our clinic. Sam's momentary oceanic consciousness and the recollection of it led to a corrective experience in the way Hans Loewald had described decades earlier:

> States of this kind have been described by mystics and are in some respects akin to ecstatic states occurring under the influence of certain drugs or during emotional states of exceptional intensity. In conditions of extreme joy or sadness, sometimes

DOI: 10.4324/9781032685151-9

during sexual intercourse and related orgiastic experiences, at the height of manic and the depth of depressive conditions, in the depth of bliss or despair, the temporal attributes of experience fall away and only the now, as something outside of time, remains.

(Loewald, 1972, p. 405)

In consequence of his reflections on the experience of eternity—drug-induced or naturalistically occurring—as well as time, ineffability and unity, and other concepts we'll discuss, Loewald's perspectives seem more than germane to the rapidly expanding contemporary discussions, in biological psychiatry and beyond, of the therapeutic action of psychedelics, especially as it potentially relates to psychoanalysis. And the more I considered his original work alongside the literature on psychedelics, the more appropriate and valuable such an analysis appeared.

A Loewaldian Perspective on Psychedelic Oneness

A core experience for those ingesting psychedelics is the achievement of a sense of oneness and interconnection with the world, and indeed, this is a common element of psychedelic experience, as demonstrated, by way of example, by narrative descriptions like these:

I was Being. I was the vibrant force that filled the room. I was the world, the universe. I was everything. I was that which always was and always would be.

(Braden, 1967, pp. 195–199)

It was as if multiple layers of thick dirty cobwebs were magically being torn and dissolved...The scenery opened up, and an incredible amount of light and energy was enveloping me and streaming in subtle variations throughout my whole being...I became the entire universe. I was witnessing the spectacle of the macrocosm with countless pulsating galaxies and was it at the same time...Everything in this universe seemed to be conscious.

(Graf, 1975, pp. 113–114)

In many such cases, psychedelic users describe themselves as being in a womb-like environment, or actually back in the womb. They see themselves as having been turned into a fetus, even experience what they perceive to be a recapitulation of their embryogenesis. This is often described as a positive, even euphoric experience—until it isn't. For example:

Michael had an experience of overwhelming cosmic ecstasy; the universe seemed to be illuminated by radiant light emanating from an unidentifiable supernatural source. The entire world was filled with serenity, love, and peace; the atmosphere was that of "absolute victory, final liberation, and freedom in the soul." The scene then changed into an endless bluish-green ocean, the primordial cradle of all life. Michael felt that he had returned to the source; he was floating gently in this nourishing and soothing fluid and his body and soul seemed to be melting in it...This ecstatic condition was suddenly interrupted, and the sense of harmony deeply disturbed. The water in the ocean became amniotic fluid, and Michael experienced himself as a fetus in the womb. Some adverse influences were endangering his existence; he had a strange, unpleasant taste in his mouth, was aware of poison streaming through his body, felt profoundly tense and anxious, and various groups of muscles in his body were trembling and twitching. These symptoms were accompanied by many terrifying visions of demons and other evil appearances; they resembled those on religious painting.

(Graf, 1975, pp. 235–236)

Related to this, in a study of Norwegian psychedelic users, published in the *International Journal of Drug Policy* and focused on analyzing "bad trip" psychedelic experiences, the key feature across these journeys was found to be, in effect, unity gone too far—severe ego dissolution and loss of self (Gashi, Sandberg, & Pedersen, 2021).

Perhaps the dangers of this would not surprise Hans Loewald, especially not the yin and yang of it. He cautioned that psychoanalysis can help the patient "recover" an oceanic unity akin to that of the original dyad, mother and child, in the womb (Whitebook, 2008, p. 1179). But at a less archaic organizational level, propelled and catalyzed by the dynamics of the Oedipal complex, because a literal return, as many a psychedelics user has found, can only result in "manic psychosis" (Whitebook, 2008, p. 1179).

While Freud and Loewald both viewed the division of psychiatric experience into "doublets" (e.g., unconscious vs. conscious, fantasy vs. reality, advanced vs. primitive, ego vs. id) as a key feature of the *analysis* in *psycho*analysis, Freud viewed "the progressive conquest of the first term in each pair by the second" as the end-goal of the process (Whitebook, 2008, p. 1175), whereas Loewald believed a more Hegelian relationship between these erstwhile opposites should apply, that their integration into "a higher synthesis" with "the optimal communication" between them (Loewald, 1980a, p. 108) should be the ultimate outcome of a successful analysis, that "the most successful moments of human flourishing occur when the archaic and advanced are united in a felicitous way" (Whitebook, 2008, p. 1175).

If mushrooms could talk—and many users of psychedelics come to believe they can—they would likely advance Loewald's position. Consider the experience of the philosopher William James, for example, under the influence of the psychedelic effects of nitrous oxide:

...every opposition...vanishes in a higher unity in which it is based...It is impossible to convey an idea of the torrential character of the identification of opposites as it streams through the mind in this experience. I have sheet after sheet of phrases dictated or written during the intoxication...God and devil, good and evil, I and thou, sober and drunk, matter and form, black and white...and fifty[-six] other contrasts figure in these pages in the same monotonous way. The mind saw how each term <u>belonged</u> to its contrast through a knife-edge moment of transition <u>it</u> effected, and which, perennial and eternal, was the nunc stans of life....

(James, 1882, p. 295)

Or these more modern examples:

> How could I be both God and man at the same time? My conventional concept of myself had been shattered in a few moments.
>
> (Van Dusen, 1961, p. 13)

> There was nothing to see but there was seeing of this nothing to see...Dualities ceased, there was just a wonderful moving in nothing...There was hearing of the sound of no sound.
>
> (Van Dusen, 1961, p. 13)

> I was swept into the core of existence from which all things arise and into which all things converge. Here there is no distinction between subject and object, space and time, or anything else.
>
> (Houston & Masters, 1972, pp. 307–308)

For Loewald, a feature of the higher unity to be achieved is also unity with nature and the natural world. As Wayne Downey put it in reviewing and discussing Loewald's *Psychoanalysis and the History of the Individual*:

> [He] engineered his own sort of Copernican, or perhaps I should say "Loewaldian," shift. Just as Copernicus proclaimed just before his death that the earth is not the center of our universe but rather that the universe is heliocentric...so did Loewald postulate that the human psyche is no longer the center of the Freudian analytic cosmos. Man is no longer the center of a conscious/ unconscious system but shares these characteristics with a much more primary cosmic natural order.
>
> (Downey, 2015, p. 993)

Downey goes on to observe that Loewald "married" psychoanalysis to:

> ...a wider evolutionary model of nature: human nature not apart from nature, with nature as its projection, but as part of a natural evolutionary order in which external influences are taken into the psyche through introjection, identification, and an active process of co-modification of both the external and the internal milieu.
>
> (Downey, 2015, p. 993)

A beautiful example, on an individual level, of the kind of oceanic unity with nature has been described by the British primatologist Jane Goodall as it transpired in the forest of Gombe, soon after she had returned from an intense six-week trip to America that had involved "fund-raising dinners, conferences, meetings, and lobbying for various chimpanzee issues":

> It seemed to me, as I struggled afterward to recall the experience, the self was utterly absent: I and the chimpanzees, the earth and trees and air, seemed to merge, to become one with the spirit power of life itself. The air was filled with a feathered symphony, the evensong of birds. I heard new frequencies in their music

and also in singing insects' voices – notes so high and sweet I was amazed. Never had I been so intensely aware of the shape, the color of the individual leaves, the varied patterns of the veins that made each one unique. Scents were clear as well, easily identifiable: fermenting, overripe fruit; waterlogged earth; cold, wet bark; the damp odor of chimpanzee hair, and yes, my own too. And the aromatic scent of young, crushed leaves was almost overpowering.… That afternoon, it had been as though an unseen hand had drawn back a curtain and, for the briefest moment, I had seen through such a window. In a flash of "outsight." I had known timelessness and quiet ecstasy, sensed a truth of which mainstream science is merely a small fraction.

(Goodall & Berman, 2000, pp. 169 and 173)

These oceanic unities can also occur unexpectedly, in moments, much as they do, as Downey notes, in analysis, "when analyst and analysand are 'on the same page' and the same association to a piece of music, art, poetry, or everyday experience occurs to them" (Downey, 2015, p. 1006). For Norwegian philosopher Arne Næss, founder of the "deep ecology" movement, such a moment occurred, wrenchingly, when he was "looking through an old-fashioned microscope at the dramatic meeting of two drops of different chemicals:"

At that moment, a flea jumped from a lemming that was strolling along the table. The insect landed in the middle of the acid chemicals. To save it was impossible. It took minutes for the flea to die. The tiny being's movements were dreadfully expressive. Naturally I felt a painful sense of compassion and empathy. But the empathy was not basic. Rather, it was a process of identification: I saw myself in the flea. If I had been alienated from the flea, not seeing intuitively anything resembling myself, the death struggle would have left me indifferent.

(Næss, 2010, pp. 83–84)

Anyone with so much as a glancing familiarity with psychedelics will have recognized familiar elements in Goodall's experience—the increased intensity of colors, the heightened senses of hearing and smell, the perception of something akin to perfection in the "voices" of the insects, "notes so high and sweet I was amazed." Grinspoon and Bakalar observe that under the influence of psychedelics "people and objects become as fascinating as if they were the first of their kind ever seen; they look like pictures created and framed in their space by a genius" (Grinspoon & Bakalar, 1997, pp. 94–95) and, of course, the merging and becoming one.

Perhaps the most striking current indication of both how common and profound the experience of unity with nature is among psychedelic users can be found in a Johns Hopkins study and survey of more than 1,600 psychedelic users, including both regular users as well as those who had only one-off experiences (Nayak & Griffiths, 2022, p. 13). Researchers found that the proportion of individuals who believe non-primate animals have consciousness rose from 63% before their psychedelic experience to 83% after. Psychedelic experience had an even more profound impact on their perceptions of plants—before, only 26% believed in the sentience of plants (somewhat higher than the general population in this regard); after experiencing psychedelics, 61% were found to believe plants have consciousness (Nayak & Griffiths, 2022, p. 13).

Psychedelics and Psychoanalysis: Shared Mechanisms Underlying Therapeutic Action

Psychedelics are reawakening interest in fields from comparative religion and art history to cognitive neuroscience and biological psychiatry. Academic journals and the popular press cover impressive outcomes in psychedelic-based clinical trials and celebrate not just significant shifts in neural plasticity but trippy expansive life-altering experiences. Classical psychedelics including lysergic acid diethylamide (LSD), psilocybin, and dimethyltryptamine (DMT) are classified most concretely by their mechanisms of actions (Carhart-Harris, 2019). They share agonist activity at the serotonin 2A receptor subtype (5-HT2AR). This has been established in several antagonist pretreatment studies (Kraehenmann et al., 2017; Vollenweider, Vollenweider-Scherpenhuyzen, Babler, Vogel, & Hell, 1998). Further, 5-HT2A receptors are densely expressed in high-level association cortex, especially layer 5 pyramidal neurons where key cortical information-integration units reside (Beliveau et al., 2017; Carhart-Harris, 2019; Deco et al., 2018; Jakab & Goldman-Rakic, 1998; Larkum, Nevian, Sandler, Polsky, & Schiller, 2009).

The association areas of our brain cortex located in the most recently evolved portion of the neocortex, are responsible for processing input from our sensory organs and translating it into action; layer 5 pyramidal neurons, in particular, are responsible for sending a variety of motor commands to the spinal cord, leading to skilled motor behavior. As the name indicates, what normally binds to 5-HT2AR receptors, whether at layer 5 or elsewhere, is serotonin, a neurotransmitter often known colloquially as our brain's "feel good chemical," but in fact playing a variety of roles beyond mood regulation, including memory and cognition, as well as regulation of body temperature, sleep, sexual behavior, and hunger.

As agonists, psychedelics can trigger actions at 5-HT2AR receptors, theoretically impacting the same functions and capacities serotonin triggers when it binds to them. It fits therefore that 5-HT2AR-induced plasticity (induced by stimulating the growth in length and number of dendritic spines, enabling the brain to make more new connections (Shao et al., 2021) is most pronounced in the cortex and that the experiential effects of psychedelics are felt at a high level, as a fundamental change in consciousness. This shift in mentation likely subserves their newfound efficacy (psilocybin specifically) in treatment of major depressive disorder (Carhart-Harris et al., 2018; Davis et al., 2021); alcohol dependence (Bogenschutz et al., 2015), obsessive compulsive disorder (Moreno, Wiegand, Taitano, & Delgado, 2006); smoking cessation (Johnson, Garcia-Romeu, & Griffiths, 2017). Beyond this, as psychologist and neuroscientist Robin Carhart-Harris elaborates:

> Current thinking around psychedelics suggests multiple scales of action of these drugs from the molecular (serotonin 2A receptor agonism) through to the anatomical and functional (heightened plasticity) and up to the dynamic (increased brain entropy), systems level (network disintegration and desegregation) as well as the very important experiential dimension. Likewise, it is proposed that psychedelics initiate a cascade of neurobiological changes that manifest at multiple scales and ultimately culminate in the relaxation of certain beliefs. Some in the field

construe that the "purpose of psychedelic therapy is to harness the opportunity for a healthy revision of pathological beliefs.

(Carhart-Harris, 2019, p. 16)

Biologist Merlin Sheldrake frames the possible implications of these substances for psychiatry in this way:

> The conventional approach was—and remains to a large degree—to use <u>stuff</u>, whether drugs or a surgical tool, to treat the <u>stuff</u> the body is made out of, just as we might use tools to repair a machine. Drugs are normally understood to work through a pharmacological circuit that bypasses the conscious mind entirely: A drug affects a receptor, which triggers a change in symptoms. By contrast, psilocybin—like LSD and other psychedelics—appears to act on symptoms of mental illness via the <u>mind</u>. The standard circuit is enlarged: A drug affects a receptor, which triggers a change of mind, which triggers a change in symptoms. Patients' psychedelic experiences appear to be the cure.
>
> (Sheldrake, 2021, p. 111)

What use to be anything but an agonist relationship between drugs and therapy has become a worldview in which psychiatric medications and talk therapy complement each other, with the former creating the conditions that make the latter possible and effective and *vice versa*. But the emergence of a fundamentally different class of medications like psychedelics raises questions about whether this paradigm needs revision, not to return to old battlegrounds, but to wonder if, perhaps, a different perspective is now possible. It's remarkable, for example, that effects of these compounds, which include the triggering of deeply profound, potentially life-changing existential experiences can be traced to an initial action at the molecular level (5-HT2AR). The direct 5-HT2AR agonist properties of psychedelics are hypothesized to "relate to enhanced sensitivity to the environment and emotional release, which, when combined with psychological support, can be therapeutically potent" (Carhart-Harris & Goodwin, 2017, p. 2105).

Loewald and the Language of Eternity

We've provided several descriptions of psychedelic experiences by users of these drugs, which we know, while on the surface engaging, can become increasingly monotonous. *In Psychedelic Drugs Reconsidered*, their survey of the psychedelics landscape, Grinspoon and Bakalar argue that this repetitiveness provides the point of consensus that undergirds the reality of the experience, by revealing the users to be "travelers to different parts of the same country" (Grinspoon & Bakalar, 1997, p. 91). The nature of the descriptive language used, which they acknowledge non-users can find "silly," "boring," "exasperatingly self-satisfied" or self-absorbed, and even "mentally disturbed," all of which are descriptors a layperson might use listening in on analysands in varying stages of analysis, has strong resonances with what Loewald might consider to be the oceanic possibilities in analysis and elsewhere.

For example, they write that:

By bringing unconscious material into awareness, the drugs give language, or, at least, symbols a grip on phenomena that are ordinarily incommunicable because they do not take a symbolic form. A psychedelic drug trip is one kind of raid on the inarticulate, and often it produces unexpected exaltation and eloquence of language. There are repeated references to a tendency to talk—usually after the experience is over—with unaccustomed poetic facility. These supposedly ineffable experiences have always engendered a strong urge to talk and write about them; it is as though words are never more necessary than when we approach the limits of language.

(Grinspoon & Bakalar, 1997, pp. 92–93)

For Loewald, both the "global mother-child interaction" of infancy (Loewald, 1980b, p. 180), in which the mother's voice is "closer to music than discursive speech" (Whitebook, 2008, p. 1180), and "the most creative forms of language, such as…authentic religious use, oratory, poetry, and dramatic art," through which he expects "new synthetic organization" (Loewald, 1980b, pp. 203–204), that is, the sought higher level of unity, to emerge—*both* these apotheoses of the oceanic, closely approach, and in the case of mother-child interaction, *live at* the limits of language.

Downey, who knew Loewald well, singles out poetry as not only ideally representative of this borderland, but also Loewald's beliefs on man's necessary relationship to and unity with nature, writing:

Poetry is an attempt to regain an earlier time when sensory fusion prevailed, and words were vehicles for unveiling preverbal, irrational primary process mysteries. Apart from poetry, feelings like this accompany sights in the natural world: sunrises and sunsets, storms and moonglow. Poetry offers us a constant if subtle reminder of our human being at the periphery, rather than the center, of nature.

(Downey, 2015, p. 1008)

At the same time, Grinspoon and Bakalar caution that the language used to describe psychedelic experiences, at least, is metamorphic, observing that to take it as definitive is akin to "preferring the confused running commentary in the mind of a participant in an historical event to his later account of it viewed in the perspective of the rest of his life and times" (Grinspoon & Bakalar, 1997, p. 92). And this, of course, has analogs not only in Loewald but psychoanalysis in general, which consists of nothing so much as iteratively, via a dyad that, like a hawk—or any bird that can soar, proceeds forward in circles, spiraling, sometimes tilting or even dipping, sometimes hanging still in the air, sometimes having to beat its wings, riding the heat of a life up like a thermal, ultimately coming, only in the fullness of time, to a mature understanding of life stories that may ultimately be told very differently than they were by the confused narrator who first related them.

Yet beyond such obvious natural metaphors, there's an aspect of the way in which this process, as realized via psychedelics, is distinctly Loewaldian, and in which both differ from what came before them. For Freud, an analysis was an end in itself; for Loewald, the analytic process merely creates the conditions and provides a jumping off point for further growth and development. Similarly, while traditional psychiatric medications are frequently taken indefinitely, psychedelics are often only used a limited number of times, even only once. Why?

A colleague who took psilocybin while taking my course told the class, after relating an experience that could only be described as very positive—and was, by her—that she wasn't planning to use it again, and when asked this question, she said she felt that it was "enough," that she had gotten what she needed from it, that to continue without a clear and compelling reason would show a lack of respect for the experience. A similar conclusion was reached by many of psychedelics' acolytes in the late 1960s and early 1970s, as cataloged by Grinspoon and Bakalar, in language that often aligns with Loewald's where analysis is concerned:

> Spokesmen very early began to refer to the danger of emphasizing LSD too much. [Ken] Kesey was one of the first: "What I told the hippies was that LSD can be a door that one uses to open his mind to new realms of experience, but many hippies are using it just to keep going through the door over and over again, without trying to learn anything from it. Ram Dass said in 1970, "I think LSD is making itself obsolete. All acid does is show you the possibility of a new type of consciousness and give you hope…after a while you dig that if you want to <u>stay</u> high, you have to work on yourself.
>
> (Grinspoon & Bakalar, 1997, pp. 85–86)

In the end, the most common reason why people stopped using LSD, they observe, was not out of worries about health or fear of legal consequences but "the belief that LSD itself had enabled them to go 'beyond' it, by transcending the need for it" (Grinspoon & Bakalar, 1997, p. 86). Along the same lines, for those who have experienced oceanic feeling without substances, the encounter has often proven so powerful, even life-altering, that sufficiency applies. My patient, for example, finds simply recalling the experience of being enveloped by those golden arms gives him the comfort and strength he needs to continue his sobriety. Arne Næss dedicated much of later years of his life to developing the ideas of ecosophy, a philosophy of self-realization in which every living thing, whether human, animal, or vegetable, has an equal right to live and thrive. He called the humble flea whose story we've included his "standard example" of the level of identification with other beings required for his philosophical framework to succeed. He "met" it in the 1940s, when he was in his thirties, and lived to the age of 96 (Næss, 2010). Jane Goodall, in considering the impact of her Gombe encounter with the oceanic, concluded:

> I knew that the revelation [what she experienced that day] would be with me for the rest of my life, imperfectly remembered yet always within. A source of strength on which I could draw when life seemed harsh or cruel or desperate.
>
> (Goodall & Berman, 2000, p. 175)

Good and Bad Trips: The Poles of Unity and Fragmentation

Candidly, not all users of psychedelics quit because they're sated and satisfied with the experience. While more than 70% of participants in studies conducted by Johns Hopkins and NYU, in which psilocybin was administered to patients suffering from anxiety, depression, or newly diagnosed with terminal cancer, rated the experience as one of the five most important in their lives—akin to the birth of their first child—other users have quit because they've experienced "bad trips." (Ross et al., 2016).

Grinspoon and Bakalar, reflecting on psychedelics' first golden age, observe that "people who used psychedelics for what they considered to be pleasure tended to stop sooner than those who had more serious and complex purposes" (Grinspoon & Bakalar, 1997, p. 85). Often it didn't, and doesn't, take much of a turn down the "wrong road," as in this account collected by Pope:

> There are like six people sitting in a room tripping, and grooving on the pretty colors, and suddenly Jane starts getting into something heavy. She begins to realize acid is a bigger thing than just seeing colors, and she begins to get deep into it and get frightened. Then someone looks over and grins and says, "Whassa matta, Jane, you freaking out?' And either she snaps back into seeing the colors thing or she gets real frightened and never takes acid again.
>
> (Pope, 1971, p. 36)

And sometimes the darkness is more serious. The same research group at Hopkins reporting the powerfully positive results above also found, in a separate study, that 39% of psilocybin users consider the worst bad trip they've had to be one of the five most *challenging* experiences in their lives (Carbonaro et al., 2016). While there are several strategies believed to reduce the likelihood of a bad trip, there's no foolproof way to prevent them—and they are common (Gashi et al., 2021).

In reviewing testimonies and aggregations of what constitutes a "bad trip," much of this raw, primary material suggests that good and bad trips are like two poles, in that not only do they represent opposites, but the "bad" is often an extreme version of the good, of the same genus, if not the same species, that if one goes too far in one direction, one can easily flip from good to bad, in an instant, as in the trip shared earlier in which the ocean the subject was happily floating in suddenly turned into amniotic fluid—and events went downhill from there. For example, one of the most reported experiences on trips is one of *timelessness*. As Grinspoon and Bakalar summarize:

> Usually it goes more slowly: people speak of years or even an eternity passing in a minute, and events may seem to be without beginning or end. But time can also pass infinitely quickly, or the events of a psychedelic experience may take place outside of time...Time may also run backward; past, present, and future events may be experienced as happening all at once; or the whole idea of temporal succession and measurement may seem irrelevant and artificial.
>
> (Grinspoon & Bakalar, 1997, p. 96)

And when one reviews the literature on "bad trips," one of the elements most often mentioned is, in fact, an extreme version of the "ordinary" psychedelic experience of time dilation, to the point where it feels as if time is "standing still," which, in turn, makes it feel as if the unpleasant aspects of the trip will never end (Carbonaro et al., 2016).

Time is, of course, an area of special interest to Loewald, and like researchers, practitioners, and users of psychedelics, he sees timelessness as a bifurcated, not unitary, phenomenon in psychic experience, taking the form of time's two "opposite poles," *eternity* and *fragmentation* (Loewald, 1972, pp. 404–406), that have what may be considered uncanny correspondence to the characteristics of good and bad trips, and moreover, importantly, have been explored in substantially greater intellectual depth than the self-reported experiences of psychedelics users, in ways that tie into psycho-analytic practice.

In the experience of eternity, the more positive of the two poles, "Time as something which, in its modes of past, present, and future, articulates experience and conveys such concepts as succession, simultaneity, and duration is suspended"; temporal re-lations vanish "into a unity in which abolishes time," albeit only for what may ob-jectively be "a small fraction of time" (Loewald, 1972, pp. 405–406). Or, as he puts it in *Psychoanalysis and the History of the Individual,* "What was lived through earlier and later, and the mental categories of secondary process mentation—all fall away, collapsing into an instant, into that one experience that then stands for all experience, although only 'for one instant'"" (Loewald, 1978,p.573).

Interestingly and importantly, it's in more quotidian psychic life, especially as it applies to the analytic process, from the analyst's perspective (at least) as much as the analysand's, that Loewald's concept of time (even) more closely represents how the temporal is experienced within a "good trip" on psychedelics. In psychic life, time is encountered:

> ...primarily as a linking activity in which what we call past, present, and future are woven into a nexus... not so much one of succession but of interaction. Past, present, and future present themselves in psychic life not primarily as one preced-ing or following the other, but as modes of time which determine and shape each other, which differentiate out of and articulate a pure now. There is no irreversibil-ity on a linear continuum, as in the common concept of time as succession, but a reciprocal relationship whereby one time mode cannot be experienced or thought without the other and whereby they continually modify each other.
>
> (Loewald, 1972, p. 407)

Loewald sees, and cites, the phenomenology of transference, as a strong example of this:

> ... not only is the present relationship to the analyst partially determined by the patient's past (which is, as we say, still active in the present) and by a wished-for or feared future (itself codetermined by the past). It is also true that the present re-lationship, and the expectations it engenders, activate the past and influence how it is now experienced and remembered. This reintegration of the past, in its turn, modifies the present relationship with the analyst (and of course with other people as well) and has a bearing on the envisaged future.
>
> (Loewald, 1972, p. 407)

Furthermore, as it happens, and independently, Loewald's overarching beliefs about transference; that its mechanism, phenomenology, and the "alteration and alterna-tion of conscious and unconscious thought" that accompanies it are "active across all domains of psychological experience," including exchanges between the individ-ual and ideas/objects, such as his/her/their "culture, history, environment, and genes" (Downey, 2015, p. 1003), would seem to have interesting implications for analyzing the dynamics and manifestations of psychedelic experience.

Loewald's other pole of time is fragmentation, an experience that seems to have much in common with the characteristics of a bad trip. On a bad trip, *time stands still*. For an individual experiencing fragmentation:

> ... one's world is in bits and pieces, none of which have any meaning. The time continuum by which we hold our world together, the interrelatedness and the connections between a past, present, and future disintegrate, are broken in the most elementary sense, so that each instant loses its relation to any other instant and stands by itself, not embraced in a time continuum... in the experience of fragmentation time has been abolished in the annihilation of connectedness....
>
> (Loewald, 1972, pp. 405–406)

In the experience of *eternity*, Loewald makes clear, it's the *unconscious id*, not the ego, that is responsible for the resulting sense of timelessness. After describing a cascade of positive oceanic experiences, he avers that:

> ...while rational processes may continue to operate...at the same time another level of our mind has been touched and activated, and the secondary, rational form of mentation loses its weight. It is overshadowed or pervaded by the timelessness of the unconscious or primary process.
>
> (Loewald, 1978, pp. 572–573)

Psychedelic experiences, in which timelessness is a common feature, would seem to support Loewald, as psychedelics' mechanisms of action "let the brain off the leash" and, "open a window of mental flexibility in which people can let go of the mental models we use to organize reality" (Sheldrake, 2021, pp. 110–111). Anyone who has used these drugs multiple times can, as in dreams, attest to myriad elements both familiar and strange that signal the unconscious coming to the fore. And as with dreams, the bizarre sights, sounds, and events experienced would seem to be a strong indication that the interweaving of time-states Loewald describes are, in fact, occurring at a breadth, depth, and velocity that's well beyond the ordinary, as well as more continuous, producing a unity that appears more deeply true, unified, and inconceivable.

By contrast, the loss of connection between the ego and id that constitutes the ultimate fragmentation produces "a chaos of fragmentation...the madness of unbridled rationality" (Loewald, 1978, p. 573). In a pointed departure from Freud, Loewald states flatly that "there is no one-way street from the id to the ego. Not only do irrational forces overtake us again and again: in trying to lose them we would be lost" (Loewald, 1978, p. 545), left with what Downey calls Loewald's "bête noir," a "frozen ego" that stands still in the river of time, "captive of the insane zeal of the id" as the latter responds to being "disavowed and denied," and "opposites, contradictions, polarities, and paradoxes" cease to be "synthesized into a creative whole" (Downey, 2015, p. 997).

When we stop to consider what kinds of events could result in fragmentation, traumas, especially complex traumas, events which psychically, in multiple respects, also become moments when "time stands still," are obvious candidates. Other common characteristics of "bad trips," such as a sudden certainty that people one has always considered to be close are no longer safe to associate with, uncharacteristically negative views on aspects of one's life always considered positive or neutral before, generalized paranoia, and associated aggression—are all likely, in part, the consequence of the *loss of connection* that occurs in fragmentation experiences.

These similarities signal wider parallels between oceanic experiences of eternity and "good trips," on the one hand, and fragmentation—to the extent that trauma is involved—and "bad trips" on the other. For example, those who have had profound oceanic experiences, like Jane Goodall and my patient, are typically able to call them back up when needed, in some cases for the rest of their lives, and many individuals who have had positive experiences with psychedelics would say the same. In fact, even within a positive trip or a positive portion of a trip, the user often seems to have some level of control over the experience. As Grinspoon and Bakalar relate, "anything in the environment—a painting on the wall, a pattern in the carpet—may become a universe to be entered and explored" (Grinspoon & Bakalar, 1997, p. 94). When a trip "goes bad," on the other hand, it's typically not something the user has willed, at least not consciously, any more than the victim of trauma has flashbacks of the traumatizing events because they consciously want to.

Both "good" and "bad" trips have a relationship with anxiety—what turns out to be a good trip is typically undertaken as a conscious measure to control or overcome anxiety, while "bad trips" are often the consequence of an overly anxious state of mind that accelerates into panic. For his part, Loewald considers *both* eternity and fragmentation experiences to be defenses against anxiety, though he wants to be clear that this "does not invalidate their status as genuine representatives of transtemporal states" (Loewald, 1972, p. 406).

We should be clear that "bad trips" are not actually considered unambiguously bad in the end by those who experience them. In fact, in the aforementioned study of Norwegian psychedelics users, most participants attested that the unpleasant experiences during bad trips had been beneficial and had sometimes given them deep existential and life-altering insights (Gashi et al., 2021). In a recent series of Johns Hopkins based studies, 84% of participants said they had found "bad trips" beneficial, and 46% said they would repeat them (Barrett, Bradstreet, Leoutsakos, Johnson, & Griffiths, 2016). Likewise, Loewald allows that "fragmentation in certain instances may be the starting point for novel linking processes which create new meaning" (Loewald, 1972, p. 409).

Making Bad Trips Good: The Work of Nonlinearity and Narrative

It's at least as important to note, however, that "making bad trips good" is not something that occurs in a vacuum. Researchers have found that "bad trips" are "often transformed into valuable experiences through storytelling," that indeed "bad trip narratives may be a potent coping mechanism for users of psychedelics in non-controlled environments, enabling them to make sense of frightening experiences and integrate these into their life stories" (Gashi et al., 2021, p. 2 of 7). Building a narrative is, of course, fundamental to the work an analyst and analysand do together. As Loewald observed in his essay on time:

...the individual not only has a history which an observer may unravel and describe, but that he is history and makes his history by virtue of his memorial activity in which past-present-future are created as mutually interacting modes of time. Psychoanalysis is a method in which this memorial activity, shared by patient and analyst...is exercised, reactivated, and promoted... A patient, after considerable analytic work had been done on his relationship to his father, once put it this way: you have to create your own history.

(Loewald, 1972, pp. 409–410)

It can be argued that this is a part of what happens on psychedelic trips, that, in fact, one not only creates a personal history, but a *topology*, bounded and shaped, as Loewald would have it, by the wider natural world. Of course, great stories almost always have a twist.

Rachel Petersen is a writer and Harvard Divinity School student who participated in a 2018 clinical research trial using high doses of psilocybin to treat major depression. Her first trip was transformative and "not a simple transformation. Not of a depressed woman cured but of a woman granted greater fullness and meaning. Not of a despair diminished but a life enlarged" (Petersen, 2022, p. 31). She has told the story of this transformation in articles, talks, and films. It is a story she acknowledged recently is "not false, but incomplete." Because it does not include the story of her second trip, which she describes as what William James would call a "reverse religious experience" (Petersen, 2022, p. 31).

If she were reading this chapter, Rachel Petersen would want us to be rightly concerned about "the medicalization of psychedelics" (Petersen, 2022, p. 32). She would want us to hear from the MDMA trial participant who said, of their experience, "it's like they did open heart surgery...they fixed what was wrong with my heart, but left my chest wide open" (Petersen, 2022). She would want us to know, when we consider the results of studies that tout the high percentage of participants who declare that a trip they experienced on psychedelics was one of the most important experiences of their lives, that their number includes, if not *Rational Mysticism* author John Horgan, then others like him, who describes his psychedelic experience this way:

I suffered from terrifying flashbacks and psychotic delusions (I thought I had discovered the secret of existence, and that reality was going to vanish as a result) for months, and then sank into a deep depression, which lasted only a year. I felt alienated from life, and from everyone I love...It was the most meaningful experience of my life...I don't regret it, but I wouldn't wish it on anyone.

(Petersen, 2022, p. 37)

Hopkins researcher Roland Griffiths, a leader in the field of psychedelic research whose work has helped fuel enthusiasm for their medical use, nonetheless observes:

Generally, mushrooms (or similar substances) are used with reverence, not used trivially or haphazardly. The use is contained within a ritual setting. Experienced individuals monitor the user and help if challenging experiences arise. In those cultures, people who participate in these ceremonies have ready access to peers and elders afterwards who can help them make sense of what happened during the experience, whether it proved challenging, insightful, emotionally taxing or uplifting, awe-filled, or transcendent, and so on.

(Griffiths)

There's clearly something to be said, when trying new approaches, for relying on traditions and approaches that have been crafted and built upon over decades, if not centuries, in implementing them. What advocates of psychedelics excitedly describe as the "rewiring of the brain" and "ego dissolution," Hans Loewald might describe as a fundamental entropy at the heart of analysis, the "interactions between patient and analyst which lead to or form steps in ego-integration and disintegration" (Loewald, 1960, p. 17). This analytic process then is fundamentally non-linear as it proceeds with starts and stops and spiraling reconsolidations.

Petersen says that one of the key lessons she has learned from her experience with psychedelics is that "trips are not arithmetic: add up the good and subtract the bad. They do not move along linear axes; rather each introduces a new dimension. They are accretive" (Petersen, 2022). She could easily be talking about the analytic process, except that in analysis the steps are smaller perhaps, and certainly less conspicuous. The question is whether, cumulatively, the relevant moments in clinical hours, the "micro-steps" or "slow medicine" of analysis, to use more 21st century parlance, might add up to a greater effect, or generate a more solid foundation, like the laying of psychic bricks.

Epilogue

For my patient Sam and the golden arms that held him, an experience that shifted the boundaries of time and space and created profound connections with self and cosmos, I am also reminded of the Mystical Experience Questionnaire (MEQ) used to evaluate Sam's experience. The MEQ, developed by Pahnke (1963) to evaluate single mystical experiences engendered by hallucinogens, was, in fact, based on Walter Stace's conceptual framework (Stace, 1960), founded on non-chemically induced experience and based in established dimensions of classic mystical experience. In validating a shorter thirty item MEQ, researchers established through factor analysis four underlying factors of a single oceanic experience. The four factors used to characterize and measure isolated hallucinogen driven experience include sense of sacredness/unity, timelessness, ineffability, and positive mood (Barrett, Johnson, & Griffiths, 2015).

The (MEQ), used in laboratories around the world, turns highly subjective oceanic experience into something objective and quantifiable. Perhaps these quantified outcomes associated with statistical significance would have finally addressed Freud's squeamishness about oceanic experience while confirming, rather conclusively, Romain Rolland's sense of the universality of oceanic experience (Freud, 1961). Still, we may imagine that these factors—of unity, timelessness, ineffability, and positive mood—which come together in hallucinogenic experience stand apart from ordinary human experience. Do they? Is it possible that the dimensions of mystical experience that are routinely measured in psilocybin experiments exist in attenuated form in a variety of therapeutic contexts in our very ordinary lives? Taken from an electronic bulletin board from a local methadone clinic, patients posted these messages:

> I have no words to describe the experience.
>
> Where did the time go? It feels like yesterday when I started.
>
> I feel so much more connected to my family and community than I did ten years ago.
>
> I want to let other people know about how positive this was about how much they can get out of this experience too.

Aren't these simple statements felicitous expressions of archaic and advanced awareness? And what about the stranger in the consulting room? The analyst whose capacity to listen and attend allows the analysand to see, hear, feel, smell, and touch the Shakespearean romance that is her own inner world. Clinical engagement in methadone treatment or, for that matter, psychoanalysis can be a long and plodding form of medicine that is sculptural by nature—as Loewald suggested—removing ways of being and thinking that do not advance human flourishing. What then is the evolutionary value of such processes that gradually bring to light the oceanic dimensions of our world?

> In analysis, we bring out the true form by taking away the neurotic distortions. However, as in sculpture, we must have, if only in rudiments, an image of that which needs to be brought into its own. The patient, by revealing himself to the analyst, provides rudiments of such an image through all the distortions—an image which the analyst has to focus in his mind, thus holding it in safe keeping for the patient to whom it is mainly lost. It is this tenuous reciprocal tie which represents the germ of a new object- relationship.
>
> (Loewald, 1960, p. 18)

As a priest at the local church suggested, "the whole point of your weekly engagement in our practice here is to help create the capacity to love yourself and your community more." This speaks to the evolutionary value of religious experience including oceanic awareness as it raises the value of self and other in a world best understood not as a dominion of objects but as a communion of subjects (Berry, 2006).

References

Barrett, F. S., Bradstreet, M. P., Leoutsakos, J. S., Johnson, M. W., & Griffiths, R. R. (2016). The Challenging Experience Questionnaire: characterization of challenging experiences with psilocybin mushrooms. *J Psychopharmacol*, 30(12), 1279–1295. doi:10.1177/0269881116678781

Barrett, F. S., Johnson, M. W., & Griffiths, R. R. (2015). Validation of the revised Mystical Experience Questionnaire in experimental sessions with psilocybin. *J Psychopharmacol*, 29(11), 1182–1190. doi:10.1177/0269881115609019

Beliveau, V., Ganz, M., Feng, L., Ozenne, B., Hojgaard, L., Fisher, P. M., …Knudsen, G. M. (2017). A high-resolution in vivo atlas of the human brain's serotonin system. *J Neurosci*, 37(1), 120–128. doi:10.1523/JNEUROSCI.2830-16.2016

Berry, T. (2006). Prologue. In P. Waldau & K. Patton (Eds.), *A Communion of Subjects: Animals in Religion, Science, and Ethics*. New York: Columbia University Press.

Bogenschutz, M. P., Forcehimes, A. A., Pommy, J. A., Wilcox, C. E., Barbosa, P. C., & Strassman, R. J. (2015). Psilocybin-assisted treatment for alcohol dependence: a proof-of-concept study. *J Psychopharmacol*, 29(3), 289–299. doi:10.1177/0269881114565144

Braden, W. (1967). *The Private Sea: LSD and the Search for God*. New York: Bantam Books.

Carbonaro, T. M., Bradstreet, M. P., Barrett, F. S., MacLean, K. A., Jesse, R., Johnson, M. W., & Griffiths, R. R. (2016). Survey study of challenging experiences after ingesting psilocybin mushrooms: acute and enduring positive and negative consequences. *J Psychopharmacol*, 30(12), 1268–1278. doi:10.1177/0269881116662634

Carhart-Harris, R. L. (2019). How do psychedelics work? *Curr Opin Psychiatry*, 32(1), 16–21. doi:10.1097/YCO.0000000000000467

Carhart-Harris, R. L., Bolstridge, M., Day, C. M. J., Rucker, J., Watts, R., Erritzoe, D. E., ...Nutt, D. J. (2018). Psilocybin with psychological support for treatment-resistant depression: six-month follow-up. *Psychopharmacology (Berl)*, 235(2), 399–408. doi:10.1007/s00213-017-4771-x

Carhart-Harris, R. L., & Goodwin, G. M. (2017). The therapeutic potential of psychedelic drugs: past, present, and future. *Neuropsychopharmacology*, 42(11), 2105–2113. doi:10.1038/npp.2017.84

Davis, A. K., Barrett, F. S., May, D. G., Cosimano, M. P., Sepeda, N. D., Johnson, M. W., ...Griffiths, R. R. (2021). Effects of psilocybin-assisted therapy on major depressive disorder: a randomized clinical trial. *JAMA Psychiatry*, 78(5), 481–489. doi:10.1001/jamapsychiatry.2020.3285

Deco, G., Cruzat, J., Cabral, J., Knudsen, G. M., Carhart-Harris, R. L., Whybrow, P. C., ...Kringelbach, M. L. (2018). Whole-brain multimodal neuroimaging model using serotonin receptor maps explains non-linear functional effects of LSD. *Curr Biol*, 28(19), 3065–3074, e3066. doi:10.1016/j.cub.2018.07.083

Downey, T. W. (2015). Hans Loewald's psychoanalysis and the history of the individual. *J Am Psychoanal Assoc*, 63(5), 993–1011. doi:10.1177/0003065115607570

Freud, S. (1961). *Civilization and Its Discontents* (Vol. 21). London: Hogarth Press.

Gashi, L., Sandberg, S., & Pedersen, W. (2021). Making "bad trips" good: how users of psychedelics narratively transform challenging trips into valuable experiences. *Int. J. Drug Policy*, 87, 103183.

Goodall, J., & Berman, P. (2000). *Reason for Hope: A Spiritual Journey*. New York: Grand Central Publishing.

Graf, S. (1975). *Realms of the Human Unconscious: Observations from LSD Research*. New York: Viking Press.

Griffiths, R. R. (2017). *Q&A with Study Authors Roland Griffiths and Robert Jesse on 'Bad Trips'*. Baltimore MD: Johns Hopkins Medicine.

Grinspoon, L., & Bakalar, J. B. (1997). *Psychedelic Drugs Reconsidered*. New York: The Lindesmith Center.

Houston, J., & Masters, R. E. L. (1972). The experimental induction of religious-type experiences (pp. 303–321). In J. White (Ed.), *The Highest State of Consciousness*. Garden City, NY: Anchor Books.

Jakab, R. L., & Goldman-Rakic, P. S. (1998). 5-Hydroxytryptamine2A serotonin receptors in the primate cerebral cortex: possible site of action of hallucinogenic and antipsychotic drugs in pyramidal cell apical dendrites. *Proc Natl Acad Sci U S A*, 95(2), 735–740. doi:10.1073/pnas.95.2.735

James, W. (1882). On some hegelisms. In *The Will to Believe* (Vol. 7, pp. 263–298). London, Bombay and Calcutta: Longmans, Green and Co.

Johnson, M. W., Garcia-Romeu, A., & Griffiths, R. R. (2017). Long-term follow-up of psilocybin-facilitated smoking cessation. *Am J Drug Alcohol Abuse*, 43(1), 55–60. doi:10.3109/00952990.2016.1170135

Kraehenmann, R., Pokorny, D., Aicher, H., Preller, K. H., Pokorny, T., Bosch, O. G., ...Vollenweider, F. X. (2017). LSD Increases primary process thinking via Serotonin 2A receptor activation. *Front Pharmacol*, 8, 814. doi:10.3389/fphar.2017.00814

Larkum, M. E., Nevian, T., Sandler, M., Polsky, A., & Schiller, J. (2009). Synaptic integration in tuft dendrites of layer 5 pyramidal neurons: a new unifying principle. *Science*, 325(5941), 756–760. doi:10.1126/science.1171958

Loewald, H. W. (1960). On the therapeutic action of psycho-analysis. *Int J Psychoanal*, 41, 16–33.

Loewald, H. W. (1972). The experience of time. *Psychoanal Study Child*, 27, 401–410.

Loewald, H. W. (1978). Psychoanalysis and the history of the individual. In N. Quist (Ed.), *The Essential Loewald: Collected Papers and Monographs* (pp. 531–579). Hagerstown, MD: University Publishing Group.

Loewald, H. W. (1980a). On motivation and instinct theory. In *Papers on Psychoanalysis* (pp. 102–137). New Haven, CT: Yale University Press.

Loewald, H. W. (1980b). Primary process, secondary process, and language. In *Papers on Psychoanalysis* (pp. 178–206). New Haven, CT: Yale University Press.

Moreno, F. A., Wiegand, C. B., Taitano, E. K., & Delgado, P. L. (2006). Safety, tolerability, and efficacy of psilocybin in 9 patients with obsessive-compulsive disorder. *J Clin Psychiatry*, 67(11), 1735–1740. doi:10.4088/jcp.v67n1110

Næss, A. (2010). *The Ecology of Wisdom*. Berkeley, CA: Counterpoint.

Nayak, S. M., & Griffiths, R. R. (2022). A single belief-changing psychedelic experience is associated with increased attribution of consciousness to living and non-living entities. *Front Psychol*, 13:852248.

Pahnke, W. (1963). Drugs and mysticism: an analysis of the relationship between psychedelic drugs and the mystical consciousness (Ph.D.). Cambridge, MA: Harvard University.

Petersen, R. (2022). A theological reckoning with 'bad trips'. *Harvard Divinity School Bulletin*, 50(3 and 4), 31–39.

Pope, H. (1971). *Voices from the Drug Culture*. Boston, MA: Beacon Press.

Ross, S., Bossis, A., Guss, J., Agin-Liebes, G., Malone, T., Cohen, B., … Schmidt, B. L. (2016). Rapid and sustained symptom reduction following psilocybin treatment for anxiety and depression in patients with life-threatening cancer: a randomized controlled trial. *J Psychopharmacol*, 30(12), 1165–1180. doi:10.1177/0269881116675512

Shao, L. X., Liao, C., Gregg, I., Davoudian, P. A., Savalia, N. K., Delagarza, K., & Kwan, A. C. (2021). Psilocybin induces rapid and persistent growth of dendritic spines in frontal cortex in vivo. *Neuron*, 109(16), 2535–2544, e2534. doi:10.1016/j.neuron.2021.06.008

Sheldrake, M. (2021). *Entangled Life: How Fungi Make Our Worlds, Change Our Minds and Shape Our Futures*. New York: Random House.

Stace, W. T. (1960). *Mysticism and Philosophy*. New York: St. Martin's Press.

Van Dusen, W. (1961). LSD and the enlightenment of Zen. *Psychologia*, 4, 11–16.

Vollenweider, F. X., Vollenweider-Scherpenhuyzen, M. F., Babler, A., Vogel, H., & Hell, D. (1998). Psilocybin induces schizophrenia-like psychosis in humans via a serotonin-2 agonist action. *Neuroreport*, 9(17), 3897–3902. doi:10.1097/00001756-199812010-00024

Whitebook, J. (2008). Hans Loewald, psychoanalysis, and the project of autonomy. *J Am Psychoanal Assoc.*, 56, 1161–1187.

Chapter 9

Origins

Oscar F. Hills

In December 1967, in the wake of the Summer of Love, The Graduate (Nichols et al. 1967) opens in movie theaters, capturing the imagination of the popular culture across the country. Benjamin, a new college graduate, is anxiously enduring a cocktail party held in his honor by his parents and their friends. He is buttonholed by Mr. McGuire, who while proud of him, is also a self-satisfied "company man" poised to impart to Ben a gnomic word of wisdom. Double-checking that Ben is listening closely, McGuire finally delivers his "just one word" with the expectable gravitas – "plastics."

A young person in those days could easily relate to the discomfort of having to pretend to welcome such incoming lightning from Mt. Olympus, however useful it might have been for igniting their own fires. And *plastic* was "everything that is wrong" with that generation, Hollywood, and the culture. Like Holden Caulfield, we "knew" the *man*, his generation, was "phony."

Today, the film is almost unwatchably "cringey," and McGuire may be the only character who got much right. "Plastics" *was* sound financial advice. Vaclav Smil tells us that the four material pillars of modern civilization are cement, steel, plastics, and nitrogen (Smil 2022, p. 84). To paraphrase Mark Twain, old man McGuire was smarter than we thought, after a half century. Plastics have come a long way since Bakelite, and modern thermoplastics are found everywhere from sewage pipes to aircraft frames.

When the film was made, no one guessed that the single word "plastics" would be the most memorable line in it. It was a film about change, active and passive. It was about the Oedipus complex, that is, the titanic passions and volatility of generational transition, amidst the vagaries of clinging and cleaving, pushing and pulling on the old and the new. Somehow, through it all, a mind takes flight, a society coalesces, the earth breathes. Somewhere in time and space, every possible shortcut, detour, and path have been taken and they are alive somewhere within each of us. The past tells us this by way of our very presence, but the future is not so easy. Plastics are still here, leaner and stronger than ever, and so is Oedipus, lurking at the ruinous center of the homogenization of three consecutive generations at a time and threatening the very fabric of society, as Oedipus is wont to do. While The Graduate did not age as sturdily as plastic, the film is here to remind us just how much promise the future can seem to hold, and yet how misadventurous we humans can be.

While individuals and societies evolve in ways we can neither predict nor control, we aspire to learn from the past and to develop principles that will carry us optimistically into the future, rife as it is with the uncertainty that thermodynamics and time impose. Despite the ever-present protestations of the popular culture, psychoanalysis

DOI: 10.4324/9781032685151-10

remains the avant-garde in our quest to embrace an artful future. But we must sustain our familiarity with how things arrive, how they stay, and how they depart our lives. We live chock-a-block with such object lessons, of course, but they flood us and we are necessarily as blind to them as we tend to be to our own characters. On the couch, though, conscious discontinuity, sometimes dissolved with a single word, confers in that transition an element of surprise, a new affect by definition, to an old idea. Perhaps this essay will deliver a dollop of that by way of a few "fun facts" drawn from the annals of human genius, but also in no small part from the long and robust history of human wrong-headedness. Several single gnomic words on the model of "plastics" will also pop up, as will the ubiquitous super-power of negativism. Freud will shepherd us through the Oedipus complex and the evolution of triadicity, and Loewald will be our guide into the non-dualism of four-dimensional psychic spacetime and our expanding universe. Perhaps Loewald's prescient work will highlight its own aptness to advance a human origin story that confers an anti-fragility to its beneficiaries (Taleb 2014).

Could an effective way to sail a tidbit of wisdom across generational boundaries during an institute graduation be "one word, just one word" ... *information*? Not the information in the candidate's manual, nor information flooding our all but implanted electronic devices, nor that of the reviled surveillance capitalism, nor even that found in the Weights and Measures of the government. Rather, it is information related to that described by Claude Shannon in his 1948 work, aimed at improving *communication* over *telephone* lines, reprinted as *The Mathematical Theory of Communication* (Shannon and Weaver 1998), and revolving around a statistical measure of degrees of freedom in the communication of data. This perspective has implications both for the kind of communication taking place in the psychoanalytic space and for our evolving model of the mind emergent therein. Images of slide rules, calculators, computers, and thick horn-rimmed spectacles notwithstanding, this alludes to a *clinical* psycho-analytic perspective. Dissecting signal from noise is an intensely personal journey in psychoanalysis, but we have the advantage of having been at it from the beginning. It is our first experience of "gainful employment" as individuals on planet Earth. The infant descends upon the world hard at work in the business of causal mapping, with an aptitude and avidity unique to the human being. While there are many enticing theories about the evolution of reason, of which causal mapping seems to be a critical component, we will take a brief look at just one proposed step, new and imaginative, to make a point about that larger world of scientific investigation.

We know that around 385 million years ago, some fish slowly evolved legs, and started living on land. But it turns out that the eyes of such creatures had tripled in size and shifted from the sides to the tops of their heads long *before* they had modified their fins into limbs. This is to say those eyes appeared evolutionarily before full-blown ter-restriality did. The beautifully named "buena vista" hypothesis suggests that the ability to see over long distances afforded new adaptive opportunities not previously available underwater where useful visibility was only a few feet. Along with this new and grand view came an adaptive advantage in favor of advanced decision-making and planning ahead. The new distance vision now allowed an organism to predict well in advance the arrival of various events, not least being predators and prey. There was now a landmark advantage to allowing decision-making to bloom in complexity. Indeed, the very de-velopment and persistence of landed tetrapods suggests that this advance in cognitive intricacy paid off, and it may well have started us on the evolutionary road to causal inference, reasoning, and probably what we call consciousness (MacIver et al. 2017).

These kinds of data suggest a relatively smooth path along the evolution of complexity on Earth, again from geochemistry to biochemistry and culminating for the moment in the human central nervous system, which in turn delivers to us the *mind*. A quarter century ago, anthropologist Steven Mithen described the "big bang of consciousness" when humans "suddenly" began burying their dead, painting on cave walls, tracking celestial movements with notches on bone, and making music (Mithen 1996). Some psychoanalysts, though, find "consciousness" itself surprisingly overrated compared to what came along with it. It is often said that if one could remove *all* the visible matter from the universe, the universe would remain at least 95% unchanged even if quite a bit darker. Might we speculate that the unconscious and conscious minds exist hand in glove in similar proportions? In fact, Loewald reminds us:

> In the course of the development of psychoanalytic thought, the id—uniting unconscious and instincts under one roof—became the concept for human nature as unconscious activity. Ego and superego represent individual developments of that activity, and human consciousness is a sporadic resultant of its further evolution.
> (Loewald 1988, p. 49)

This is in line with Freud's work, rooted in 19th-century scientific naturalism, and advancing the principle that progressive internalization is at the heart of the evolution of biological life and therefore, isomorphically, of the mind. From the beginning, when an environmental element encounters another that confers to it a selective advantage, selective pressure will favor the first's subsuming the second physically rather than having to depend upon coming across it and harnessing it again further afield. The naturalistic view of the mind is that while the mind seems to be an abstraction layer emergent from the central nervous system, its evolution too is certain to have proceeded by way of selective pressures including those along lines of progressive internalization. Freud:

> The antiquity into which the dream-work carries us back is of a double aspect, firstly, the individual antiquity, childhood; and, secondly (in so far as every individual in his childhood lives over again in some more or less abbreviated manner the entire development of the human race), also this antiquity, the philogenetic. That we shall be able to differentiate which part of the latent psychic proceeding has its source in the individual, and which part in the philogenetic antiquity is not improbable. In this connection it appears to me, for example, that the symbolic relations which the individual has never learned are ground for the belief that they should be regarded as a philogenetic inheritance.
> (Freud 1920, p. 167)

A naturalistic construction of the psyche foregrounds two dualities. The first is inside versus outside, each most broadly a data source. And the second, a little more obscure and not unrelated to the first, is past versus present. The further distinction is between the phylogenetic and ontogenetic past, each residing within and thus both carried forward into our futures. It is the ontogenetic mind, of course, that takes in data emanating from both inside and out, over time, and sets itself to the task of causal mapping and prediction via Bayesian reasoning (incorporating conditional probabilities and updating them in the face of new evidence) (Pinker 2022). This activity is ferociously advantageous, furthering adaptive functioning over the life cycle. Adaptation here is based ideally on ever deepening and progressively refined distinctions between what emanates from within and what from without. A good deal of *psychoanalytic* theory itself has emphasized an additional and vital duality of analyst and analysand in a two-person ego psychology in which transference interpretation becomes the cognitive instrument for shoring up the analysand's emotional ability to distinguish self from other, and thus inner from outer. All these dualities catalyzed remarkable progress in psychoanalytic theory and practice over the decades and they led many analysts and their institutes to a level of *certainty* about what they were doing. In an ideal psychoanalytic world, of course, certainty itself should raise the proverbial red flags warning that defensive activity might be afoot, in proportion to that of the certainty. Indeed, many young analysts now hear "ego psychology" the way Ben heard "plastics" in *The Graduate*.

Whatever disinclination to loosen one's grip on the old and to make some room for the new our fictional characters encounter in film and literature pales by comparison to the extensive recorded history of generalized human disinclination. Whenever we think about evolution and "progress," we might bear in mind our own obstinacy. Even in the halls of psychoanalytic Institutes and convention centers, of course, most of us have heard muttered the occasional negative, "*that's* not psychoanalysis." Unsurprisingly, territoriality fueled by fear is as ubiquitous in medicine and in the life of the mind as it is anywhere in nature.

A particularly vivid historical example of negativism, to remind us how people are, surrounds the number *zero*, the only *real* number that is symmetric under a change of sign, is also a complex number at the same time, and is further symmetric under rotation of argument. Zero stands at the center of things, a beautiful point of rotation and of rest, and it is a reassuring beacon of symmetry in the universe, is it not? Well, not to the Sumerians at the dawn of civilization around 3,000 BCE, it was not. They had revolutionized accounting by emancipating numerals from objects themselves so that instead of drawing five fish in a column to denote a sale; they were now able to use something like a 5. It took another *thousand years* to create numbers that could be manipulated by any operators other than addition and subtraction, and priests executed many mathematicians and accountants because they felt cheated by the lack of economic balance a mere placeholding zero would have conferred to some arithmetical shortcuts like multiplication. But to Christians, the idea of zero represented the void, the absence of God, and thus the domain of the devil. The Arab world accepted the void and zero somewhat more easily, but it still took *13 centuries* for zero to come up to its full power when accountants of the Republic of Genoa invented double entry bookkeeping in about 1,340 CE to account for the evolving complexities of trade (Padilla 2022, p. 173). Follow the money was the rule then as it is now. Because until then, zero? *That's not a number.*

The acceptance of zero propelled mathematics and physics forward, but there remained abundant conflict over other fundamental principles. Newton thought of light as a stream of particles. Niels Bohr formulated his original model of the hydrogen atom much later, and it was an elaboration of an old planetary model with electrons as little balls in orbit around a larger sun-like nucleus which was designed to account better for the light *actually* emitted by the atom. Thomas Young's original double slit experiment showed interference patterns that revealed light to be a *wave-like phenomenon* in contrast to Newton's view. Within a hundred years, though, it became clear that light could show *both* wave-like and particle-like behavior, and by 1927, it had been demonstrated that this was *also* true of electrons and eventually even molecules. That is, they *all* show *both* granularity and undularity. Physicists came to realize that if objects had some properties of *both* waves *and* particles, then those objects must actually *be* neither thing. They are now best thought of as quantum objects and they are best described by the branch of quantum mechanics called Quantum Field Theory in which quantum fluctuations in fields account well for the behavior of quantum objects. Outside of physics, one regularly hears, "*that can't be true!*"

In the analyst's office, it is tempting to liken Freud's thinking about the structure of the mind to the definitive dualities of Newtonian physics, and then Loewald's to the fields and matrices of the quantum mechanical understanding of the smallest objects in our universe, and in fact some *do* see things that way. But, there are not good analogues in physical or psychoanalytic theory to support any direct mapping of this kind.

Still, current day physics is downright bizarre. We should let it sink in that a particle can indeed be in *two places at once*, and even *molecules* as large as 2,000 atoms can be co-located as above. The wave-like component of all objects has extension in space and allows for this quantum superposition. We know this to a staggering degree of experimental validity, and it is only one of many strange physical facts. Curiously, there is even a *relational* interpretation of quantum mechanics that posits that there are no objects in the universe apart from the relations between them. Physicist Carlo Rovelli says, "Quantum mechanics is a theory about the physical description of physical systems relative to other systems, and this is a complete description of the world" (Rovelli 1996). Once again, the kind of terminology we find in advanced physics bears a remarkable similarity to that of much current psychoanalytic theorizing, which further points up the importance of remaining clear-headed about what we do and do not understand, especially in light of psychoanalytic naturalism, which is now in my view, consistent with modern physicalism, a less opaque term.

The intoning "information" instead of "plastics" in fact finds its origin and ideological true north in frank physicalism. In support of physicalism, we will keep in mind that we know a *lot* more about some things such as quantum field theory than we do about other things such as the neuroscience of consciousness. We understand the physical laws that govern the *constituents* of our world as well as we understand anything. In December 1980, Carl Sagan said in an interview in *Rolling Stone Magazine*, "*We* are the representatives of the cosmos; we are an example of what hydrogen atoms can do, given 15 billion years of cosmic evolution" (Cott 1980). Sagan poetically implies that humankind evolves in accordance with the laws of physics and that all activity, uniquely human though it may be, supervenes on that framework. This is disturbing to many in the same way that the concept of zero once was, namely, "*there's no there there*" and possibly worse.

Why no there there? Think of young people making beautiful music in mother's basement with an inexpensive laptop computer. A mere twenty years ago, the same sound would have required a room full of expensive signal processing hardware stuffed with wires, resistors, capacitors, transistors, and even vacuum tubes. Now, circuit for circuit, these devices and their components are simulated precisely in the random access memory of a computer and could be said to have no physical instantiation at all, and yet, the output is the same. There is little complaint about this unless you are in the recording studio business, but it is not a huge leap to imagine a near future in which a human being is either simulated in an electronic space or copied and assembled particle for particle in our current space. What do we have on our hands *then*? Did a human mind arise from it? Well, let us recognize a lose-lose when we see it. If yes, then what happened to the human part of a being that we can now manufacture in a machine? If no, then what exactly *is* it that is standing before us and so uncannily human that we are nearly or completely fooled? This sort of brain teaser, the philosophical Zombie problem, came to this name in the 1970s but predated that in concept and has reared its head regularly throughout the history of mind-body arguments. The zombie concern has attracted more intense opprobrium and/or disbelief in recent years, however, as artificial intelligence has begun to feel less artificial every day. People are now using AI chat-bots to write their work-related emails, to write children's books, and even to write college term papers, upsetting your everyday human to no end when they are informed that their trust has been betrayed by a machine. *That's not a person.*

Some discomfort right about now that we are not yet savoring the work of Hans Loewald in this essay may be even worse than just that. Our anxiety mounts. "Maybe those ancients *were* on to something about that whole *the devil is in the void of zero* business, and maybe the chat-bots *are* coming for our analytic couches – could we please find a little humanity with Dr. Loewald?"

Fortunately, there is yet another gnomic word that could rescue us from becoming mired in a philosophical mind-body row when we are *trying* to think about psychoanalysis, to wit, *complexity.* And maybe that will land us on Loewald's theoretical doorstep.

What has come to be called Complexity Science, or the "science of complex systems" has been with us since Aristotle. It took massive leaps forward in the 1960s and 1970s with an increasing understanding of chaotic complex systems and non-linear computer weather modeling. It is exploding with exciting work right now, particularly in adaptive systems and artificial intelligence, led by scientists and mathematicians. It has shed significant light on the complexity of biologic, social, and economic systems as well. But, even so, it is a challenge to define precisely what complexity *actually* is. Happily, complex systems *do* have some clear attributes. One of those is *structure*, occurring at differing scales, and made up of moving parts. Now, in some systems that are *not* complex, there are only a few moving parts, and the system is easily characterized by explaining exactly what every moving part is doing, while in cases of greater complexity there can be a large number of moving parts. And in *some* of *those* cases, such as the study of a gas, you can average over all the vast number of identical atoms or molecules to minimize or smooth out the contribution of the behavior that any individual one makes to the overall behavior of the gas. What emerges are collective variables such as pressure or temperature which once again attain a newer, perhaps "higher" level of simplicity. That is, they can account for the behavior of the gas as a whole based on collective behavior.

Complexity is captured then by saying it exists when you find *neither* a *small* number of parts whose behavior can be described, *nor* a *large* number of parts over which individual idiosyncrasies can be smoothed out, but rather a large number of parts in which the behavior of each of the individual parts *matters* in some difficult to determine ways to the outcome. *And*, most importantly after that, you are left with a structure that does some sort of interesting work. Complexity describes the fact that such systems give rise to *near* unpredictability or often only statistical predictability. Studying, modeling, and predicting the weather is a good example. A tornado cannot be easily understood on the basis of particle physics because of its emergent higher order properties. And needless to say, a study of human society is almost infinitely complex. Trying to predict and, say, curtail phenomena such as gun violence, to name only one, is an extraordinarily difficult task. There we must consider individual beliefs and behavior, gun ownership, cultural and subcultural influences, network theory, economics, politics, and the list goes on, and that is just at the macro level. There is nothing to be gained and much damage to be done by the naïve application of principles which confuse the individual with the whole or the whole with the individual. To the best of our knowledge to date, the human brain is by far the most complex physical entity in the universe, and the human mind, physicalism tells us, is an emergent property thereof. This is formidable epistemological as well as practical territory.

Philosophers will recall that Gilbert Ryle's work in 1949, *The Concept of Mind* (Ryle 1949), concerned itself with, among other issues, a critique of Cartesian mind/body dualism. Ryle coined the term "the ghost in the machine" to deride the idea of some immaterial mental substance existing alongside the machinery of the body. Remarkably, in the same book, Ryle introduced the term "category mistake." This idea too was marshaled by Ryle against Cartesian dualism, stating in essence that it made no sense to think of mind and body as two different things from a linguistic perspective, and further, that a *causal* connection explaining how a separate mind would be able to act on a body could not be found. This was viewed by philosophers as a *behaviorist* point of view, and it might be obvious to say that it did not put to rest the mind-body problem. Over the decades, the term found its way out of philosophy and it was no longer constrained to its original meaning. It has most recently found its way into critical theory and into politics, becoming even more confusing, also needless to say. Nonetheless, Ryle's original idea is of enormous importance to Complexity Science. His own illustrations of category mistakes at the time were, for example, a visitor who sees lots of colleges, laboratories and libraries in Oxford asks, "But where is the University?" Or a child watches a military parade and after seeing marching squadrons and battalions asks, "But where is the division?"

In other words, the category mistake confuses the properties of the whole with the properties of a part. It is made up of the logical fallacy of *composition* which is to assume the whole has the properties of the part, and/or the logical fallacy of *division* which is to assume the part has the properties of the whole. In Ryle's examples, the problems are primarily linguistic only, but he makes clear that:

> The theoretically interesting category-mistakes are those made by people who are perfectly competent to apply concepts, at least in the situations with which they are familiar, but are still liable in their abstract thinking to allocate those concepts to logical types to which they do not belong.

> (ibid., p. 15)

Just this sort of category mistake plagues scientists to this day. For example, it can take the form of "because large objects are made of atoms, large objects have the properties of atoms, and atoms have the properties of large objects." This drives most of us to distraction when we try to understand even rudimentary quantum mechanics. How can a particle travel through two different slits simultaneously? They can because they are *not* little tennis balls and they are governed by different physical laws. It is exceedingly difficult for us to recede from the macro world of classical physics and to inhabit, in our minds, that of the micro quantum world. Freud asks us to do the same in Two Principles of Mental Functioning (Freud 1925, p. 215) when we are to imagine a theoretical failure of primary hallucinatory wish fulfillment and the necessarily subsequent advent of the reality principle, or in Instincts and Their Vicissitudes when he asserts:

> If now we apply ourselves to considering mental life from a biological point of view, an 'instinct' appears to us as a concept on the frontier between the mental and the somatic, as the psychical representative of the stimuli originating from within the organism and reaching the mind, as a measure of the demand made upon the mind for work in consequence of its connection with the body.
>
> (Freud 1915, pp. 121–122)

This is the quantum mechanics of psychoanalytic psychology. We are all guilty, via the category mistake, of transporting instincts at this level of abstraction to the impulses, feelings, and behaviors of "macro" adult life, analogous to confusing the laws and domain of quantum mechanics with the laws and domain of classical physics.

The proposal that understanding category mistakes saves psychoanalysts from some of the philosophical problems of naturalism and physicalism is primarily that as we travel up the complexity hierarchy from say the phospholipid bilayer to the cell to the fish to the tetrapod to the hominin to the human and then to the mind, we also traverse a route of causal exponentiation and emergent levels of organization that render the output of an individual system almost completely unpredictable on the first pass. Some of our cherished notions such as free will (downward causality) and consciousness (a feeling of being that extends beyond qualia alone and participates in free will) can be viewed as category mistakes in that their complex properties are given short shrift by an underappreciation of the emergent properties of each step. Somewhat impoverished higher order concepts then emerge from an unconscious smuggling of simpler sets of properties from "lower" levels of organization to higher. This in turn seems to simplify the higher levels but in fact degrades their accuracy or more precisely, their usefulness.

The idea that we *know* consciousness and free will to be illusory would be deserving of the very red flags of certainty we alluded to earlier. Instead, we note that they belong to a universe of discourse surprisingly unimportant to clinical and theoretical psychoanalysis, or more accurately, they are so complex that the distinction as to whether they have some "reality" that we would assume to have causal properties has negligible impact on the psychoanalytic endeavor, as understood in the work under consideration here. It should be made clear that "consciousness" for these philosophical purposes is a concept different in kind from notions about what is conscious or unconscious in the psychoanalytic mind, again the former is different by dint of its oft presumed downward causal capacity in violation of what we know of thermodynamics and the arrow of time.

Everything we have covered so far, while not new, has been of renewed interest in many disciplines in part riding the wave of stunning confirmatory physical findings made possible by the high energy of the Large Hadron Collider in Switzerland, and in part because of the ever eye-opening advances in robotics and artificial intelligence we have witnessed in recent years. Loewald, in his 1988 paper *Psychoanalysis In Search of Nature* (Loewald 1988) addresses the scope of psychoanalysis in the context of the science of his lifetime as though he were standing here today. While he does not address free will and causal consciousness directly, one can surmise he too finds such concepts orthogonal to psychoanalytic inquiry.

> The traditional theory of nature is changing, and with that change the theory of knowledge of nature is changing. Nature is no longer simply an object of observation and domination by a human conscious mind, a subject, but an all-embracing activity of which man, and the human mind in its unconscious and sometimes conscious aspects, is one element or configuration, albeit of uttermost importance to that human mind.
>
> (ibid., p. 50)

Loewald de-emphasizes the inner versus outer duality of mind and nature, and as well he de-emphasizes a disequilibrium or antagonism along an active-passive duality where man is either victimized by or dominant in nature. As he indicates, those dualities are well-trodden paths in psychoanalysis and in science, thus reflecting at least a rigidity of stance that can limit access to a less bellicose and more creative, participatory perspective toward nature whence we came and of which we are.

The subjects of being "*of* nature" and of "knowing a great deal about its fundamental constituents if less about its complexities" all but compel the good physicalist to turn some attention to the science of the *origin* of life itself on Earth. Our origins were simplest when we believed God put us here whole, but once biochemistry and evolution appeared in science, we began contemplating how early macromolecules and the phospholipid bilayer may have come about in the first place. Exogenous factors, often violent, were frequently contenders. Were we fertilized in a shower of extraterrestrial debris carrying new molecules of uncertain origin themselves? Such origins would suggest the presence of a sudden surge in life on Earth after some inoculation, and for a long time, the guess that something sudden had happened was as good as any.

More recently, however, there is evidence that the transition from geochemistry to biochemistry may have been quite smooth if still rapid, and that deep sea warm alkaline vents may have acted as substrates for the formation of semi-permeable membranes, later internalized and used independently out away from the vents. In this theory, Nicholas Lane posits that warm hydrothermal vents created ridged, iron and sulfur rich walls of small pores that baffled off warm alkaline fluid in the vent from cooler, acidic seawater, creating a natural charge gradient, not unlike a battery (Lane 2015). One beautiful facet of this idea is that it involves *all* of Mother Earth in the process of giving life via hydrothermal vents made alkaline without the participation of volcanoes, magma, or external deliveries – one might say without any localized big bangs.

There is something soothing about this origin story despite the gargantuan forces it is perched upon, and it squares well with Loewald's assertion that the origin of individual psychic life is

> a transindividual field, represented by the mother/infant matrix, not an individual unconscious and instincts residing in an individual. The objectivity of traditional modern science is an outcome of the gradual differentiation of this field culminating in individual consciousness. Yet. it disregards (represses) the transindividual matrix which continues to actively originate, in ever-widening spirals, the various transformative internalizations of individual psychic life, i.e., endopsychic life ... a deeper understanding of nature will widen the horizons of a science of nature and increase, one may hope, its power of mastery, a mastery that involves yielding no less than dominion. Such deeper understanding subordinates the traditional view to a more comprehensive perspective on nature as unconscious activity (*"natura naturans"*). Psychoanalytic theory is on that path, and so are the physical sciences themselves (Freud remarked on the parallels). Indeed, "classical" psychoanalysis fights a rearguard action against such a wider framework, a battle in which theoretical physics is no longer immobilized.
>
> (Loewald 1988, pp. 50–51)

If quantum mechanics has taught us nothing else, we should have at least the sense that any simple-minded, intuitive notions about how nature is wired can be utterly out of alignment with nature at its most fundamental level. Loewald says that

> unison and reverberation, as regards other human beings, is called empathy. But it would be erroneous to assume that this empathic resonance stops at the frontier of human mentality. Our knowledge of organic and so-called inorganic nature is likely to derive from similar attunements; these are in themselves not defensive projections, but they most often have been altered by the model of consciousness to conform to its structure. It may indeed be claimed that in traditional natural science, too, the objectivity achieved in human consciousness was projected onto the universe and to what we call, then, physical material reality, and that this nature, so structured by us was now perceived as ultimate reality, in the same vein as the "ultimate reality" of metaphysics, mythology, and religion.
>
> (ibid. p. 50)

It is easy to overdo *natura naturans*, that is, nature not as an objective entity, but rather as one co-created by our participation in it, by over-simplifying the quantum measurement problem and imagining such macro-phenomena such as "the moon is not actually there until someone looks at it." This is another category mistake in which a macro level object is thought to behave the way quantum objects *seem* to. This is different from Loewald's point that the human unconscious *is* nature, and thus, unconscious processes within the individual must also be found in nature. The moon problem could be viewed as an egocentric projection of the human conscious mind onto nature, thus limiting our conception of nature now mistaken for a hard external reality.

Technology is growing and expanding explosively with only about thirty years between the advent of home computers and the current information/digital age! There were thousands of years between the Stone, Bronze, and Iron Ages. We envision an accelerating Sisyphus, pushing higher and faster with each cycle. Astronomical time is linear, but socioeconomic time is speeding up, driving us to work longer, harder, and faster (West 2018). Since these realities do not favor gradual processes such as classical education or psychoanalysis, it helps at least frame them in some current ideas. Updating "plastics" to "information" reflects first our living squarely in the Information Age, but also the value of considering information to be the "Shannon Information" of communication rather than a tally of elements in external "reality." Shannon realized, remarkably, that the formerly deterministic process of coding and decoding a signal over a telephone line was actually probabilistic and best understood from the perspective of uncertainty, without which the word "communication" would not even need to exist. He called the minimum number of bits per second it took to represent a piece of information on its entropy, and he developed an entire complex mathematics to address it. The higher the entropy, the greater the uncertainty. Without Shannon's work, there would be no Internet today. Further, his information theory has also become one of the finer precision tools available in quantum physics, the epicenter of probabilistic reasoning, as well as to quantum computing, the future of "artificial" intelligence.

Information transfer and its complexities are necessarily central to psychoanalysis, which one hopes is obvious, and they have been since its origin, long before the pandemic-related massive exploration of psychoanalysis in virtual space. In all cases, whether the geographical distance is from couch to chair or of international proportions, analysts promote the transfer of information, some of which can be labeled Shannon information, highly uncertain communication, frequently unconscious, and transduced by way of Loewald's unison, reverberation, and attunement. But there is also anamnestic information, traditional knowledge, know-how, memory, futurity, and even space itself, to name just some of the more complex forms information may take. The free flow of information will eventually bring the analysand's umvelt, if you will, into focus between the dyad. The analyst in that position of visiting a new world, will feel many of the tensions between its constraints and its comforts as did its originating dyad. Loewald's thinking promotes an openness to a dynamic equilibrium of information of all flavors which, while reflecting an earlier such transpersonal field, also holds the potential of a comparable but novel matrix in light of the newness of the analyst to the scene. That this state of transpersonal nature emanates from an embrace of oneness reduces the danger posed by its sharp edges and allows fluidity to fulfil its potential to nourish revitalized and unexpected new lines of growth, most especially at the level of the simpler psychic constituents of the tangle of complexity that is the individual person.

We might note that this openness and oneness achieved by the analyst may be mistaken for a tranquil, meditative state of passive receptivity which it is not. Perhaps we can agree first that "passive receptivity" is an insulting contradiction in terms, which Mother Earth will probably demonstrate to humankind soon enough if we do not watch our P's and Q's, as it were. Next, let us recognize that the fluidity, attunement, and oneness of *natura naturans* is an active creation in a supremely fertile field of complexity potential. To embrace nature actively is to embrace uncertainty, an act of courage in all instances. We do not know what we do not know, and science is not a science. Facing this demands Keats's "negative capability" – "of being in uncertainties, mysteries, doubts, without any irritable reaching after fact and reason" (Rollins 2012, pp. 193–194). To bring this courage to psychoanalysis takes two, and whatever is passive about it is balanced by what is active. The result is an uneasy zero point. It is said that learning to hover-taxi a helicopter is like trying to ride a bicycle balanced along a single railroad track … upside down. The analyst's chair can be such an unparalleled but demanding mode of transportation into the transpersonal matrix in a co-created nature if one is receptive to that world and can handle the journey. To express this in more accessible and up-to-date terms, a broad perspective on Loewald's work is to appreciate that it aims to deemphasize "othering" whether that be of analysands, mothers, or the earth itself. Again, one could mistake that goal for normopathy when in fact it constitutes a *decentralization* and *distribution* of focus across the broad expanse of causality that participates in our human granularity and undularity. In the macro world, those two attributes are individuation and socialization.

To imagine why this stance is so difficult, we might examine our own anxiety about the idea of having a future AI agent as an analyst. "*They will never know the human experience!*" Really? Perhaps not, but in this moment the reader *now* knows what it is to "other" an entity that will have evolved through us and will be therefore *of* us. It takes some doing to accept even that *possibility* much less to find the requisite *openness* to embrace it.

Let us mercifully touch down briefly in the consulting room for a more experience-near moment. The analytic work here is suffused with Loewald's influence, and perhaps in the context of this brief snippet will adumbrate something clinically Loewaldian about it. If so, it is likely to emerge from the spaces and not the black-letter content.

An older professional man, an only child who was eight years old when his father died, had begun an analysis a decade ago complaining of a sense of hollowness and detachment despite a rich external life. Driving to our first session, he had had a near hallucinatory recollection of a comedy recording he knew from college. "You are now embarked upon a journey that must certainly lead you to change your life forever! If you were never a special person, you are a special person now!" He and I recognized this as the Firesign Theater, a surrealist radio comedy group of the 1960s who made an album entitled "Everything You Know Is Wrong." This was the first line of that recording. At the time, he dutifully saw the line as referring straightforwardly to his beginning a trip designed to focus on his life and a trip in which he was indeed a special person. After some celebration of the fascinating phenomenon of an unbidden psychic experience actually having *to do* with something, he seemed available for observation number two which was that there can be *more* facets to a thing. We noted that he was recalling a futuristic absurdist comedy troupe, so maybe there was another message too. He said he had also heard the message as mocking him for trying to change his life, but even worse for looking to fulfill a babyish wish to feel special.

Now, a decade later, with termination in the air, he came in astounded that I did not seem disturbed by the unfinished remodeling in the building. Perhaps, he thought, such an analyst was obliviously prepared to cut him loose unfinished and in a state of disrepair himself, an image that panicked him. He had aggressively declared himself ready to leave me and I had passively gone along with it, and now where was he going to be? He remembered the first day, and the Firesign Theater. He was now stuck on the *name* of the album, Everything You Know Is Wrong, and stuck on what term grammatically modified what else in the title. His first inter- pretation was that "Everything" modified the rest of the phrase as a single term. This would catalog everything in the set of things he "knows to be morally wrong." It was as though I were saying "now let's go over everything in your life where you should have known better." But this was not his only thought. He said analysis was also the only place he could come and enjoy recounting his love of forbidden pleasures, sexual and destructive, to a man who he felt might be against them in theory, but who could secretly and vicariously enjoy them too. This to him was the ideal father, unlike his own who had instead died. Next, he wondered "what if Wrong modified Everything You Know?" He imagined I would tell him he knew nothing of the world and he was all wrong. He decided that this was more *his* way than mine, and saw that *he* would love to tell *me* how wrong *I* am about everything, placing that interpretation back in the guilty pleasures column. Then, easing his aggression, he wondered whether "you know" could be a collegial bonding phrase, as though I would say, "hey, you know, *everything* is wrong." This would be him and me against the world. We'll show them! We both fell silent for a couple of minutes, as though to rummage around in the results of the mighty linguistic cer- ebration that had been going on, or perhaps to take some distance from it. After a while, he said,

> I was just taking a step into all this, instead of a step back. This isn't really about which of us is right or wrong about anything, factually or morally or even who would win in a fight ... we've been to all those places here many times ... this is about relativism ... of knowledge itself. Nothing stays right over time, not even science. No wait, it's not even knowledge. Knowledge is not the culprit. Not everything either one of us knows is *wrong*, it's just that everything we *think* is wrong. We *know* plenty, just by being alive, but the second we think a thing, it is well on its way to being wrong. My father left me early, but I also *am* my father. As much my father as anyone on earth is. And you are some of him now too, knowing me. Thinking isn't quite where we *live*, good as it is. Being alive is a *knowing*. Being alive is a *feeling*.

> (He wept silently)

> These tears contain everything I just said, the pain of both growth and loss, in fact, they contain this entire analysis. It's raining outside right now, and I am alive. In Jamaica the rain is called liquid sunshine. See you tomorrow.

He was on point, we *had* been to these places, enough that they were familiar even from a distance and less full of surprises than they once were. Today we had seen Everything You Know Is Wrong in many of its quantum superpositions, and then the last one – the one that says everything you *know* is *right*. We were able to manage those manifestations, all occupying the same psychic real estate, while still open to a moment of renewed expectancy. The rain *held* the son.

References

Cott, Jonathan. (1980). [C] The Cosmos: An Interview with Carl Sagan. *Rolling Stone.*

Freud, Sigmund. (1915). Instincts and their Vicissitudes. *Standard Edition* 14:121–122.

Freud, Sigmund. (1920). *A General Introduction to Psychoanalysis*, New York, NY: Thirteenth Lecture, Bonnie and Liveright Publishers.

Freud, Sigmund. (1925). Formulations on the Two Principles of Mental Functioning. *Standard Edition* 12:218.

Lane, Nick. (2015). *The Vital Question: Energy, Evolution, and the Origins of Complex Life.* New York, NY: W. W. Norton & Company.

Loewald, Hans W. (1988). Psychoanalysis in search of nature thoughts on metapsychology, "metaphysics," projection. *Annual of Psychoanalysis* 16:49–54.

MacIver, Malcolm A., Lars Schmitz, Ugurcan Mugan, Todd D. Murphey, and Curtis D. Mobley. (2017). Massive increase in visual range preceded the origin of terrestrial vertebrates. *Proceedings of the National Academy of Sciences* 114 (12):E2375–E2384.

Mithen, Steven J. (1996). *The Prehistory of the Mind: A Search for the Origins of Art, Religion, and Science.* London: Thames and Hudson.

Nichols, Mike, Charles Webb, Anne Bancroft, Dustin Hoffman, and Katharine Ross. (1967). *The Graduate.* Los Angeles, CA: Embassy Pictures Corporation.

Padilla, Antonio (2022). *Fantastic Numbers and Where to Find Them: A Cosmic Quest from Zero to Infinity.* New York, NY: Farrar, Straus and Giroux.

Pinker, Steven. (2022). *Rationality: What It Is, Why It Seems Scarce, Why It Matters.* New York, NY: Penguin.

Rollins, Hyder Edward. (2012). *The Letters of John Keats: Volume 1, 1814–1818: 1814–1821.* Cambridge: Cambridge University Press.

Rovelli, Carlo. (1996). Relational quantum mechanics. *International Journal of Theoretical Physics* 35 (8):1637–1678.

Ryle, Gilbert. (1949). *The Concept of Mind.* London, New York: Hutchinson's University Library.

Shannon, Claude E., and Warren Weaver (1998). *The Mathematical Theory of Communication.* Champaign, IL: University of Illinois Press.

Smil, Vaclav. (2022). *How the World Really Works: The Science behind How We Got Here and Where We're Going.* London: Penguin Random House Ltd.

Taleb, Nassim Nicholas. (2014). *Antifragile: Things That Gain from Disorder.* New York, NY: Random House Trade Paperbacks.

West, Geoffrey. (2018). *Scale: The Universal Laws of Life, Growth, and Death in Organisms, Cities, and Companies.* New York, NY: Penguin.

Part II

Personal Loewald

Chapter 10

Brief Thoughts on My Father, Language and Attachment, and Life's Generational Vicissitudes

Caroline Loewald Farnham

History and Family

My father was fifty-three years old when my sister Kate was born in 1959, and fifty-eight when I was born in 1964. Most readers are likely familiar with the years of his life that occurred way before his two daughters were ever a notion in his mind – his birth in Colmar (which in 1906 was part of Germany, and is now part of France), his early life in Berlin, his move to Italy in 1933, how the rise of Hitler and the Third Reich shaped the choices he made in his life and the necessity of certain decisions that he otherwise might not have had to make.

I begin here with some family history because it is so much a part of the narrative about my father, in both his public and private lives. Perhaps because I came so late to the party (his youngest child, born only when he was closing in on sixty), my understanding and my experience of my father is intimately entwined with the narrative of his history, his Jewish ethnicity – though he was a self-proclaimed atheist and never, to my knowledge, overtly identified as "Jewish" (or Christian for that matter). Nonetheless, I have felt throughout my life a quiet resonance with Jewish culture, and the source for this can only be the generations of Loewalds and Landshuts (my Oma's maiden name) that came before me. At Dad's memorial service at The Western New England Psychoanalytic Institute in New Haven after his death, a man (I can't remember who it was), walked up to my family and handed us VHS tapes of interviews that Dad had secretly participated in, for the Yale Holocaust Archives. Dad had not told any of us, not even my mother, that he had done this. I was stunned. Over the decades, by way of my own psychoanalysis, further therapy, conversations with family members and others, ancestral research, and lots of reading on the subject, I have come to really understand how generational trauma travels – through language, through stories, through affect(s), through dynamics, and through DNA (as some research indicates now). I am so glad that Dad was spared from living through four years of the Trump Administration. And its aftermath.

I doubt he ever conceived early on (who does?) that he would have a second set of children – two daughters – in a second marriage. My parents, who originally met in 1948 through friends, started dating in the Autumn of 1953 in Baltimore, and were married (in the Minister's study of a Unitarian Church with just two witnesses and no photos taken) three months later, according to my mother. It was a second marriage for both; my mother had just turned thirty and my father would have been forty-eight years old, with two teenage sons already in tow. It was a long, happy and fruitful

DOI: 10.4324/9781032685151-12

marriage (coming up on forty years when my father passed in 1993), from what I know from my parents and from what I experienced as their child.

My mother told me that she wanted very much to have children (and to have two, so that Kate would not be an only child as she herself had been), but that Dad would have been content with not having more children; there was an unspoken understanding that she would be the primary caretaker. From my father I felt love, sometimes tenderness, humor most certainly (in a quiet way), and a powerful valuing of intellect and expansive thoughtfulness (in the sense of thinking about things philosophically, reflectively). There was a part of him that was a humanist, in the sense that he held a respect for the dignity of human beings and a belief that each individual has the freedom – *really the responsibility* – to think for him or herself and to shape his or her life accordingly. He also had a good ear and eye for the absurd and the ridiculous, and I think this infused his sense of humor. And, I think, another part of him operated around the belief that suffering is the matrix around and within which human experience is shaped.

Other characteristics of my father that I loved: He did NOT like to be categorized. He would not have liked to be co-opted by any one faction of anything, and I feel strongly protective of his "name" and his work around this. I think that this is also a characteristic – or a stance? – that he passed on to me. He did not directly dictate to me how I should be or what was the way to go through the world; it became part of my character through osmosis. Or, perhaps, through generational trauma. He was a trauma survivor in that he lost relatives to the fate of being murdered in concentration camps. He had to leave his own country because he was Jewish. He lost his father (to disease) when he was only a month old, thereby having a loving but surely grieving mother in his infancy. He lost his older sister (to disease) when she was in her early thirties.

As far as I can remember, he did not talk about the family members that were deported and murdered. I have found through my own research and connecting with distant relatives in Israel and elsewhere, that he did indeed lose a number of aunts and uncles as well as second cousins, and there are probably more that I have not yet discovered. I wonder whether he was not aware of these events because by the time they happened he was already living in the United States? Did my Oma not talk about this with him? Or did he know but dissociate the information (and the feelings connected)?

He was also distant, depressive, sometimes unapproachable, lost in his writing and a seemingly impenetrable cocoon of cigarette smoke and ideas, in his parquet-floored study. He was often not very in tune with my needs, including a very basic need for him to be more present and interested in my life, more affectionate, less critical. I experienced him, at times, to be overly critical, judgmental, as if not able to see the forest for the trees, in terms of what I needed, reflected back to me. As a young teen in junior high, if I showed him a poem, he would focus on one word that I might have used that he didn't think quite right or would challenge me on why I used that word, rather than simply showing me that he was proud that I was writing a poem, almost as if I was a small adult rather than a child. On the other hand, he instilled in me (as did my mother) a huge love of the arts, and this is a way that I feel deeply connected with both my parents. From my perspective, Dad seemed most comfortable in the arena of the life of the mind, and through this we could connect. But in crucial ways (culminating with his expressed wish to die, when I was 28, not yet married, not yet with kids), as a father, he left important chunks to be desired, which took me some time to work through. Given Dad's own history, this is of course (intellectually speaking) easy to understand.

On a visit to Germany within the last couple of years, my half-brother, Francis, did some research and explored the neighborhood within which the Loewalds supposedly lived. My nephew was apparently able to find some actual addresses. My brother wrote to us:

> The addresses (Dernberg Strasse 46, Reichstrasse 104, Suarez Strasse, Neston Strasse 4) are all in the Charlottenburg and Wilmersdorf areas in West Berlin. Several of the houses still exist, some do not and have been replaced by other structures or in one case a small park like area. The addresses are all relatively in the same area. A section of Berlin that was then and now considered upper middle class populated by professionals and business people. Liz [my mother; Fran's stepmother] had recently related that Dad did not like geraniums because he associated them with the train line that ran near their home in Berlin and these were apparently the only flowers that would survive the train smoke/fumes. Our guide mentioned that a train line ran through the neighborhood. The area lies east of the Charlottenburg Palace (summer home of Frederic III) and west of the large Tiergarten park. The area was built up in the 19th century because Frederic wanted wealthy and middle class folks in the area. So, the sense I got was that it was a pleasant and comfortable area in which to live at least when Jews were welcomed or tolerated. Our guide indicated that the history of Jews in Germany since the middle ages was one of being welcomed when the powers that be in any particular area needed a merchant class and bankers and being thrown out when that need was no longer deemed to exist. It was only in the 19th century that Jews were allowed full citizenship rights. Jews had to buy the right to use non-Jewish names and this was done to assimilate into German society. Great grandfather Caspar Landshut is a case in point. Caspar being a very Germanic name of that era. I should add that older Jewish areas were mostly in the eastern part of Berlin.

A story related to me by my father that is etched into my mind is that he "knew it was time to leave Germany" when he gazed down at the street from the window of the hospital where he was working as an intern and saw the Brownshirts (Braunhemden) marching down the street. He had already been fired from his original internship because he was Jewish, so this current position was one that he had found in another hospital following that. I imagine that this was not truly the first inkling that he had that things were desperate enough to necessitate leaving, but that some sort of focus or presence of mind that he experienced in that moment at that window was powerful enough to pierce the membrane of denial or disbelief of what was happening in the country. He and my half-brothers' mother both left Germany in 1933, she apparently to Palestine and my father to Italy, by way of France; he had wanted to make a life in Paris, according to my mother, but was unable to for various reasons. He took a year in Bologna to get his medical license in Italy, then moved to Padua to practice in a hospital. My brothers' mother joined him there in 1935. They were married in Italy, according to my brother, who along with his fraternal twin was born there in 1936. Somewhere around 1936–1937, Mussolini joined forces with Hitler and a treaty of cooperation in foreign policy between Italy and Nazi Germany was created. I remember Dad telling me that every day at the hospital someone would deliver the daily newspaper and say "here's the day's fresh pack of lies!" – (because the papers were, apparently, so full of propaganda). Dad and his family then emigrated to the United States in 1939 on the ship Isle de France. According to my brother, they traveled from France rather than from Italy or as German citizens. He writes,

> Back in the 1920s, the U.S. enacted quotas for immigrants from various countries (the 1920s was a period of anti-immigrant fervor). The German and Italian quotas were fully booked. The French considered Dad to be French even though he was born in Alsace during the period it was part of Germany. Alsace was then ceded by the French to the Germans as part of the peace negotiation to end the Franco-German war of the 1870s. It became France again at the end of WWI [Following the defeat of Germany in WWI, Alsace was returned to France under the Treaty of Versailles along with part of the région of Lorraine]. That accident of history was critical to our being able to make it to the U.S. in 1939.

Of course, before all of this, when my father was still a formal student of philosophy in Freiburg and had not fully switched to the study of medicine, he experienced a devastating disappointment when, as he put it to me, he "had to cut [Heidegger] off," when he discovered writings of Heidegger's that apparently were sympathetic to Nazism. This I believe was a formative turn of events in his life. I often wonder whether he had to shut down parts of himself to deal with that loss (and the echoes then of the early loss of his father), and my fantasy has been that, if it were not for that, he would have surely been a philosopher, outright. He was indeed a philosopher in his soul even in the life that he ultimately created, and expressed that, of course, through his psychoanalytic writings.

Influences and Echoes

In graduate school at New York University (for English, before returning to school six years later to get my MSW at Smith) my concentration was in literary theory. Jacques Derrida (Derrida, 1978, 1986, 1987) as is well known, had a particular relationship in his writings with psychoanalysis and Freud's writings. In both deconstructive theory and in the practice of psychoanalysis, there is a drive to unpack, a tireless seeking of emotional authenticity (although Deconstruction might say there is no "emotional authenticity"). Both question and look to the meaning(s) and operations of language; both practice a continual engagement with symbolism, the signifier/signified/object/subject dialectic.

Peter Benson (2014) writes here about Derrida's term "the *grammè*":

> *the minimal unit of language (the* grammè*) [is] always* an iterable trace. A 'trace' is *a mark remaining after the moment of its inscription. In French, the word 'trace' also carries as one of its connotations the idea of a trail left by an animal that a hunter might follow. These footprints or flattened foliage indicate the animal (the producer of the* grammè*) that has now passed; they remain there whether the hunter (the receiver of the* grammè*) arrives on the scene or not; and it is always possible that their*

significance may fail to be read (by an inexperienced tracker). So the trail, like the gramme, *conjures forth what is absent (producer, receiver, message). This is a strik-ing quality for any entity to have. In general, things are what they are, and nothing else – self-contained elements of existence. But a* gramme *(once it's recognised as being a* gramme) also brings with it the shadows of things it is not (my italics).

And my father, writing about symbolism and symbolization:

> Symbolization may be described as an imaginative act: Two different items of experience are linked in the mind in such a way that one represents the other…A symbol seems, in a special way, always to be a symbol for us… I begin with one example of symbolization. In writing down (or voicing) my thoughts I give them visibility (or sound) in the form of symbols. Through my sensory-motor acts of writing, and reading what I wrote, the flow of my thinking acquires a materiality, a presence it did not have before. They are "communicated" to me myself by these sensory-motor acts and can be communicated to others. …Words and sentences are embedded in a linguistic tradition of which I partake and which I share with others… It seems that whatever is represented by a symbol does not remain quite the same as before it was symbolized…and its representational import varies… with each occasion and with each writer (or speaker).
>
> (Loewald, 1988, pp. 45–52)

At that time, in the late 1980s and early 1990s, the relentless questioning and seeking stance that literary theory posed resonated deeply; looking back on this now, I can identify the emotional linkages to the themes with which my father was so engaged. There was also a kind of atheism, or anarchy, so to speak, in deconstructive theory – or at least that is how I experienced it then – that was to me, at the time, another identifier of my father (the atheism part, not the anarchy part), as well as a needed expressive outlet for me, developmentally, as an early adult. I think for me deconstruction was (not consciously) a kind of loving referent to psychoanalysis *and* a possible expression by which to disassemble and invalidate psychoanalytic theory – all at the same time.

Now decades later, I think of my father as more spiritually connected – like looking at the negative of a photograph – you are looking at the same image, but you are seeing the opposing proportions of light, the absences and presences of light and shadow. In the negative was the spiritual. But I conceive of this part of him as something that he was not fully conscious of and so again, if he were here to read this, he might very well dispute my perceptions. My own spirituality resurfaced (I have memories of it being there in early childhood) later in life, not in the sense of any religious affiliations or structured practice but in other varied ways in daily life and over the years.

My training in social work from the beginning has been in community mental health both with children and families as well as with adults. The work is with families with histories of or with active trauma including sexual abuse, physical abuse, domes-tic violence, incarceration, drug abuse, racism and community violence, generational trauma. For twenty-two years, I have also maintained a private practice working with adults and late adolescents. When working with community mental health popula-tions, I have been keenly aware that my knowledge of psychoanalytic thinking, and my early training in a psychodynamic approach is always present, is a starting place for me – even in a world of mental health that increasingly sees psychoanalysis as something from the past, part of the history of psychology but not an active, useful framework. This has been especially true over the last, say, ten to fifteen years, with the rise of Evidenced Based Practices/Treatments (EBPs/EBT) in community mental health, with funders such as Department of Children and Families, Medicaid and Health insurance companies dominating the system and mandating these practices in return for funding that keeps agencies running.

In the arena of a community family agency, there is an external complexity (involving poverty, absence of privilege, multiple needs, etc.) that requires a collaborative approach to supporting individuals and families, which is of great value and necessity. Social work education is infused now with considerations of intersectionality, implicit bias and the impact of privilege and white supremacy. These frameworks are somewhat commonplace – at least to the extent that people "talk" about it – in agency settings as well (although this of course varies widely). In my role as teacher and supervisor of graduate students I have been overjoyed that these frameworks – which were so very much lacking in the study of psychology generally speaking – twenty to thirty years ago – are so much part of the discourse now. At the same time, I have been dismayed and saddened, even angered, that the proverbial throwing out of the baby with the bathwater seems to have also evolved in the sense that psychoanalytic and even psychodynamic theory and discourse is, at best, on the back burner, generally speaking, in social work education. There are of course exceptions, but this is my anecdotal observation. I think this is to a large extent a result of the systemic changes in healthcare, funding, and the economics of mental health in the United States. As usual, marginalized populations are on the receiving end of this evolution, to the extent that those who have money or other forms of privilege are the only ones who are able to seek out private psychotherapy that has less (not zero) of a requirement to conform to funder mandates. More recent efforts to have a living dialogue and attempt to create language (as imperfect as it is) around psychoanalytic thinking, intersectionality and racial trauma feels hopeful and crucial (Cheng, 2000; Lewis, 2012, 2020; Radhakrishnan/Cheng 2021; Walton, 1995; among others).

As a clinician/therapist with a specialization in trauma-focused work, I have integrated body-centered approaches such as sensorimotor psychotherapy (Fischer, 2019; Ogden, 2006; Van der Kolk, 2015; etc.) and polyvagal theory (Dana, 2018; Porges, 2011; etc.) into the clinical work. The impact of trauma on the brain and nervous system is fundamental to working with trauma survivors. This includes racial trauma and the particular configurations of language and bodily experiences, endemic to racism, that are impactful. For me, these lenses are always woven into a foundation of a psychodynamic framework. I often think about language and its function and energy in the therapeutic process. I think I understand my father, in some of his writings, to imply that language connects people, that it can facilitate the working-through of lived experiences and even early, pre-verbal sensorimotor experiences. It follows then that finding language, *in dialogue with the therapist or other*, is fundamental to the working through of traumatic experiences that need still to be integrated into the structure of the adult "self," that are held in the body and have not yet found a verbal narrative. Creating that verbal narrative for trauma is one manifestation of healing, along with, I would argue, reinstating or creating, in the therapeutic process, an awareness of body sensations and movements that the trauma long ago disavowed or dysregulated. Returning for a moment to symbolism: my father writes:

> But it is unwarranted, I think, to maintain that any differentiation of symbol and symbolized is the work of repression and defense, or to hold that true symbolism, understood psychoanalytically, is not present unless repression is involved and the representational relationship of symbol and symbolized is disrupted... Repression, far from bringing symbolism about, disguises symbolism by interfering with the symbolic linkage and hiding the symbolic function of the symbol. Defense is responsible not for creating symbolism, but for disrupting it, disguising it, and distorting it.
>
> (pp. 52, 54, Sublimation...etc.)

Developmental trauma and significant early attachment disruptions such as physical or sexual abuse (perhaps particularly if perpetrated by a caretaker or significant attachment figure) robs the victim of her capacity to symbolize her sensorimotor experiences, disrupts the development of secondary processes and instigates distortion around the victim's symbols through the resulting repression, disassociation, and fragmentation of self that can become so very necessary as a defense against the perceived annihilation that abuse perpetrates.

How can language *not* be intricately bound up with attachment? The unborn baby hears the resonances of language through the mother's body that it lives in; can hear the cadences of the voices outside the mother's body when they are close enough. Speaking, as has been stated, is a physical act. Acts of compassion and empathy – so core to the healing process in the therapeutic relationship, dialogue, and process – is expressed through language, *both* verbal and bodily. This points to the vital need for psychoanalytic practitioners, theorists, and writers to continue to rigorously acknowledge, explore, and challenge the Whiteness (white narrative, white space, white bodies) that Stevens (Stevens, 2021) has identified as "a structural phenomenon built into the law, politics, and psychoanalysis itself as both an institution and clinical practice." The parameters of my essay here do not encompass a larger examination of the history of White narrative in psychoanalysis; for further reading see bibliography.

My father refers to a passage written by Hellen Keller, to illustrate "symbolization in action." This is again from his book on Sublimation, in the chapter on Symbolism.

> Hellen Keller in The Story of My Life (1903) gives a vivid and moving description of symbolization in action and its impact on her emotional-intellectual life.
>
> 'One day, while I was playing with my new doll, Miss Sullivan put my big rag doll [an old familiar one] into my lap also, spelled "d-o-l-l" and tried to make me understand the "d-o-l-l" applied to both. Earlier in the day we had a tussle over the words "m-u-g" and "w-a-t-e-r". Miss Sullivan had tried to impress upon me that "m-u-g" is mug and that "w-a-t-e-r" is water, but I persisted in confounding the two....I became impatient of her repeated attempts and, seizing the new doll, I dashed it upon the floor. I was keenly delighted when I felt the fragments of the broken doll at my feet. Neither sorrow nor regret followed my passionate outburst.

I had not loved the doll. In the still, dark world in which I lived there was no strong sentiment or tenderness...

[Later that day] We walked down the path to the well-house, attracted by the fragrance of the honeysuckle with which it was covered. Someone was drawing water and my teacher placed my hand under the spout. As the cool stream gushed over one hand she spelled into the other the word water, first slowly, then rapidly. I stood still, my whole attention fixed upon the motions of her fingers. Suddenly I felt a misty consciousness as of something forgotten-a thrill of returning thought; and somehow the mystery of language was revealed to me. I knew then that "w-a-t-e-r" meant the wonderful cool thing that was flowing over my hand. The living word awakened my soul, gave it light, hope, joy, set it free!... I left the well-house eager to learn. Everything had a name, and each name gave birth to a new thought. As we returned to the house, every object which I touched seemed to quiver with life.' (Pp 36-37).

(Loewald, 1988, pp. 62–63)

This passage so beautifully illustrates the dialectic between the senses, between sensory experience and thought, and between all of that and the exigencies of safety and attachment. My father's choice to use a passage from Helen Keller's autobiography here (which he states was brought to his attention by other authors who wrote, in the 50s and 60s about symbolism and symbol formation) moves me probably in part because he has chosen a passage about a young girl's experience, as well as because the writing itself is so vivid (I see images as I read her passage) and the moment, of course, so apparently epiphanous.

I end here with a poem that I wrote in the spring of 1993 (the season in which my birthday falls), some months after my father died in January 1993, ten days before what would have been his eighty-seventh birthday (Figure 10.1).

Birth Countries

-for my father

It's late spring now, the air heavy with Lilac.
The leaves of the tall elms and the sheltering copper beeches
Are open. Pollen sifts from the trees onto the sidewalk
As a fine, green dust.

You and I, we agreed: The particular season of one's birthday
Feels most akin to *oneself,* a kind of natural valley of time,
The climate again familiar, the layout of the days instinctively known,
Like the lines on the inside of your own hands or
The hands themselves. My first birthday with you not in this world
Came and went. But I still see you

Briskly stepping out with the tan, light jacket,
Your black leather wallet in the big pocket, your keys
In your hand, some quick trip to the store, perhaps for a pack

Of cigarettes. The unfiltered end's tobacco bits stick
To your bottom lip, which you then spit off.
After dinner the smoke turns blue as it winds
Upward, above the wisps of your grey hair, white at the ends,
And the hazel of your eyes still clear.

You know things.
You say the smoke will keep the mosquitoes away.
The heels of your shoes scuffle in the gravel driveway as
You shift your legs, crossing them loosely, easily, left over right,
While we sit on the low stone wall. I, so much smaller,
Could sit with you forever, you protecting me
From flying bugs with your graceful smoke, and pointing out
The fireflies in the woods, over the yard, darkness coming.

Your voice, accented, different from everyone else's, was
The most particular thing, of which I was before the first word
Unconscious. You translated the near future
Into the present tense: "After we eat, we go outside,"
- these misconjugations always signifying to me
Germany, that old place where you were born and lived, where
What you were saying presumably did not miss its semantic occasion.
I forever forgot *Colmar,* and so had to ask its name
over and over, as if the place of your birth
was a bit too obscure.

I memorized: was *then* Germany, is *now* France, imagining
The border just slightly pushed over after some territorial
Dispute. And did this make you French? or
Did you get to keep the *Germanness* of you, taking it with you
Where you moved, like your own bones, or a birthright?

There were always flowers from you on my birthday,
The tiny card reading, "*All my love,*" in barely comprehensible script,
Your writing practically as flat as if you had simply drawn a horizontal line,
But the capital "A" in "All" signaling the proximity of your love
And then your name, just below.

Your mouth approached an "O", open, the last time I saw you,
Minutes after you ended, your death, after eighty-seven years
An absolute shock in the moment, and again and again,
Despite the foreknowledge, the preparing and the time.
You lay flat under the covers, having died quietly,
Your face, for me, the ripple in the horizontal line, the sign.
I stroked the soft underside of your forearm and thought
How I could sit with you forever.

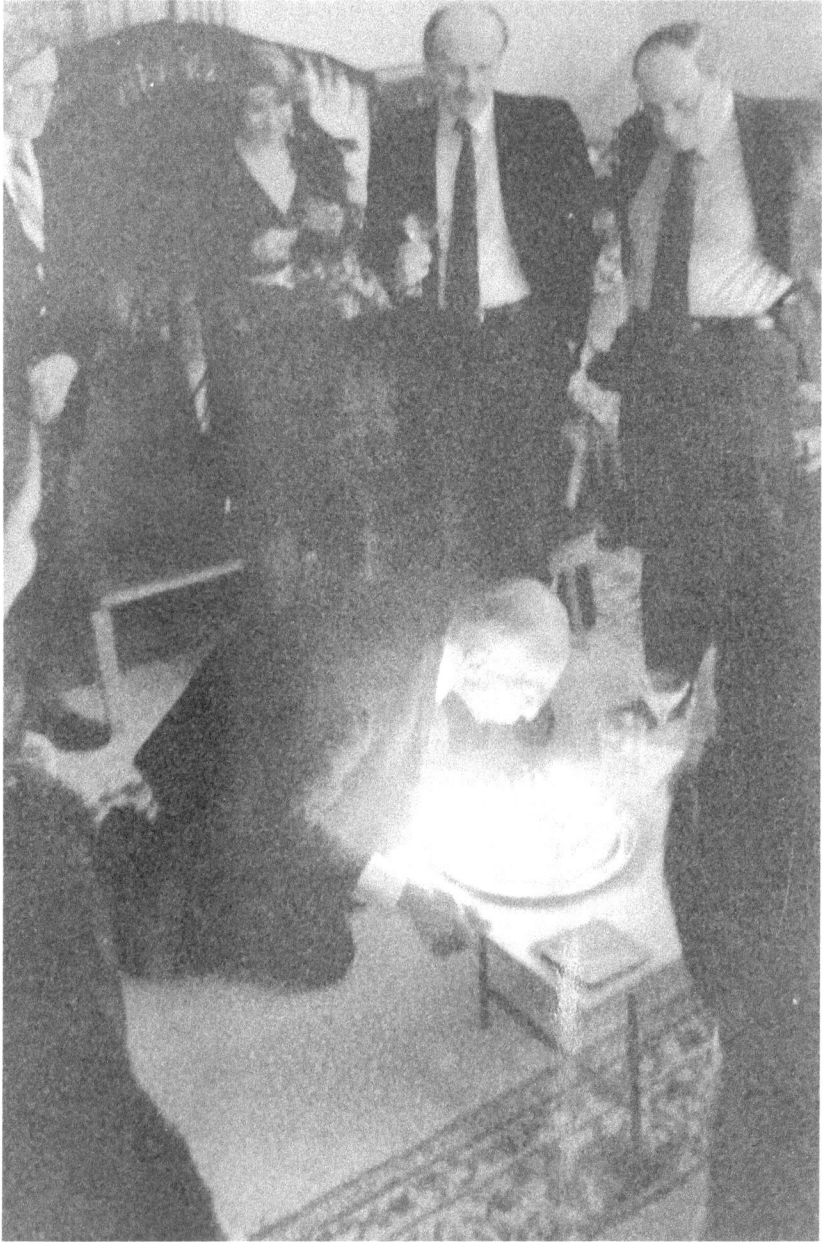

Figure 10.1 My father blowing out candles at party celebrating his 80th birthday, 1986, Hamden, CT. Photograph by the author.

References

Benson, Peter. (2014). https://philosophynow.org/issues/100/Derrida_On_Language

Fischer. (2019). Sensorimotor Psychotherapy in the Treatment of Trauma Janina Fisher, Ph.D. Published in Practice Innovations, 4:3, 156–165, 2019.

Cheng, Anna Anlin. (2000). *The Melancholy of Race*. New York, NY: Oxford University Press.

Dana, Deb. (2018). *The Polyvagal Theory in Therapy*. New York: W. W. Norton and Company.

Derrida, Jacques. (1978). *Writing and Difference*. Chicago, IL: University of Chicago Press. Trans Alan Bass.

Derrida, Jacques. (1986). *Of Grammatology*. Baltimore, MD: Johns Hopkins University Press. Trans Gayatri Chakravorty Spivak.

Derrida, Jacques. (1987). *The Postcard*. Baltimore, MD: University of Chicago Press. Trans Alan Bass.

Keller, Helen. (1903). *The Story of My Life*. New York: Doubleday, pp. 36–37.

Lewis, Gail. (2012). Signs: Journal of Women in Culture and Society; 'Where Might I Find You': Popular Music and the Internal Space of the Father', (2012) Psychoanalysis, Culture and Society.

Lewis, Gail. (2020). Once More with my Sistren: Black Feminism and the Challenge of Object Use, (2020) *Feminist Review*.

Loewald, Hans. (1988). *Sublimation: Inquiries into Theoretical Psychoanalysis*. New Haven, CT: Yale University Press, pp. 45–63.

Ogden, Pat. (2015). *Sensorimotor Psychotherapy; Interventions for Trauma and Attachment*. New York and London: W.W. Norton and Company.

Porges, S.W. (2011). *The Polyvagal Theory: Neurophysiological Foundations of Emotions, Attachment, Communication, and Self-Regulation*. New York: Norton.

Radhakrishnan/Cheng. (2021). https://bombmagazine.org/articles/anne-anlin-cheng/

Stevens, Michelle Ann. (2021). Collisions in the Dark: Invisible Intersectionality and the Black Female Psychoanalyst. *Contemporary Psychoanalysis*, Vol. 57(2), pp. 165–197.

Van der Kolk, B.A. (2015). *The Body Keeps the Score: Brain, Mind and Body in the Treatment of Trauma*. New York: Viking Press.

Walton, Jean. (1995). Re-Placing Race in (White) Psychoanalytic Discourse: Founding Narratives of Feminism. *Critical Inquiry*, Vol. 21(4), pp. 775–804.

Chapter 11

Analyst and Teacher

*Richard L. Munich, Barbara Rosen Garber
and Tsilia Glinberg*

Supervision with Hans

By Richard L. Munich

As the celebration of Hans Loewald's career and contribution to psychoanalysis grows, it has led to my reflecting on supervisory work with him over forty years ago. I had four supervisors at the Western New England Institute for Psychoanalysis, all of whom were excellent. Rebecca Solomon helped with a very difficult, more than neurotic patient. Stan Leavy supervised my beginning patient and Dr. Loewald supervised a classically neurotic patient. Each of the supervisors opened a wide doorway into the intricacies of the field. But Rosemary Balsam, a classmate and co-analysand, had to invite me three times to write something about my supervision, before I was comfortable doing so.

And why was this the case? What was at stake? I believe that the work with Dr. Loewald was a very private experience, at the same level of intimacy but more comfortable than my personal analysis. He was simultaneously utterly available and non-intrusive. I felt being held, while at the same time very much on my own. And most importantly, he was both practical and down to earth as well as a spiritual presence. And what do I mean by spiritual? It refers to that part of me that first of all wanted to be a Rabbi, then looking to not having an authoritarian presence in my life so that I could truly be a person and connect, then discovering in my first two months of internship at an ER assignment that by asking the right question I rarely had to examine the patient, and then diving into Psychiatry and Psychoanalysis where I found my way to Hans Loewald. And back to my connective soul that he helped me begin consolidating.

DOI: 10.4324/9781032685151-13

Analysis with Dr. Loewald

By Barbara Rosen Garber

I started analysis with Dr. L when I was 31. I had a three-year-old daughter. I was a fledgling artist and was teaching art part time. My work with L ended when I was 35. So, forty-six years later, my memories are few, but I do have several, some of which are quite vivid.

I remember the waiting room with a painting hung over a large, wood Victorian mantel. It was a landscape of a red farmhouse in a field of very white snow, somewhere in New England perhaps. I looked at it often, maybe wondering why it was there.

I recall my first visit with Dr. L. I wore a miniskirt and boots. Sitting opposite at his desk, he wore glasses and a gray suit. He looked old. He did not smile. The only thing I think I remember him saying at that first meeting was, "You change only the things you want to change" (or something to that effect).

Perhaps my most vivid memory was walking into his office, several years later, the day after I learned of my father's sudden death. I sat on the edge of the couch and talked and cried. He was very kind and sympathetic, listening carefully to what I said. I think now, in retrospect, it was then that I began to open up about my father.

My final memory is when I was terminating. My husband and I had decided to move to Vermont with our seven-year-old daughter. I remember I gave Dr. L a small black and white abstract line drawing. Leaving was hard, but I took with me the conviction that I was an artist. My path felt clear.

At the Mailbox

By Tsilia Glinberg

A blue mailbox was conveniently located on Whitney Avenue, in New Haven, between Bradley and Trumbull Streets, part of the square block, nicknamed "the triangle of analyzed dreams." This was a well-deserved name, since many training analysts and their students occupied offices housed in buildings on that block. An office on Bradley Street belonged to me, and I made frequent trips to that blue mailbox on Whitney.

Being in analysis was kind of an unusual experience since one is forced to travel back, forth and sideways into previously unfamiliar corners of the mind. All of it was being done with a stranger, the analyst, who was chosen as the "tour guide" through the turbulent, surprising terrain of the unconscious mind.

Hans Loewald was my analyst. As quite a young, naïve and green person, a recent newcomer from the Soviet Union, I imagined all training analysts to be Supreme Beings, not in a religious sense, but as having supreme knowledge and understanding of the human psyche. It also implied high authority. Growing up in a totalitarian state, my perception of authority was infused with a great sense of danger and intimidation, so the prospect of analysis was pretty scary.

At least in the Soviet Union, there were strict rules and regulation, that we all learned and practiced in order to avoid conflicts with authorities. The analytic rules were of little help, free association implied suspending all censorship and mind control, I learned so well to practice growing up in the Soviet Union. With all these complications, my life, training and analysis went on. The notion that my analyst was a "supreme being" persisted, implying a large, imposing being, a primitive notion, living in my unconscious mind. I never thought much about that, but at one point, it had to be confronted.

On a warm Fall afternoon, I ran quickly to the blue mailbox on Whitney to drop some letters. As I turned the corner, I noticed an older man with gray hair in a suit, kind of fumbling with the mailbox, pulling the handle to open the box, letting go, trying again. I began to feel irritated, wondering if I left enough time for this errand to avoid being late for my next appointment. Just as I got closer, I realized who that was and I felt so embarrassed about my disparaging thoughts that I almost turned back to my office with all the letters in hand.

Well, I did not turn back, but slowed my pace and before my last step to the mailbox, Dr. Loewald turned to leave and as he had seen me stepping up said, "Oh, hi," and went on. I must have realized that he had no idea about my short- lived disparaging thoughts, but so many others replaced them. The chance meeting at the mailbox set off a real conflict in my mind between the vision of the little gray older person fumbling with his letters at the mailbox turning out to be the "Supreme Being" – my analyst.

Perhaps that's a perfect metaphor for the analytic work, since most everything we believe on the way into analysis, gets analyzed, interpreted and reinterpreted during the analytic process. It all ends up being something quite different. On the surface nothing much changes, but underneath there may be an avalanche of memories, dreams, fantasies swirling around and eventually landing into an interpretation. Since analytic perception and understanding of the events in one's world is quite a bit different from the analysand's own, I often wondered how does Dr. Loewald come up with those few precious words or sentences he would say from time to time. In later years, my understanding of the analytic process expanded to a point where psychody-namics, unconscious motivations of aberrant behavior and various compulsions had reasonable explanations. Despite my innate stubborn nature and well-learned distrust of authority, the analysis progressed, resistances crumbled or diminished, and certain interpretations took up permanent residence in my mind. One was an interpretation in the form of a Marx Brothers joke: "You would never want to belong to a club, that would admit you." It took me by surprise but turned out to be very true over and over again.

The struggle to shed the thorny cape of "safe distance" from the world around me and my attempt to find a spot to belong and fit in, turned out to be a monumental task. At times it felt impossible, but we both persevered; even so Dr. Loewald told me in a moment of exasperation that I was the most stubborn creature, he ever encountered. He may have used different words, but that is how I remember it. From the long dis-tance of over thirty years, I do not remember how far along that struggle was by the time my analysis ended, but I know it still goes on and on.

After all, that is a fitting way to live for a wandering Jew. The venom of anti-Semitism was ever present in Europe and reached very dangerous levels during Hitler's rise to power. Work and personal life of Jews moved from understated restrictions to outright danger of extermination. The Soviet Union was very instrumental in destroying fas-cism and freeing Europe from Hitler. A large number of Soviet Jews were soldiers and officers in the Red army fighting on the front line against the Germans. Many perished in the battles. However, after the war, anti-Semitism did not disappear in the Soviet Union. Jews remained stigmatized and endured various restrictions. No matter how advanced an expert he or she was or how high a position in science or art one achieved, if the person was Jewish, they stood on shaky grounds and could easily be demoted or disappear. To some extent that may have been true for "high achievers" of all ethnic groups, but to a much greater extend for the Jews.

Since Dr. Loewald lived and practiced psychiatry in the mid- to late-1930s in Germany and Italy, before leaving for the United States in 1939, he was very familiar with the marginalization of Jews in Western and Eastern Europe as well as the impact that had to have on the pattern of relationships both at work, school and personal life. At the time I heard the interpretation in the form of the Marx Brothers' joke, it struck me as quite true, but I was not aware that Dr. Loewald may have lived in a time and place very conducive to that particular defense. So he was particularly well attuned to my struggles with connecting to any community or joining a group/club, that would admit me.

Chapter 12

Hans W. Loewald: Quiet Revolutionary, Creative Synthesizer, Inspiration for 21st-Century Psychoanalysis

An Introduction to The Hans W. Loewald Center[1]

Margery Kalb

Welcome to the inaugural conference of The Hans W. Loewald Center. It is my privilege and pleasure to introduce you to this venture honoring and extending Loewald's "quietly revolutionary" thinking.

We are thrilled to share our dream and hope that you, too, will find it exciting and meaningful. Speaking of dreams....

Growing up, my sons were passionate baseball and movie fans. One of their favorite baseball films was *Field of Dreams* (1989). While thinking about what I wanted to say today, my mind frequently turned to a line from that movie: "If you build it, they will come."[2] A dream that at first seems an illusory flight of fancy holds the potential to grow into a reality that is deeply and personally meaningful for many. Loewald might call it an integrative experience, but more on that, later. By the movie's end many come, from far and wide, to connect to the fullness of the dream's meaning in their own personal ways. Dreams don't always come true, of course. But here we are – we're building it and nearly 450 of you came to help us transform the dream into a meaningful reality.

But what *are* the meanings embedded in our dream – *Why* a Loewald Center? And why *now*?

The Loewald Center strives to be, in Loewald's words: "ahead of ourselves, in-so-far as we recognize potentialities in ourselves which represent more than we are at present" (1962a, p.501). Our psychoanalytic field of dreams, as "represented" by the Loewald Center, recognizes "potentialities" that lie in Loewald's seminal, both/and thinking as a rich point of departure for the ongoing development of becoming "more than we are at present" – clinically, theoretically, and as a field. In his spirit, we wish to both honor and extend Loewald's bountiful legacy by bringing a broader array of analysts into meaningful contact with the ongoing potentialities that lie within his integrative-synthetic mode of thinking.

Let me elaborate by first telling you something about my own way into this project.

DOI: 10.4324/9781032685151-14

"Potentialities": The Personal and the Dream

There are those of us involved in establishing the Loewald Center (LC) who knew Loewald quite well – as analyst, supervisor, friend, husband, father. There are those who met him a few times. And there are those – like myself – who know him only through others' anecdotes and his writing. But what a knowing! I was first introduced to Loewald's work in graduate school (Loewald 1960, 1962a, 1975, 1979b).[3] I was immediately drawn to – enchanted, really – by the freedom of his deeply open, humanistic, and artistic attitude toward psychoanalysis – the symphony of his thinking humming in my mind and heart. Here was an analyst exploring topics that touch me, my patients, my loved ones: growth, love, loss, ghosts, sublimation, the soul. An analyst writing rigorous and nuanced meta-psychology, with living, breathing clinical resonance – and poetry. An analyst whose voice sparkles with oceans of wisdom, grace, and goodness; with moral integrity and decency; with feeling. An analyst whose voice embodies, too, the bold independence of the original iconoclastic spirit of psychoanalysis. An analyst who offers the nuance the human psyche-soul deserves.

My contact with Loewald's work was, of course, deepened by discourse. I was taken by his capacity to hold conflicting ideas while also reaching toward his own personal synthesis, to embrace Freud with love even while at times deconstructing him – re-interpreting as well as integrating in a radical (rather than rebellious) melding of tradition and innovation. I recall literally laughing aloud in one class during my analytic training while musing over Loewald's (1960) ideas about ghosts and therapeutic action, feeling tickled by the breadth, depth and clinical consequence of his distinctive stretch toward imaginative integration. Loewald manages to lace together drives, topographic and structural models, as well as social interactions; an intricate interpenetration of compassion, containment, and interpretation; a mingling of intrapsychic, interpersonal, and interpsychic (one-person and two-person, internal and external) levels of contact and meaning; different forms of time and memory; nonlinear, fluid lifelong cycles of growth that contain the destruction, disorganization, and disintegration required for reconstruction, reorganization and progressive reintegration, and much more – all through the lens of early development and object relations. Here is theory that is both cohesive and clinically lush. And Loewald does it so poignantly. His writing and thinking exemplifies, and pulls on us for, the very kinds of interpenetrations he is exploring. And so I was naturally drawn to teachers, supervisors, colleagues and authors who were thinking and working clinically in the spirit of Loewald's work. In my final semester of analytic training at NYU Postdoc, my ongoing interest in Loewald-inspired integrations led me to initiate a pluralistic clinical study group. Although Loewald was not a focus of the group's attention, a profusion of ghosts materialized, and I heard Loewald reverberating in our experiences.[4]

Loewald, I discovered over and over, gave me meaningful thoughts and flexible clinical tools for "unthought knowns" (Bollas, 1987) and "absent presences" (Bollas, 1994; Caruth, 1996; Gerson, 2009; Kalb, 2015; Ogden, 1992) – for experiences previously beyond my grasp.

Loewald profoundly shaped my understanding of development: love, internalization, ghosts, separation, mourning, sublimation, and the sacred. His concepts of "creative repetition" (1960), "new discovery" (1960), and the "interpsychic" (1970, 1979a) clarify how the "essence" of therapeutic action is embedded in integrative experience nurtured by the patient-centered, restrained love of the analyst (1960). He helpfully accentuates that development is unending, marked by ongoing grieving and working-toward. Loewald envisions psychoanalysis as a potentially capacious amalgam of theories and techniques. Personally, and with patients, it all rang so true, so wise. Despite a humbling certainty that I could never reach anywhere near Loewald's level of sophistication, I think it fair to say I sensed a kindred spirit. The ethos of Loewald's thinking resonated.

That is what gifted artists do: They create – and thus inspire – fullness and freedom out of a particular ethos and disciplined structure. Dancers, for instance, find structure in psychic-somatic centeredness: in proprioception; in physical vocabulary, bodily limitations, and expressiveness. They find it in choreography and improvisation. In speed and stillness. In musicality and its cadences and silences. In the fourth wall of a performance space. And so on. For clinicians, this structure lies in the flexible centeredness of our theoretical-clinical frame. The very possibility of affective freedom lies in the disciplined but shifting subtleties of structure and frame itself, for therein awaits the potential centeredness and space that releases freedom: freedom to risk and play with the dangerous primal energies touching the vulnerable human in us all. I think here of the astonishing accomplishments of the choreographer George Balanchine, who, like Loewald, was born outside the United States into a world steeped in classical traditions. Once in the United States, his internalized classical values coupled with his embrace of American culture such that his creative talents were uniquely suited to integrating the past with the present. In so doing Balanchine honors, preserves, yet also utterly reinvents and revolutionizes classical as contemporary. Loewald, I think, potentially does for classical psychoanalysis something similar to what Balanchine does for ballet: Standing squarely on the shoulders of ancestors, integrating theories, and cultures virtuosically to discover new intelligibility and contemporary relevance, he honors and preserves the old while simultaneously inventing something exhilaratingly new – a "new discovery." Loewald was a psychoanalytic artist, freeing new creative potentialities in theory, in clinical work, and – ongoingly in the form of the Loewald Center – in psychoanalysis itself.

I am so grateful for my internal dialogue with Loewald and his abundant contributions to my growth. At the same time, a couple of things bothered me.

First, while his influence has increased since his death, I nevertheless felt Loewald's contributions were often underrecognized in the United States and downright neglected internationally (Mitchell, 2000; Moscovitz, 2014). Chodorow (2008) points out how much Loewald's views intersect with international as well as North American thinking – particularly with the British independent tradition – and form the basis for an American independent tradition. So why is Loewald not more explicitly influential?

Friedman (2008, p.1115) points out that, in his time, Loewald's linkages "bridged too many worlds and fit too few comfortable niches for popularity." Perhaps (despite our wish to think of ourselves as more open-minded and enlightened) that discomfort persists. Lear (2012, p.168) notes that while Loewald writes "gently but firmly against the grain of an age," he is also a writer who "will challenge any serious practitioner" in any age.

A good deal of what is "new" in contemporary psychoanalysis is substantially rooted in Loewald without giving him due credit. And much of what Loewald espoused is now so accepted that it's unremarkable and unremarked upon. I think here, for example, of internalization of infantile interpsychic interactions and its extension into the clinical relationship. Loewald conveyed his prescient attention to the dyadic interaction in statements such as: "To discover truth about the patient is always discovering it with him and for him as well as for ourselves and about ourselves" (Loewald, 1970, p.298). Loewald anticipated the ascendancy of the here-and-now emotional connection between patient and analyst, integrating the significance of the therapeutic relationship with classical theory and early development. This is a monumental contribution that is rarely acknowledged. Other conceptualizations, such as Loewald's overarching tendency to think in flexible, dialectical – potentially synthesizing – both/and ways, continue to be a struggle for us but hold significant potential for growth in our field. In his balanced integration of, for instance, external and internal (of the social, drives, self, and internal life) Loewald takes account of each aspect without giving any one of them decisive primacy. Rather, he emphasizes the complex interactions amongst these elements. Groundbreaking and quite breathtaking in their time, these ideas deserve credit and continue to hold potential for us to develop further.

Which brings me to the second thing that bothered me: it's been thirty-five years since Loewald's last writings (Loewald, 1987), and psychoanalysts have continued to work and think and grow. I wondered how I could use Loewald and also use – integrate – myself and what speaks to me of what we've added to our psychoanalytic repertoire since Loewald's time, an approach that would link up with how Loewald himself approached Freud and others.

Each of Loewald's geographic moves, from Germany (where he trained as a philosopher, with Heidegger as his mentor) to Paris and Italy (psychiatric training), to Baltimore (interpersonal training), and to New Haven (Freudian and object relational ego psychology training), only *seem* to reflect ideological shifts. Although he manifestly leaves former places and ideas behind in that he does not explicitly write of most of them much, Loewald's exposure to multiple intellectual and cultural views widened his perspective and facilitated a remarkably individual integration of what felt valuable to him.[5]

Today, recent and future analysts come to their professional field of dreams much as Loewald himself did: with significant exposure to multiple theoretical-clinical orientations, and receptivity to using our personal selves. We all grapple with the contemporary proliferation of different ways of thinking. Thus, most of us are faced with questions: Do we allow multiple views to simply co-exist? Do we try to adopt one singular way of thinking and practicing? Do we continue to create yet more new schools?

I recall Martin Bergmann (personal communication) saying that new schools of thought are typically founded on militantly throwing out the old. What a sad state of affairs. Must it be so? Must we abandon the past in order to grow? Must we identify with one particular group and split from others? How is the fantasy of one truth so seductive? How much space is there for individuality? For interconnectedness? How binary are our schools of thought, really, and how much is projection and caricature? Can we engage in gentler self-critique rather than attacking the "other?" (Aron, Grand, & Slochower, 2018; Slochower, 2022). It seems to me we are impeded by what often comes down to a theoretical "narcissism of small differences" (Freud, 1930).

What kind of thinking and feeling really inspires us to give ourselves over to the uncertainties and vulnerabilities – and vitalities – of deep clinical engagement? How much space is there for knitting together both tradition *and* innovation? Loewald felt that he had "fallen through the cracks" theoretically (Balsam, 2008). But since his death Loewald has managed to fill gaps by becoming quietly influential in the thinking of analysts from diverse orientations (Aron, 2019; Bach, 2001; Balsam, 2008; Chodorow, 2008; Fogel et al., 1996; Friedman, 2008; Lear, 2012; Mitchell, 2004; Orange, 2014a, 2014b, 2017; Poland, 2011, 2017; Vivona, 2013; Whitebook, 2004; and numerous others). I felt Loewald's generous and kaleidoscopic, integrative-synthetic attitude signaled potential for something different, something that could be better.[6]

Consciously and unconsciously, each of us, like Loewald, comes to our own unique conglomeration in how we think and practice. Granted, most of us do not approach the sculpted clarity and cohesiveness of Loewald's integration, and therein lie risks. Nevertheless, especially clinically, analysts today are inevitably influenced by the plethora of what we learn, and thus we inevitably pick and choose what we use (sometimes an unconscious hodgepodge). *Now* – a time of greater theoretical-clinical exposure and cross-pollinization than ever – the time is ripe to engage even more explicitly and intentionally with the Loewald-like potentialities of relatively greater integration and synthesis. Doing so can expand space for greater mutual trust and interchange; it can clarify as well as deepen our approach (reducing some of the risks of those unconscious hodgepodges). Such an approach can serve, too, as tonic to our professional history of internecine splintering. Loewald's philosophy can nourish our own efforts – and yes, struggles – to cultivate such an environment. The seed of an idea was taking root.

In 2016, Gil Katz and I met at a favorite Italian restaurant for one of our frequent lunches. As usual, we chatted away about all things psychoanalytic including our mutual appreciation for Loewald. The seed sprouted: Could there somehow be a center dedicated to the fundamentally integrative-synthetic ethos of Loewald's thinking? Gil was quickly and enthusiastically on board and we began brainstorming. By the end of lunch, we had a shared vision, copious notes and a plan to invite Seymour Moscovitz, a friend, colleague and Loewald scholar, to join us. And so the first seeds for our field of dreams were sown. Gil and Seymour have been an absolute dream team – thank you both, from the bottom of my heart.

We quickly decided that we wanted to collaborate with Loewald's family and his home institute, the Western New England Institute for Psychoanalysis (WNEIP), and with The Institute for Psychoanalytic Training and Research (IPTAR) in NYC. We were galvanized by the support of both institutes. Abundant thanks to our Executive Board members from WNEIP and IPTAR: Rosemary Balsam, Larry Levenson, Betsy Brett, Doris Silverman, Chris Christian, and Matthew von Unwerth for being so receptive and invested. You have wholeheartedly joined us in making this wished-for LC a reality. Immense gratitude also to our Program Committee Co-chairs: Natasha Black, Barbara Marcus, Masha Mimran and their committee members, who have likewise become an integral part of this dream team. Special thanks to our resourceful tech team, deftly led by Program Committee member Joe Giardino. It is absolutely essential to us to be generative and authorize this next generation of leaders. And of course, thank you to the Loewald family, without whose support we would still be merely dreaming. Many thanks, as well, to our keynote speakers today: Nancy Chodorow and Jonathan Lear, and our Roundtable speakers: Matthew von Unwerth, Adrienne Harris, Warren Poland, Betsy Brett, Doris Silverman, Chris Christian,

Larry Friedman, and Jeanine Vivona – much gratitude in advance for what I know will be a tremendously enriching day inaugurating the LC. I feel so very lucky to have so many extraordinary teammates.

"Potentialities" and Parameters: The Dream and Its Definition

But. And it's a big "but": It is well known that Loewald stood strongly against the divisive competing schools that have haunted our field and saw yet another school of psychoanalysis as a recipe for yet another false certainty, another false God – another schism. Thus, he resolutely opposed discipleship or anything resembling a "Loewald school."

So let's be crystal clear: Like Loewald himself, the Loewald Center stands definitively against any "Loewald school." Reflexive veneration of Loewald's work, or espousal of any one school of thinking and its attendant certainties, is the antithesis of what we have in mind. *Indeed, it would be the spiritual antithesis of the freedoms of open-system, dialogic and integrative "new discovery" that Loewald epitomizes.*

How do we factor this antipathy toward another school of thought into refining the "whys" of our vision for the LC? How do we rise above discipleship and strive even beyond pluralism - toward integration? These are complex and challenging questions that deserve attention.

The Loewald Center website blurb telegraphs the "whys" of our mission, so I quote from the statement itself before trying to amplify some of its most salient themes:

Hans W. Loewald:

Quiet Revolutionary, Creative Synthesizer, Inspiration for 21st Century Psychoanalysis

Among the challenges facing 21st-century psychoanalysis is the task of integrating our various theoretical schools. Hans Loewald is a pioneer of this endeavor.

Loewald's emphasis on the fundamental role of internalization combines object relations, drive theory, self-concepts, and the sociocultural history of an individual. Throughout his writing, Loewald views mind as an open system and the analytic relationship as an interpsychic experience developmentally grounded in the mother–infant matrix.

He conceives of the analyst's task as holding in safe keeping the image of the individual that he or she can become. In his model of therapeutic action, Loewald understands the analyst's interpretations as conveying not only insight, but also a new object relational experience. The original objects – the ghosts that haunt present day life – are thus gradually transformed into ancestors.

Loewald's ongoing, internal dialogue with Freud and others brought him to his remarkably prescient synthesis. His visionary thinking is a profound legacy and a rich *point of departure* for the ongoing development of psychoanalysis.

Toward that end, the mission of the Hans W. Loewald Center is to promote and *develop a dialogue around Loewald's legacy, by bringing a broader array of analysts into meaningful contact with his integrative thinking and its implications for contemporary psychoanalysis.*

The Loewald Center will work toward this mission by sponsoring...professional activities inspired by Loewald's *integrative* vision.

[My italics]

Loewald was indeed a "quiet revolutionary and creative synthesizer" whose work holds still-untapped possibilities. Casting a clinical eye on our professional history can help elucidate his pioneering approach to psychoanalysis as well as our vision for the potentialities of the LC. Toward such understanding, I will apply some of Loewald's open system clinical conceptualizations – such as ghosts, internalization, integration, destruction and "new discovery" to ongoing professional development.

In thinking about how human beings grow and thrive, Loewald is faithful, always, to himself and his own internalized version of psychoanalysis. To his own reading and rereading of Freud and others, to his own clinical experience. Loewald is aware that new is not always improved. Today's truth is not necessarily truer than past truth. Rather than throw out the proverbial baby with the bathwater – and thus remain haunted rather than enriched by the past – Loewald honors the old as well as the new by explicitly rooting his thinking in the psychoanalysis that was itself, at its inception in turn of the century Vienna, a revolutionary way of thinking. Loewald, who by all accounts saw himself as elucidating Freud and psychoanalysis generally, was quieter about his innovations than was Freud (or others, subsequently). Perhaps as neither insider nor outsider in any of the places and theories he immersed in, Loewald was able to cultivate freedom and space – a third area – to think critically and creatively, and so conceive his in-between formulations. Ultimately, listening to the theoretical music of his ancestors combined with a receptivity to the new to enable Loewald to develop a rich, reformulated integration that goes beyond discipleship. His unique approach facilitated an understanding that was – is – radically open, flexible, and fuller than any one understanding alone – and is thus radically humanistic in its dimensionality and potentiality.[7]

Such an approach cannot flourish within the confines of any one school of thought and cannot be static – cannot be mired in the certainty that accompanies single school thinking or stasis. Such engagement requires an open, fluid system rooted in the love and vitality of holding internalized ancestors in mind while continually and thoughtfully integrating new developments and conversations from a wide array of sources, ever renewing.

With Freud as a profound inner presence and guide – but definitely not an idol – Loewald unassumingly yet inventively rereads others' contributions as well as features they overlooked, transforming them into his emphatically singular integrative-synthetic voice. As deeply as he respects Freud, Loewald aspired to find a way to break free from the closed system that emerged in the wake of Freud, as well as to build on Freud himself.[8] And so we read Loewald reading himself into Freud, lovingly using but also integrating and extending Freud's different models (aspects of drives, topographic, economic, and structural models) and building on ideas such as eros/love, unconscious to unconscious communication (Loewald's "interpsychic"), the preoedipal dyad, memory as construction, time as non-linear (après coup and the re-emergence of early experience in the transference-countertransference interaction), the fundamental nature of containment and processing of the too-muchness of painful experience, and much more. As Loewald (1978, p.193) put it,

> What psychoanalysis needs might not be a "new language" but a less inhibited, less pedantic and narrow understanding and interpretation of its current language, leading to elaborations and transformations of the meanings of concepts

and theoretical formulations, or definitions that may or may not have been envisaged by Freud.[9]

In explicitly using and also extending Freud's ideas, Loewald brings his 20th century imagination to bear on the classical canon, moving beyond coexistence and also sowing seeds for postmodernism and beyond.

Even beyond Freud, there are so many giants in our rich field. While Loewald steadfastly considered himself a Freudian and an ego psychologist, extended linkages abound. First, the interpersonalists, including Sullivan, with whom Loewald trained prior to his move to New Haven certainly contributed to Loewald's emphasis on interaction. Second, some of Loewald's contemporary developmental theorists were (more or less simultaneously) exploring overlapping themes. For example, Kohut's attention to the self shares similarities with Loewald's thinking. Object relational theorizing of the time, particularly the notion of the analytic relationship grounded in earliest mother-infant interactions, also intersects with Loewald's views. Winnicott (1982a, 1982b) and Mahler (1975), were, like Loewald, creative developmentalists who emphasized the early environment, loss and separation. They too underscored how destruction is necessary for new construction (although it seems to me that Loewald centers his attention more – or at least more unambiguously – on the unconscious and on the dialectical value of undifferentiated primary process experience throughout the lifespan than does Winnicott). There was some mutual influence among these theorists, and each extended or significantly modified existing theory and practice. But all have received significantly more overt attention and credit than Loewald. Moreover, Winnicott modified classical thinking without explicitly acknowledging he was doing so, while most others developed their theories in open (often avid) opposition to classical thinking. Loewald alone among these giants intentionally held onto his identity as a Freudian while also explicitly acknowledging that he was integrating and extending our theoretical-clinical framework. He believed in quietly revolutionary nonlinear growth from the inside, from deepening and developing our visionary roots while also thoughtfully knitting new ideas into our theoretical-clinical fabric.

Some insist on seeing Loewald as a Freudian (Fogel et al., 1996; Friedman, 2008). Others claim Loewald as object relational or Relational (Aron, 2019 and private communication; Mitchell, 2004). But he was not a conventional Freudian Ego Psychologist, nor was he a standard bearer for any orientation. Loewald does not emphasize drives *or* relationships, internal *or* external, preoedipal *or* oedipal, containment *or* interpretation, one-person *or* two-person, tradition *or* revision. He shuns dichotomies and instead strives openly for the creative both/and complexity that results in quietly revolutionary integration and balance.

There is no one true psychoanalysis (though the fantasy it exists is seductive). The building of any theory is a process characterized by uncertain evolving rough approximations. Each school and generation, including ours, has blind spots. It is only later that the faults in our theories and clinical work can be seen and revised.

Loewald was better than most at taking this into account. In refusing to become another school and instead working in deep dialogue with multiple theories, in systematically moving toward integrating and extending, and in adding his own emphasis on love and the sacred in humanity, Loewald created an invaluable legacy: he espoused not an ultimate truth or "Loewaldian" theory but rather an open approach involving ongoing, intergenerational processes of disorganization that can lead toward reorganization and discovery – individually and in our clinical theory building.

In welcoming creative tensions and building from them, Loewald's is a "radical conservative" (Whitebook, 2004) vision that can serve as a model for us.

To draw further on Loewald's (1960, 1979b) theory of assimilation and development and extend it into the realm of our own professional development, Loewald lovingly "destroys" Freud and others in order to grow toward internalization, individuation and integration. Toward actualizing the potential to re-discover and re-create. In contrast to "discovery of new objects," "new discovery of objects" (1960, p.18) offers a re-discovery of the old that promotes integration. Such "new discovery" facilitates both a new way of relating to others and a new way of relating to oneself – in this instance Loewald's internalized dialogue with Freud plus his dialogue with contemporaries facilitates his unique rediscovery, his capacity to integrate his theoretical-clinical past and present to create his own way of relating to psychoanalytic theory and practice. What makes such destruction loving (a life force) is that in building internalizations one paradoxically and creatively connects as well as differentiates, honors as well as re-creates – this is relational ancestry. It is a form of laying of ghosts to relative rest by way of enhanced internalizations that are generative. And it is an approach we believe offers ongoing promise for laying our collective theoretical-clinical ghosts to greater rest, helping us to grow. The Loewald Center aspires to model itself on such imaginative integration, developing Loewald's approach for our times and beyond.[10]

"Integration" is an oft-used, preferred term for Loewald. His prominent usage of the word is, of course, not accidental. A unique core of Loewald's thinking lies in his revolutionary emphasis on creatively and overtly integrating – and thus innovating – tradition.[11] He uses the term "integration" to convey robust internalization and growth rooted in the binding force of love. Loewald highlights integration not only at the level of theory building but also at the developmental, clinical, and social levels. He centers on nonlinear potentialities inherent in rhythms of integrative and disintegrative – and re-integrative – experiences, and poignantly portrays such consolidative enrichment as a process of laying ghosts to (relative) rest.[12]

I offer just one of Loewald's many visionary statements, this one from his paper on *Therapeutic Action*: "Analytic interpretations represent, on higher levels of *interaction*, the *mutual recognition* involved in the creation of identity of experience in two *individuals.... Insight* gained in such *interaction* is an *integrative* experience" (p.25; italics mine). In the classical psychoanalytic world of 1960 this was revolutionary indeed.

By supporting mutually interactive integration and synthesis where possible, Loewald's approach can inspire growth and the best in us. In a space of open and supple theoretical-clinical reflectivity and generosity, we read Loewald creatively wondering, holding conflicting thinking in mind, breaking it down, parsing, internalizing and integrating so much of what he learned and experienced, personally and professionally. In so doing, he holds onto the Freudian bedrock of the internal world while also developing in new directions – broadening and deepening and ultimately revolutionizing the wisdom of our thinking. Today, to be a Freudian or an interpersonalist, relationalist, self-psychologist, Kleinian, Lacanian, and so on, is to be multiple. Internalization and integration are inherently multiple. Loewald exemplifies an attitude of integrative multiplicity that we believe offers ongoing promise for laying our collective theoretical-clinical ghosts to greater rest, potentiating our ongoing growth. Growth that springs from freedom of independent thinking and can shift the locus of our attention away from our largely counterproductive history of factional discipleship, and toward what's most sacred: development of the psyche-soul. This is the attitude the LC strives to embrace.

Controversial Dream Potentialities: Toward Loewald's Spirit of Integration

As always, there are alternate points of view. Controversies over integration can only be touched on here but given its centrality to our endeavor I attempt to sketch some of the most salient themes.[13]

Some urge a greater purity and clarity of technique that springs directly from theory. Then again, even some of those who counsel greater purity note that some theories are better than others at accounting for a broader range of human experience (Boesky, 2002). It is clear to us that Loewald is such a theorist. His deep understanding and assimilation of Freud, Interpersonalists, Winnicott and others allowed an internal discourse in his creative mind that fostered linkages and inclusion of aspects of each in an unusually expansive developmental theory.

Others argue that integration is not the best approach, that the best we can do is to work with a set of independent or alternative theories that co-exist, without trying to integrate them. For example, Aron (2017) argues for what he calls "critical pluralism," suggesting that psychoanalysis move beyond tolerance to critical dialogue among alternative viewpoints. In his quiet and often internal way, Loewald engages in just such a process – but also moves beyond such dialogue. Loewald subtly offers a potential both/and: engaging – deeply, thoughtfully, generously, imaginatively – with differences and then using that engagement as a basis for finding links and integrating where it makes sense to him to do so. The two approaches, in creative yet thoughtful oscillation and combination, can exponentially sharpen and deepen our work – potentiating our development.

We do not wish to deify integration or synthesis. Tensions between engaging differences and striving toward integration, between the dual realities of divergence and convergence, are inevitable. We recognize the need to think critically and hold conflicting ideas in mind, and do not believe that psychoanalysis can – or should – be synthesized into anything approaching one overarching theory.

Same time, Loewald goes beyond accounting for a broad array of human experience and beyond holding and engaging difference: His theory *both* engages with the broad array of human experience and with alternative viewpoints, *and* also strives to accommodate conflicting points of view by creatively integrating where possible. Indeed, Loewald's integrations sprout directly from his respectful (often internal) discourse with others and differences. He holds, considers, critiques and appreciates otherness while also moving in the direction of integrating some of the false dichotomies that have beleaguered psychoanalysis. In so doing, he creates a mutual enhancement of multiple theories and techniques that meaningfully deepen our work and lays a template for ongoing paradigmatic potentialities.

Numerous contemporary thinkers highlight Loewald's integrative-synthetic ethos, and hint at its enduring potentialities. To cite a few [italics added for emphasis],

Chodorow (2003) dubs Loewald an "insistent synthesizer." She also (2008) states that Loewald "provides a unique *synthesis*, a comprehensive and original account that seamlessly *integrates* apparently contradictory claims and approaches, while at the same time moving beyond and *transforming its initial components*." Balsam (2008) notes that "Loewald's work has successfully *transcended the era of theoretical plural-ism*. I predict that because of the *open, integrative nature of his thought, and its abiding clinical aptness*, he will only gain stature in the years to come." Fogel (1989) writes that, "Interpretation and continual reworking – a kind of theoretical working through – may then lead to new *synthesis, integrity, and integration*. This *boldly integrative approach* to theoretical concepts is what Loewald calls the 'authentic function' of psy-choanalytic theory." Greenberg (1996) points out that,

> Hans Loewald's….passion was Freudian psychoanalysis; in virtually every pas-sage of his writings we encounter Freud as a living presence, as a participant in Loewald's inner dialogue. But Loewald engages Freud with a vision shaped by his early exposure to Sullivan and other interpersonal and object relational analysts. Although these theorists remain a background presence…Loewald clearly be-lieved that reconciliation and synthesis are needed if psychoanalysis is to develop conceptually.

Whitebook (2004) notes that

> Loewald's work is characterized by a degree of systematic rigor and a *synthetic thrust* generally absent from contemporary psychoanalysis. Indeed, not only is the *concept of synthesis central to Loewald's theory*, the activity of *synthesis is also manifested in his work*. He methodically attempts to *transcend the binary oppositions—the theoretical splintering* —into which psychoanalytic controversies regularly become frozen. For example, both the relational analysts and the struc-tural theorists try to claim him as their own. But Loewald's analysis should have done much to obviate the opposition between the two positions.

And Mitchell (2004), shifting toward Loewald near the end of his life, felt that,

> Perhaps the greatest joy in my reading of the psychoanalytic literature in recent years has been my immersion in the work of Hans Loewald….I began to realize just how powerfully Loewald's vision had influenced my own *in many ways I had not directly recognized*…. As Loewald's ideas developed within the context of his love of Freud and of his extremely idiosyncratic and creative reading of Freud's work, reading Loewald *led me back to reread and reconsider Freud. I've found this kind of continual cycling back as probably the best way to both preserve and revitalize analytic traditions*.

I wonder whether Mitchell would have taken this line of thinking in the direction of greater integration, had his life not been cut short.

Personally, when asked my orientation I often describe myself as an Interpsychic Freudian. I am attached to Loewald's prescient (though underused) term "interpsy-chic" (1970, 1979) as a word that refines, clarifies and balances my personal brand of

"Freudian" – it is shorthand that captures something of the reach toward the integrative-synthetic attitude I find so theoretically and clinically valuable.

Loewald's thrust is quite clear: He engages difference yet also moves, where possible, toward creating linkages and integrating one and two-person psychology, insight and relationship, trauma and fantasy, individual and social, philosophy, spirituality, creativity, and a broad array of human concerns. Interactive integration and synthesis are conspicuously central themes throughout Loewald's thinking and writing, suggesting they held particular aspirational meaning and potentialities for him – and thus for our ongoing dialogue with him. Loewald's thinking can serve as an invitation to expand beyond yet another school of thought, even beyond pluralism, toward a relatively more integrative-synthetic way of developing psychoanalysis for our times and the future.

Further, independence of theories is simply no longer tenable (if it ever was). While schools of thought each have their differences and their place, they are far from pristine or discrete. Most of the theories we study and assimilate today are *already* to some degree blends. The splendor of the theoretical buffet before us guarantees that we imbibe theoretical multiplicity (whether and how we contend with this varies, of course). Even if theories could be taught in pure independent form, the simple fact of their multiplicity means they would become blended internally for each individual. Thus, whether or not we "should" be, as analysts we are influenced by all we have absorbed, and we use what is at our internal disposal. Especially clinically, purity or parallel co-existence of theories is simply not viable: Our absorption of a multitude of approaches to some extent (consciously or not) infiltrates and interpenetrates. In the heat of the moment with a patient, we are, ipso facto, reacting in a way that is colored by the diverse array we have at our internal disposal – albeit often in an underreflective muddle rather than an integration.

I wonder whether some of the opposition to cultivating an integrative-synthetic attitude may reflect a threat of identity diffusion. Our attachments to schools – splintered as they often are – serve as "home" and "tribe" and thus provide a seemingly clearer sense of identity and belonging. Differences or integration may thus feel disequilibrating or even subversive. Yet as analysts we know that what is threatening is also frequently worth exploring and can tame the muddle. We wish to explore the questions: Where is dialogue with difference valuable? Where is integration and synthesis possible – and where is it desirable?

Integration and synthesis are, of course, extraordinarily ambitious, ultimately unreachable ideals. In another context, Lear (2012, p.167) notes that Loewald requires "patience," "playfulness" and a readiness to absorb the complex unfamiliar, allowing "it to take root in one's own psyche, to return to it after some time and see how it *now* looks, from the changed perspective that has become one's own." We, at the LC, also have our differences that are difficult to absorb and beg patience and playfulness in our interactions. Each of us is an "other" with our own real and imagined relationship to Loewald and our own vision for the LC. We do not always agree on things or come as near as we would like to mutually interactive integration (much less synthesis). And I imagine that many readers of this chapter disagree, or at least feel skeptical, about some of what I am saying. Unfamiliar or different views can indeed be unsettling, inhibiting our receptivity. Sometimes we find it useful to seek dialogue around discord without aiming for integration. Further, the dissonance between seemingly irreconcilable demands for appreciation of otherness and the promises of integration can be daunting. It is asking a lot of ourselves.

Yet we can strive. Unsettledness signals potential for growth. Critical thinking does not need to be hostile or bitter. Differences, lightly held, do not need to be lodged as perpetual splits. Cumulative wisdom can be seen as an asset rather than a threat. Existing splits and allegiances can be softened. Let's try to hear one another out, to allow otherness to "take root" so that we can "return to it" over time from our own – possibly somewhat revised and more integrated – perspective. Á la Loewald, who was able to absorb and develop his integrations from differences, we have faith that the more generously we can listen to one another and sustain meaningful dialogue, the more we can grow.

Crucially, in Loewald's spirit we can strive toward a paradigmatic both/and: we can engage with differences where integration is not possible or desirable and move toward thoughtful integrations where possible. With an attitude of mindful playfulness, we have the opportunity to minimize the muddle of our integrations and maximize the deepening of our thinking and our work.

We are not the only ones to support an aspirational integrative view. Sandler, for example (1983) takes the position that although the many theories which comprise our corpus are often contradictory, they can all be useful clinically, provided the analyst remains unruffled by theoretical discrepancies. Like us, Sandler holds that such personal mixtures and integrations actually enrich the practice of psychoanalysis. Pine is well known for his theoretical-clinical integration, which he dubbed "post pluralism" (2011). Like Pine, Cooper (2016) advocates "post pluralism," although unlike Pine, Cooper sees post pluralism not as integration but rather as an "interpenetration" of theory and technique wherein we allow the unconscious play of theories to inform our work. The salient differences between interpenetration and integration are not entirely clear to me; perhaps the LC can sponsor activities that explore that line of thinking. Levine's view of analytic work as an orchestral symphony of instruments – theories – that we take in, and which then emerge from our conscious as well as our unconscious as we work, dovetails well with our vision for the LC (Levine, H.B., 2021, personal communication).[14]

It is plain that regardless of whether epistemological assumptions can or should be woven together it is to some degree inevitable they will be. We believe that there is an alloy of ideas that each analyst can – and does – use, to improvise their own integrations. We believe that listening and integrating as thoughtfully as possible to avail ourselves of the fertile resources offered by the multiplicity of mutually influencing theories and techniques can help us to clarify, to counter factionalism, to repair and build. Particularly clinically and socioculturally – where theoretical difference recedes – we have work to do that is impeded by what often comes down to a theoretical "narcissism of small differences" (Freud, 1930, p.114). What unites us as analysts is more fundamental than what divides us. To paraphrase Sullivan, we're more simply psychoanalysts than otherwise.

Loewald epitomizes such an approach. He finds the sweeping freedom to weave strands from a diverse array of models together, creating a theoretical-clinical tapestry of his own. His commitment to putting dialogic pressure on ideas and emotions in order to move toward a reformulated integration is a vital gift with much ongoing potential. Loewald synthesizes where he can by attending to internal life and the social surroundings and then using that attention to balance theoretical-clinical interrelationships amongst interpretation, containment, interaction, and mutual recognition (his integration of one-person and two-person models). In so doing, he interrupts the familiar and moves toward transcending hollow binaries imposed by rivalrous models. Loewald instead centers on the synergies of what matters: The multifaceted and still mysterious depths of how the psyche-soul works and can grow.

We are the inheritors and future of this legacy. Much as we respect Loewald, our project is greater than homage to an admired psychoanalyst. For beyond the unique eloquence and nuance of Loewald's own integration, beyond discipleship, Loewald provides an exceptional *point of departure* – an invitation to build on his attitudes. It is in his spirit of thoughtful dialogue, integration, synthesis and centering on what matters that we seek to take up his legacy by engaging with Loewald for *our* time and *our* future.

In respecting the past, Loewald imagined the future. Let's both honor and build on Loewald's legacy by lovingly – to use his language[15] – "destroying" (1973a, 1979b) him so that we can internalize our interaction with his imaginative ways of being and thinking, as part of us. To quote Loewald again, the aim toward, "….active re-creation….is repetition with its face towards the future while aware of the past" (1971, p.64).

Our dream is to make use of Loewald's ideas toward such a supple present and future – to strive toward a "radically integrative vision for our theoretical and clinical work" that suits 21st-century sensibilities. And – crucially – let's aspire to pass that mode of thinking along to the next generation.

In the film *Field of Dreams*, the hero – haunted by a fraught relationship with his baseball-enthusiast father – acts on a dream-voice he hears saying, "If you build it, he will come" by destroying his cornfields (his home and livelihood) to build a baseball diamond in the middle of his farm. The film can be construed as a mythical-magical-realism passage through the process of what Loewald called laying ghosts to rest as ancestors (Loewald, 1960). One might say the farmer is destroying creatively in order to rediscover and remake the ghost of his father, a process of internalizing and re-integrating that lays the shadowy ghost relationship to relative rest.

We see the Loewald Center as a potentially actualizable dream for our field. Whether ghosts are those of our personal lives, our splintered professional field or other socio-cultural realms (Chodorow, 2019; Harris, Kalb, & Klebanoff, 2016a, 2016b; Holmes, 2021), whether they are theoretical or clinical, individual or collective, laying ghosts to rest is always relative – a "waning" (Loewald, 1979b), bittersweet and incomplete (Kalb, 2015, 2021). But with mourning, reflection and imagination, "new discovery" (Loewald, 1960) – and the internalization and integration that grows with it – can help rebuild and recreate the past, potentiating the present and the future.

The process of mourning loss – laying ghosts to relative rest – thus endows a potential for more fully building upon the work of our ancestors to actualize the potentials of our field. Every one of us is an agent of such transmission. Such a developmental process is, at its essence, a triumph of love and life. A la Loewald, let's aim to lay some of our professional ghosts to relative rest in order to enhance *our* development and our legacy.[16]

Making the Dream "Future Present": Hopes and Strivings

For my part, I feel deeply, deeply honored to be linked in any way with Loewald and the LC. Also, I confess, rather nervous – humbled by striving to follow in Loewald's venerable footsteps even in a small way. I am satisfied enough in believing Loewald himself would have been pleased to know he has generated a Center devoted to continually striving toward such open conversation and potentialities and satisfied enough if I have kindled in you any inclination toward dreaming with us.

Ultimately, the Loewald Center is an act of love and optimism. We plan to, "Go the distance" (*Field of Dreams*, 1989) in building this field of dreams. We promise to try our best to honor and extend Loewald's vision. We do not ask for more than trying our best, but we accept no less. We have faith that in doing our best – in working toward, reaching for, trying, striving – we can help nurture the meaningful contact and freedom that stimulates rich "potentialities."

In conclusion, I quote again from Loewald himself: "Anticipation makes the future present" (1962b, p.264). In such anticipation, we challenge ourselves to be open and nimble enough to work toward following Loewald's spirit, and we ardently hope you can find your own unique way of reaching with us for this field of dreams.

Notes

1 This chapter is an expanded version of a talk given originally on the occasion of the inaugural conference of the Hans W. Loewald Center, on April 30, 2022. I am grateful to Gil Katz, Seymour Moscovitz and Joyce Slochower for their valuable comments on earlier versions of this essay.

2 The actual line in the movie is: "If you build it, *he* will come," but an online search shows that my mistake is a common one. I suspect that I, and others, 'remember' it as, "If you build it, *they* will come" because by the end of the movie it is abundantly clear that the hero's dream is a shared dream of laying ghosts to rest as ancestors and many do, indeed, come to take part in that dream.

   Interestingly, the quote originates in the bible where God answers Noah's question of where he will find all the animals to fill his ark (Genesis 6–7, Hebrews 11:7); in the biblical story it is indeed "they" – the animals – that will come to Noah's ark.

3 I will always be immensely grateful to Beth Hart, for introducing me to Loewald and for our wonderfully rambling, stimulating conversations about his writing, and to Norbert Freedman for generously nurturing that introduction.

4 I was drawn particularly to Shelly Bach and Steve Solow's clinical style, Gil Katz's thinking on the "enacted dimension of analytic process," Seymour Moscovitz's insights into Loewald himself, Nancy Chodorow's thinking about Loewald as the basis for an American Independent Tradition, the writings of Jonathan Lear, Rosemary Balsam, Warren Poland, Steve Mitchell's late writings (2000), Gerald Fogel et al.'s 1996 paper, Nields on the spiritual potential in Loewald's thinking (2003), and others. The pluralistic study group consisted originally of Adrienne Harris, Galit Atlas, Heather Ferguson, Michael Feldman, Arthur Fox, Susan Klebanoff, and myself.

5 It is self-evident that previous experiences and cathexes significantly informed Loewald's work. However, given Loewald's preference for privacy it seems to me gratuitously intrusive – as well as speculative – to take the next step and guess at the ways in which these cathexes and subsequent moves may have imbued Loewald's work as ghosts or as ancestors.

6 Particularly in a contemporary climate often so hostile to psychoanalysis, I passionately believe our best future lies in playing with the more harmonic possibilities that lie in trying to move beyond distrustful splits, distortions of the other, ruptures – even beyond pluralism – and stretching toward a more tolerant, richer, integrative-synthetic approach.

7 For Loewald, as for Fairbairn and numerous others, being slightly on the psychoanalytic and cultural margins can allow seeing and conceptualizing somewhat differently from those who are more fully insiders. These theorists and clinicians often seem to be able to fit in just enough to be part of the conversation (at least peripherally) while developing and sustaining their own unique voice. For Loewald, his "falling through the cracks" (Balsam, 2008) may have been part of what potentialized his integrative-synthetic thrust.

8   Interestingly, in building on Freud in this way Loewald can be seen as elaborating Freud's own attitude toward theory-building and its clinical implications: There are multiple Freuds as well as multiple post-Freudian and "non-Freudian" models (ego psychologists, conflict theorists, self-psychologists, Kleinians, Bionians, Winnicottians, field theorists, interpersonalists and relationalists, Lacanians, intersubjective Freudians, pluralists, and on and on). The last thing we need is another 'new' theory. Freud – himself a revolutionary thinker in his time and place – recognizes that in its newness his theory is fundamentally fluid, an imprecise framework on which to reflect and build (although Freud's authoritative early 20th-century writing style as well as some of his personal-professional encounters can camouflage this fact). Freud's trajectory affirms his recognition: Early Freud is very different from middle Freud, which is different from late Freud. Little in Freud is fully worked out, and he knows it. To read Freud is to read Freud thinking aloud (Bergmann, private communication).

    Just one example of Loewald building in this way upon Freud's shoulders is Loewald's elaboration of preoedipal mother-baby dynamics and their clinical consequences. Never having been in analysis himself, Freud was deprived of the regressive transference experience that could have informed his understanding of earliest dynamics. Moreover, personal hauntings limit everyone's work, and the absent presence of the maternal suffusing Freud's oeuvre may also indicate that a personal ghost interfered with his capacity for attention to the impact and implications of early maternal relationships. To the degree that one is haunted one is limited. And so, others, like Loewald, build to fill in the gaps.

9   According to Moscovitz (private communication), this quote was a direct reference to Roy Schafer, who was proposing a "new" action language for psychoanalysis to replace the metapsychology of drives, forces, and closed system hydraulics. Schafer, Merton Gill, and other close colleagues of Loewald's were impatient with him for what they saw as his clinging to outmoded Freudian metapsychology, rather than taking the hermeneutic turn with them. Loewald "rediscovered" this metapsychology, by expanding and reinterpreting Freud's drive theory as an open system model with Eros as a life force based on integration rather than stimulus reduction, the Nirvana principle, and the death drive. I wonder if perhaps Loewald was also in part reacting to the fact that the new language that emerges along with new schools can obfuscate rather than illuminate: While fully new concepts deserve new vocabulary, some of the idiosyncratic new language overlaps with existing concepts in ways that can muddle and erect barriers to dialogue and understanding. More common language and definitional clarity might smooth the exchange of ideas.

10   This form of destruction differs from mere rebellion in that rebellion is often a form of stagnated attachment resulting in ghostly repetitions, rather than in enhanced internalizations. Of course, the two forms of destruction – that driven by love and that driven by stagnated attachment – are not always so easy to distinguish in vivo, and can also be intertwined (for example, rebellion may be a stepping-stone that is part of the nonlinear process of development, as if often seen in adolescence). For Loewald (1960, 1979b), the wish to experience and discover ways to cope with the past and its difficulties is destruction driven by love and mourning – individuation and internalization; simple rebellion is driven by a wish to undo or get rid of the past, which results in haunted repetitions.

11   Loewald's mother was a pianist who it is said often played Beethoven for her son when he was young (Mitchell, 2000, 2004), so perhaps this is one way that Loewald absorbed, early on and deeply, something about love and respect for classics alongside the harmonies of integration.

12   To cite just a few examples of how Loewald can be extended to apply to sociocultural phenomena, Holmes (2021) pulls from Loewald's concept of ghosts to gorgeously lay out how split-off whiteness returns as a ghost that interferes with therapeutic work of symbolization and mourning. Others use the concept of ghosts and demons to illuminate dynamics around the Holocaust, gender, political environments, and many other sociocultural phenomena (Gerson, 2009; Harris, Kalb & Klebanoff, 2016a, 2016b). Loewald's theories can be easily extended to offer valuable insights on how to heal collective as well as clinical divides.

13   Quite a bit has been written on the themes of pluralism, integration, synthesis, and alternate models. For example, Fred Pine (multiple psychologies), Charles Hanly, Leo Rangell (composite theory), Robert Wallerstiein, and Lew Aron (critical pluralism) have all written

on the theme of integration of theory. Valuable as a more in-depth discussion could be, it is beyond the scope of this chapter but we hope it will be pursued in future LC activities.

14 See also Lament (2020), who is among those who write about pluralism and integration, in the context of the "complexity of truth" (p. 195). She recognizes the challenge of including alternate perspectives, noting that "people tend to select one theory over others, all the while knowing that such a singular perspective is but an idealization or useful fiction of what the fuller truth is if one eventually includes....[a] multiplicity of inexact models." (p. 195).

15 As previously noted, Loewald and Winnicott influenced one another and use similar language to describe similar processes of developmental destruction that facilitates growth.

16 Sprengnether (2018) captures the essence of Loewald and the Loewald Center when she writes: "Mourning Freud does not mean disparaging, ignoring, or forgetting him. Nor does it mean elevating him to a position that demands discipleship or submission to unquestioned authority. Rather, it means digesting his body of thought in a way that resembles the process of assimilating the memory of a departed loved one as an internal source of support and inspiration. Hans Loewald's concept of transforming 'ghosts into ancestors' eloquently articulates this process. Whereas ghosts haunt us in ways that terrify and transfix us, preventing us from moving forward in our lives, ancestors act as internal guides and sources of wisdom." In his ongoing dialogue with Freud, Loewald did just this, internalizing and using Freud as a source of wisdom and springboard from which he built, elaborated, extended, and integrated. We at the Loewald Center wish to continue just this mindset of psychoanalytic thinking.

References

Aron, L. (2017). Beyond tolerance in psychoanalytic communities: Reflexive skepticism and critical pluralism. *Psychoanalytic Perspectives*, 14:271–282.

Aron, L. (2019). Discussion of "bread and roses: Empathy and recognition". *Psychoanalytic Dialogues*, 29:92–102.

Aron, L., Grand, S., & Slochower, J.A. (Eds.) (2018). *Deidealizing relational theory: A critique from within*. London: Routledge.

Bach, S. (2001). On being forgotten and forgetting one's self. *Psychoanalytic Quarterly*, 70:739–756.

Balsam, R. (2008). The essence of Hans Loewald. *Journal of the American Psychoanalytic Association*, 56:1117–1128.

Boesky, D. (2002). Why don't our institutes teach the methodology of clinical psychoanalytic evidence? *Psychoanalytic Quarterly*, 71:445–475.

Bollas, C. (1987). *The shadow of the object: Psychoanalysis of the unthought known*. London: Free Association Books.

Bollas, C. (1994). Aspects of the erotic transference. *Psychoanalytic Inquiry*, 14:572–590.

Caruth, C. (1996). *Unclaimed experience: Trauma, narrative, and history*. Baltimore, MD: Johns Hopkins Press.

Chodorow, N.J. (2003). The psychoanalytic vision of Hans Loewald. *International Journal of Psychoanalysis*, 84:897–913.

Chodorow, N.J. (2008). Introduction: The Loewaldian legacy. *Journal of the American Psychoanalytic Association*, 56:1089–1096.

Chodorow, N.J. (2020). *The psychoanalytic ear and the sociological eye: Toward an American independent tradition*. London: Routledge.

Cooper, S.H. (2016). *The analyst's experience of the depressive position: The melancholic errand of psychoanalysis*. New York: Routledge.

Fogel, G.I. (1989). The authentic function of psychoanalytic theory: An overview of the contributions of Hans Loewald. *Psychoanalytic Quarterly*, 58:419–451.

Fogel, G.I., Tyson, P., Greenberg, J., McLaughlin, J.T., & Peyser, E.R. (1996). A classic revisited: Loewald on the therapeutic action of psychoanalysis. *Journal of the American Psychoanalytic Association*, 44:863–924.

Freud, S. (1930). *Civilization and its discontents*. Standard Edition XXI: 57–145. London: Hogarth Press.

Friedman, L. (2008). Loewald. *Journal of the American Psychoanalytic Association*, 56(4): 1105–1115.

Gerson, S. (2009). When the third is dead: Memory, mourning, and witnessing in the aftermath of the Holocaust. *International Journal of Psycho-Analysis*, 90:1341–1357.

Greenberg, J. (1996). In Fogel, G.I., Tyson, P., Greenberg, J., McLaughlin, J.T., & Peyser, E.R. (1996). A classic revisited: Loewald on the therapeutic action of psychoanalysis. *Journal of the American Psychoanalytic Association*, 44:863–924.

Harris, A., Kalb, M., & Klebanoff, S. (2016a). *Ghosts in the consulting room: Echoes of trauma in psychoanalysis*. London: Routledge.

Harris, A., Kalb, M., & Klebanoff, S. (2016b). *Demons in the consulting room: Echoes of genocide, slavery and extreme trauma in psychoanalytic practice*. London: Routledge.

Holmes, D.E. (2021). "I do not have a racist bone in my body": Psychoanalytic perspectives on what is lost and not mourned in our culture's persistent racism. *Journal of the American Psychoanalytic Association*, 69(2):237–258.

Kalb, M. (2015). Ghosts in the consulting room: Reluctant ancestors. *Contemporary Psychoanalysis*, 51(1):74–106.

Kalb, M. (2021). On ghosts: An aspect of the universal infantile & its theoretical-clinical perils and promises. Presented July, 2021 at the Congress of The International Psychoanalytic Association.

Lament, C. (2020). Useful untruths: Another look at pluralism in the clinical setting. *Psychoanalytic Quarterly*, 89(2):195–218.

Lear, J. (2012). The thought of Hans W. Loewald. *International Journal of Psycho-Analysis*, 93(1):167–179.

Loewald Center. (2021). loewaldcenter.org.

Loewald, H.W. (1951). Ego and reality. In: *Papers on psychoanalysis*, 3–20. Hagerstown, MD: University Publishing Group, Inc.

Loewald, H.W. (1960). On the therapeutic action of psychoanalysis. *International Journal of Psycho-Analysis*, 41:16–33.

Loewald, H.W. (1962a). Internalization, separation, mourning, and the superego. In: *Papers on psychoanalysis*, 257–276. Hagerstown, MD: University Publishing Group, Inc.

Loewald, H.W. (1962b). The superego and the ego-ideal. *International Journal of Psycho-Analysis*, 43:264–268.

Loewald, H.W. (1970). Psychoanalytic theory and the psychoanalytic process. In: *Papers on psychoanalysis*, 257–276. Hagerstown, MD: University Publishing Group, Inc.

Loewald, H.W. (1971). Some considerations on repetition and repetition compulsion. *International Journal of Psycho-Analysis*, 52:59–66.

Loewald, H.W. (1973a). On internalization. In: *Papers on psychoanalysis*, 69–86. Hagerstown, MD: University Publishing Group, Inc.

Loewald, H.W. (1973b). Some considerations on repetition and the repetition compulsion. In: *Papers on psychoanalysis*, 87–101. Hagerstown, MD: University Publishing Group, Inc.

Loewald, H.W. (1975). Psychoanalysis as an art and the fantasy character of the psychanalytic situation. In: *Papers on psychoanalysis*, 352–371. Hagerstown, MD: University Publishing Group, Inc.

Loewald, H.W. (1978). Primary process, secondary process, and language. In *Papers on psychoanalysis*, 174–206. Hagerstown, MD: University Publishing Group, Inc.

Loewald, H.W. (1979a). Reflections on the psychoanalytic process and its therapeutic potential. *Psychoanalytic Study of the Child*, 34:155–167.

Loewald, H.W. (1979b). The waning of the Oedipus complex. In: *Papers on psychoanalysis*, 384–404. Hagerstown, MD: University Publishing Group, Inc.

Loewald, H.W. (1987). Sublimation. Inquiries into theoretical psychoanalysis. In: *Papers on psychoanalysis*, 439–525. Hagerstown, MD: University Publishing Group, Inc.

Mahler, M. (1975). *The psychological birth of the human infant: Symbiosis and individuation.* New York: Basic Books.

Mitchell, S.A. (2000). *Relationality: From attachment to intersubjectivity.* New York: Psychology Press.

Mitchell, S.A. (2004). My psychoanalytic journey. *Psychoanalytic Inquiry*, 24(4):531–541.

Moscovitz, S. (2014). Hans Loewald's "on the therapeutic action of psychoanalysis" initial reception and later influence. *Psychoanalytic Psychology*, 31(4):575–587.

Nields, J.A. (2003). From unity to atonement: Some religious correlates of Hans Loewald's developmental theory. *International Journal of Psychoanalysis*, 84:699–716.

Ogden, T. (1992). The dialectically constituted/decentered subject of psychoanalysis. *International Journal of Psycho-Analysis*, 73:517–526.

Orange, D.M. (2014a). "A psychotherapy for the people: Toward a progressive psychoanalysis," by Lewis Aron and Karen Starr: A book review essay. *International Journal of Psychoanalytic Self Psychology*, 9:54–66.

Orange, D.M. (2014b). What kind of ethics?: Loewald on responsibility and atonement. *Psychoanalytic Psychology*, 31:560–569.

Orange, D.M. (2017). Review of ghosts in the consulting room: Echoes of trauma in psychoanalysis and demons in the consulting room: Echoes of genocide, slavery and extreme trauma in psychoanalytic practice. *Psychoanalysis, Self, and Context*, 12:91–96.

Pine, F. (2011). Beyond pluralism: Psychoanalysis and the workings of mind. *Psychoanalytic Quarterly*, 80:823–856.

Poland, W. (2011). Self-analysis and creativity: Views from inside and outside. *Psychoanalytic Quarterly*, 80:987–1003.

Poland, W. (2017). *Intimacy and separation in psychoanalysis.* New York: Routledge Press.

Sandler, J. (1983). Reflections on some relations between psychoanalytic concepts and psychoanalytic practice. *International Journal of Psychoanalysis*, 64:35–45.

Slochower, J. (2022). Are we nicer now? Paper given at the IARPP conference, Los Angeles, CA, June 2, 2022.

Sprengnether, M. (2018). *Mourning Freud.* London: Bloomsbury Academic.

Vivona, J.M. (2013). Psychoanalysis as poetry. *Journal of the American Psychoanalytic Association*, 61:1109–1137.

Whitebook, J. (2004). Hans Loewald: A radical conservative. *International Journal of Psychoanalysis*, 85:97–115.

Winnicott, D.W. (1982a). *Through Pediatrics to psychoanalysis.* London: Hogarth.

Winnicott, D.W. (1982a). *The maturational processes and the* facilitating *environment.* London: Hogarth.

Chapter 13

Meanings of These Books and the New *Loewald Center* to the Family

Elizabeth Loewald

When we the remaining family first heard that a Hans Loewald Center was being formed to encourage discussion and dissemination of Hans's work, I had two swift reactions. The first—thought it's now twenty-seven years since his death—was, "But what about his privacy?" His children said just the same thing, in our first flurry of conversations. Over his lifetime, Hans had schooled us! We knew that when he was drawn to think and write, he wanted solitary time without discussion and with lots of quiet. He must reread the works of others that bore on his subject. When he'd followed the thread of a new insight as far as possible, his next step was to invite one or another good analyst-friend to spend some evening or weekend hours with him—to talk in privacy, make notes, sometimes in turn scribble odd diagrams or phrases on a yellow pad. When these thoughts had found their best-possible written expression, he'd present the new paper to his familiar colleagues at the Western New England Psychoanalytic Society. Would a Loewald Center be too large scale, too non-reclusive a place to please him? Would too bright a spotlight be trained on him there? This he'd always discouraged.

Then there was another thought. Perhaps this Center would be the very place for demonstrating one of Hans's favorite ideas. He spoke, once, of his sense of having the company of thinkers past available, when he needed them for his work. Whatever their discipline—psychoanalysis, biology, philosophy, literature—he could feel them ready and welcoming when he opened their books and brought up his questions. Socrates and Aristotle, mentors in his youth, were as pleased as he was to be talking again. Sigmund Freud was less eager to be disturbed—but he'd left many versions, many examinations of his own thoughts, for this younger psychoanalyst and others to consider.

Hans liked to call up an image of each generation of scholars standing on the previous one's shoulders.[1] Giant ancestors like Socrates and Shakespeare offered *very* broad shoulders. But many a more modest, persistent seeker of truth could give his scholarly descendants a hand up to a wider view. I have no doubt Hans would welcome this change to offer his shoulders, just as they are, to those who come after. And present generations of psychoanalysts—some of them designing this Center—still include some of his friends and students whom he knew honored and resonated to his "ways of knowing." I think he would allow himself to be pleased to be honored.

Hans was a modest man. Or as he expressed it, he felt himself to be on a long, often solitary, pilgrimage in life, and tended to keep to himself. In his family, though, we sometimes glimpsed his pleasure in being seen and appreciated. One such time his son Francis and I remember. Sometime in his seventies, Hans had been given a prestigious

DOI: 10.4324/9781032685151-15

psychoanalytic award, and would go to New York City to receive it. He was to present a paper, one evening, in a lovely Manhattan building, to a handsome assembly of psychoanalysts and their wives from New York City, New Haven, Boston and even elsewhere. There would be a reception. He would wear his tuxedo. We remember his saying to Francis—who would attend, with his wife—"Do you think the boys," three young grandsons, "would like to come too?" His eyes twinkled. We all immediately imagined the misery of those boys as the long lecture droned on and they understood not a word of it. Francis declined for them. But Hans had said enough that we'd discovered his wish. He'd like his grandsons to see their mysterious grandfather in his tuxedo. (He wore it in his ceremonial European way.) They'd see his shining black shoes. He'd speak gently and measuredly, just as he did with them, but to a big crowd of people who'd listen to him very, very respectfully. When these boys later became grandfathers, they would be able to tell their grandchildren that they had witnessed all this. For the émigré Hans Loewald, who'd been harshly uprooted from his original family life by Adolf Hitler, the continuity of generations had in many ways been broken. (Even the family's old name, Lovald, had needed revision for use in the several countries in which Lovalds began new lives, in the 1930s.) I think this solitary pilgrim did wish to settle again; and add new stories to the family lore.

The subject of sublimation is on my mind as I write this.

When news of the Center's conception reached us, I thought again about that knotty subject which Hans had so regretted abandoning in his last years, when he'd become too ill to go on writing. He'd felt, even as his book, *Sublimation* (1988), was being published, that he'd failed to find answers to many questions crucial to both 'theoretical psychoanalysis' and to his understanding of and peace with himself. He lists some of these in his epilogue to the book: "...the relationship of sublimation to guilt, expiation, and atonement and to celebration and self-liberation, as well as to love and hate..." "...the questions of the sublimation of aggressive impulses..." "...the frequent, hardly coincidental concomitance of overt homosexuality or bisexuality with creativity..."[2]

I'd imagine that these puzzles and many others have been addressed in psychoanalytic writings since Hans's death. I know that other scholars will be standing on the shoulders of recent writers too—and *their* writings will be read at Loewald Center meetings. I would like to contribute one remembrance of Hans that may suggest how richly interlaced were needs, disappointments, renunciations, and experiences of the sublime from which *he* wrote.

Hans was telling me the tale of his life throughout our courtship. He added vignettes through many years of marriage. Especially in the beginning, most of these he told in a semi-detached but slyly pleased way. (His ancestors, he told me, were a rabbinical scholar on one side of the family, and a bishop on the other. No *wonder* he'd turned out as he had.) Darker memories he told calmly, but with a hint of drama. (His paternal grandmother, in Germany, was a clinically depressed, angry old lady who wore black dresses and sat always in a darkened room. She was the mother of his father who had died in Hans's infancy; so, as a little boy he must have been brought to see her now and then. It was an ordeal.)

I was seventeen years younger than Hans. I was a native Californian. Like Hans, I'd tried to keep my own lapses and difficulties hidden, and as a girl had lived my happiest life in reading and writing and listening to music. These are all reasons I felt I understood Hans' special mix of soft mockery and inner pride about himself. He told me that as an adolescent in Berlin during the great inflation, he'd rushed to an art store with his last precious marks to buy prints and art books: the prices would be tripled by the next day, and he *needed* these! That seemed only sensible to me.

We married in 1954. The next year, we took our first trip together to my native San Francisco. I wanted Hans to love my city as I did. He wanted that too, but also brought along his own special enchantment with California. His intellectual friends in Italy had told him that all innovative and profound thought was now coming out of California! His mother had said that her grandfather Landshut had sired half a dozen children in East Prussia, then went to California to sell provisions to miners in the Gold Rush, then returned to Europe to sire eight more! And it seems his mother had offered Hans a bowl of Kellogg's Corn Flakes every morning as a boy in Berlin, because some German experts at the time lauded their purity and their benefit to the bones of growing children. The Kellogg factory was located in Oakland, California.

The keen pleasure of that trip was surely related to our being in love. But one afternoon, something additional must have been at work.

We'd driven past one cemetery, then another, on the outskirts of the city. At a third one—large, green and venerable by California standards—Hans stopped the car and suggested we look around. "Let's look for 'Landshut" on a tombstone here. I just have a feeling." He was not joking. We did that; in an unhurried, but expectant, sort of way, down many a row of graves. After a long while, we walked back thoughtfully to our car.

What were we doing? I can tell you that I'd lost all connection to my "real" knowledge, that day. Hans's great-grandfather's body would not be found in a California cemetery. He had returned to Europe from the Gold Rush, and he'd had his last eight children there to prove it. But I did not see in Hans's face or manner that he believed that "reality" either. He'd perhaps had a true vision of an alternate family history. Hans was, in it, a Californian. At home, deeply connected, in this vibrant beautiful place.

We were not drunk or drugged. Was it a touch of *folie a deux*? Had Hans told himself a story so poignant he got lost in it? And I was drawn to follow? Were we actors, for an afternoon, enacting to the point of forgetting that we were?

We never, later, talked about it. I wonder whether he too had the odd sensation of almost creating a new reality but failing.

Look at chapter headings in *Sublimation*, the book Hans published thirty-three years later. There is "Transformations of Passions and Their Vicissitudes." There is "Symbolism; Illusion; Subjectivity." (Loewald, 1988). All of these pathways—in ways not then all mapped, nor are they yet—I know we walked on, that California afternoon.

Notes

1 See Isaac Newton's letter to Robert Hooke.
2 Sublimation (1988), H.W.L., p. 82.

Reference

Loewald, H (1988) *Sublimation: Inquiries into Theoretical Psychoanalysis.* New Haven: Yale University Press.

Index

Note: Page numbers followed by "n" denote endnotes.

For Product Safety Concerns and Information please contact our EU
representative GPSR@taylorandfrancis.com
Taylor & Francis Verlag GmbH, Kaufingerstraße 24, 80331 München, Germany